Big Data and Smart Service Systems

Big Data and Smart Service Systems

Xiwei Liu
The State Key Laboratory of Management and Control for
Complex Systems, Institute of Automation,
Chinese Academy of Sciences, Beijing, China;
Qingdao Academy of Intelligent Industries, Qingdao, China

Rangachari Anand
IBM Watson Group

Gang Xiong
The State Key Laboratory of Management and Control for
Complex Systems, Institute of Automation,
Chinese Academy of Sciences, Beijing, China;
Dongguan Research Institute of CASIA, Cloud Computing Center,
Chinese Academy of Sciences, Dongguan, China

Xiuqin Shang
The State Key Laboratory of Management and Control for
Complex Systems, Institute of Automation,
Chinese Academy of Sciences, Beijing, China;
Qingdao Academy of Intelligent Industries, Qingdao, China

Xiaoming Liu
North China University of Technology, Beijing, China

Jianping Cao
Information System and Management College,
National University of Defense Technology, Changsha, China

ZHEJIANG UNIVERSITY PRESS
浙江大学出版社

AMSTERDAM • BOSTON • HEIDELBERG • LONDON
NEW YORK • OXFORD • PARIS • SAN DIEGO
SAN FRANCISCO • SINGAPORE • SYDNEY • TOKYO

Academic Press is an imprint of Elsevier

Academic Press is an imprint of Elsevier
125 London Wall, London EC2Y 5AS, United Kingdom
525 B Street, Suite 1800, San Diego, CA 92101-4495, United States
50 Hampshire Street, 5th Floor, Cambridge, MA 02139, United States
The Boulevard, Langford Lane, Kidlington, Oxford OX5 1GB, United Kingdom

Notices
Knowledge and best practice in this field are constantly changing. As new research and experience
broaden our understanding, changes in research methods, professional practices, or medical treatment
may become necessary.

Practitioners and researchers must always rely on their own experience and knowledge in evaluating and
using any information, methods, compounds, or experiments described herein. In using such information
or methods they should be mindful of their own safety and the safety of others, including parties for
whom they have a professional responsibility.

To the fullest extent of the law, neither the Publisher nor the authors, contributors, or editors, assume any
liability for any injury and/or damage to persons or property as a matter of products liability, negligence
or otherwise, or from any use or operation of any methods, products, instructions, or ideas contained in
the material herein.

British Library Cataloguing-in-Publication Data
A catalogue record for this book is available from the British Library

Library of Congress Cataloging-in-Publication Data
A catalog record for this book is available from the Library of Congress

ISBN: 978-0-12-812013-2

For Information on all Academic Press publications
visit our website at https://www.elsevier.com

Working together
to grow libraries in
developing countries

www.elsevier.com • www.bookaid.org

Publisher: Glyn Jones
Acquisition Editor: Glyn Jones
Editorial Project Manager: Naomi Robertson
Production Project Manager: Kiruthika Govindaraju
Designer: Greg Harris

Typeset by MPS Limited, Chennai, India

Contents

List of Contributors

R. Anand
IBM Thomas J. Watson Research Center, Yorktown, NY, United States

J.H. Bauer
IBM Thomas J. Watson Research Center, Yorktown, NY, United States

N. Bertolazzo
University of Pavia, Pavia, Italy

F. Carini
University of Pavia, Pavia, Italy

S. Chen
The State Key Laboratory of Management and Control for Complex Systems, Institute of Automation, Chinese Academy of Sciences, Beijing, China

X. Dong
The State Key Laboratory of Management and Control for Complex Systems, Institute of Automation, Chinese Academy of Sciences, Beijing, China; Qingdao Academy of Intelligent Industries, Qingdao, China

Y. Duan
The State Key Laboratory of Management and Control for Complex Systems, Institute of Automation, Chinese Academy of Sciences, Beijing, China

H. Fan
Cloud Computing Center, Chinese Academy of Sciences, Dongguan, China

D. Fang
IBM Thomas J. Watson Research Center, Yorktown, NY, United States

B. Hu
The State Key Laboratory of Management and Control for Complex Systems, Institute of Automation, Chinese Academy of Sciences, Beijing, China

W. Kang
Qingdao Academy of Intelligent Industries, Qingdao, China

J. Karjalainen
Aalto University, Espoo, Finland

Q. Kong
The State Key Laboratory of Management and Control for Complex Systems, Institute of Automation, Chinese Academy of Sciences, Beijing, China; Qingdao Academy of Intelligent Industries, Qingdao, China

M. Laine
Aalto University, Espoo, Finland

H. Li
IBM Thomas J. Watson Research Center, Yorktown Heights, NY, United States

Y. Li
The State Key Laboratory of Management and Control for Complex Systems,
Institute of Automation, Chinese Academy of Sciences, Beijing, China

X. Liu
The State Key Laboratory of Management and Control for Complex Systems,
Institute of Automation, Chinese Academy of Sciences, Beijing, China;
Qingdao Academy of Intelligent Industries, Qingdao, China

Y. Lv
The State Key Laboratory of Management and Control for Complex Systems,
Institute of Automation, Chinese Academy of Sciences, Beijing, China;
Dongguan Research Institute of CASIA, Cloud Computing Center,
Chinese Academy of Sciences, Dongguan, China

T.-y. Ma
University of Pavia, Pavia, Italy

A. Mojsilović
IBM Thomas J. Watson Research Center, Yorktown, NY, United States

G. Motta
University of Pavia, Pavia, Italy

M. Nelson
Stanford University, Palo Alto, CA, United States

W. Ngamsirijit
National Institute of Development Administration, Bangkok, Thailand

T. Nyberg
Aalto University, Espoo, Finland

G. Nyman
University of Helsinki, Helsinki, Finland

J. Peltonen
Aalto University, Espoo, Finland

B. Qian
IBM Thomas J. Watson Research Center, Yorktown Heights, NY, United States

D. Sacco
University of Pavia, Pavia, Italy

X. Shang
The State Key Laboratory of Management and Control for Complex Systems,
Institute of Automation, Chinese Academy of Sciences, Beijing, China;
Qingdao Academy of Intelligent Industries, Qingdao, China

T. Teng
Cloud Computing Center, Chinese Academy of Sciences, Dongguan, China

H. Tuomisaari
Aalto University, Espoo, Finland

K.R. Varshney
IBM Thomas J. Watson Research Center, Yorktown, NY, United States

J. Wang
IBM Thomas J. Watson Research Center, Yorktown, NY, United States

K. Wang
The State Key Laboratory of Management and Control for Complex Systems, Institute of Automation, Chinese Academy of Sciences, Beijing, China

G. Xiong
The State Key Laboratory of Management and Control for Complex Systems, Institute of Automation, Chinese Academy of Sciences, Beijing, China; Dongguan Research Institute of CASIA, Cloud Computing Center, Chinese Academy of Sciences, Dongguan, China

Y. Yao
The State Key Laboratory of Management and Control for Complex Systems, Institute of Automation, Chinese Academy of Sciences, Beijing, China

L.-I. You
University of Pavia, Pavia, Italy

F. Zhu
The State Key Laboratory of Management and Control for Complex Systems, Institute of Automation, Chinese Academy of Sciences, Beijing, China; Qingdao Academy of Intelligent Industries, Qingdao, China

Z. Zou
Dongguan Research Institute of CASIA, Cloud Computing Center, Chinese Academy of Sciences, Dongguan, China

Introduction

CONCEPTS

Big Data is not a germ, as was reported in *Nature Special Report* on September 4, 2008. It has actually been utilized for years in scientific fields such as physics, biology, environmental ecology, automatic control, military, telecommunications, finance, and other industries. In recent years, with the rise of social networking, telecommunications, e-commerce, the Internet and cloud computing, audios, videos, images, and logs, data volume has increased exponentially. According to McKinsey's prediction, global new data stored in hard disks currently exceeds 7 exabytes (EBs) (2^{60}bytes) in 2010, and the global total data will reach almost 35 zettabytes (2^{40} bytes) by 2020. In general, Big Data with variety, mass, and heterogeneity is involved in all domains (Xu, 2012).

In early 2012, the *New York Times* announced the arrival of the "age of Big Data." Decision-making increasingly relies on the collection of data and its analysis in commerce, economics, and a variety of other fields, while predictable capacity of Big Data comes to prominence in healthcare, the economy, and forecast fields (Ren, 2014).

It could be said that data processing, application models based on cloud computing and data sharing, cross-tabs develop intellectual resources and knowledge service capability have transformed the traditional service system into a smart service system (Zhu, 2014).

AGE OF BIG DATA

"When we haven't understood the PC era, Mobile Internet comes; when we haven't known Mobile Internet, age of Big Data is here." sighed Ma Yun, the chairman of Alibaba Group, at the 10th-year anniversary celebration of Taobao on May 10, 2013 (Li, 2013).

In fact, Big Data is being hotly debated across the board, from the United States to China, Silicon Valley to Zhongguancun, in scientific research, healthcare, and even in banking and on the Internet. With the emergence of smartphones and wearable devices, our behavior, location, and even seemingly inconsequential changes in our everyday life can be recorded and analyzed (Liu et al., 2014).

In a drastic departure from traditional data, Big Data allows the exposition of the intentions, character, hobbies, and other information of the data producer. By analyzing massive data about "you," a more real "you" can even be revealed that you have not known before.

The "Big Data revolution" arrived quietly and 2013 is now known as "the first year of Big Data" (Guo et al., 2014).

Big Data, also known as massive data, are data sets which have massive volumes, complex structure, and varying types. Despite the superficial phenomena of

Big Data, we can begin to understand and appreciate the exciting potential of Big Data through the following three examples (Xu, 2012; Li, 2013; Ren, 2014).

- Data thought. Big data provides us with a new way of thinking. We can analyze overall data rather than individual samples, focus on the data's correlation rather than causality. Commercial reform has always been begun with a shift in society's way of thinking and Big Data thought will become a mainstream concept for the next-generation manufacturers. A subverted industrial revolution is coming.
- Data assets. The concept of assets has changed in the age of Big Data and assets can now be classified as extending from physical property into the less tangible data field. In our daily lives, goods with smart and networking functions such as routers, household appliances, and vehicles can produce large amounts of data when they are being utilized. These data can therefore be considered as part of our assets and perhaps even as the most crucial. This redefinition of the concept of assets will have a significant impact on our lives.
- Data liquidity. The value of assets could be converted into owner, shareholder, even social value through data mining.

SERVICE SCIENCE AND SYSTEM

Service science is an emerging subject which forms the backdrop of the modern service industry and its research concerns phenomenon, data, and information relating to service (Zhu, 2014). The structure and behavior of the service system are described using techniques of computer science, operational research, industrial engineering, business strategy, management, social cognition, and jurisprudence. A set of strict, complete, theoretical service models is finally established based on a distillation of information abstracted from all kinds of service systems. These models are able to provide useful insights and comprehension of service knowledge vital to the operations of service providers and users. They can then utilize scientific methods to guide the service system's design, construction, and operation. Service science has four essential characteristics: inseparability, heterogeneity, intangibility, and perishability. The definition of service is as shown in Fig. 1.

A service system is a kind of sociotechnological system. In this system, service providers and users should follow an established and specialized protocol. A specific customer's request is satisfied via data interaction and value is created. The essence of the service system is cooperative production relations built by a system provider and demander. Service objectives can be various: ranging from serving an individual such as architect, entrepreneur, to a government department or enterprise such as tax authority, post office, bank, hospital, university, a multinational corporation, for example, FedEx or KFC. Fig. 2 indicates a socio-service system.

A service system is a complex system made up of various elements. Connections between the elements are complex and interactions between those involved in the system are positive. The system's control right is not mastered by a certain element

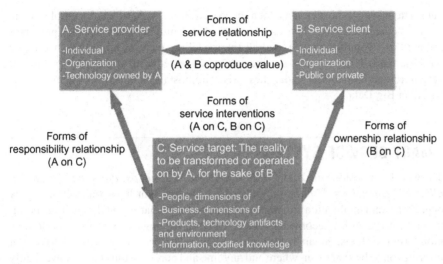

FIGURE 1

The definition of service.

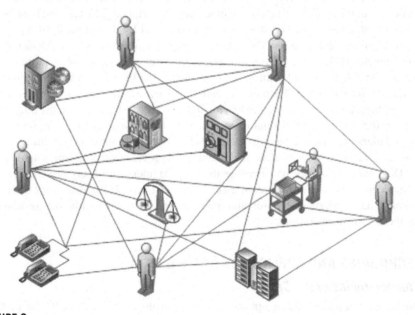

FIGURE 2

A socio-service system.

but scattered in all the elements, then the system forms a distributed control system. If one element changes, then all elements alter simultaneously. All the processes produce vast volumes of data, and all the modeling analyses are established based on these data. These courses are inevitably connected with Big Data. The service system research operating under these new circumstances must, to some extent, be based on Big Data.

SMART SERVICE SYSTEM

The world can be described as "*6 billion people× 24 hours per day× 365 days annually× 183 countries× 43 billion application software.*" Our lives, transactions, daily operations, and application software are all becoming smarter. Intelligent transportation means that cities become less congested with the dawn of real-time traffic-flow monitoring systems. Smart healthcare creates a platform for cases and treatment information to be shared anywhere and anytime and cures are thus more conveniently accessible. Smart education supports e-learning and resources-sharing to allow more people access to learning and knowledge. Additionally there is smart finance, manufacture, communication, grid, and production, as well as smart service. Healthcare providers need to store lots of medical images; cities collect the data relating to vehicles and traffic flow; retailers ought to keep the detailed information about interactions with customers. The storage volume required by digital media is rising by about 12 times each year and the data relating to the film Avatar's production were 1.6 petabytes (PBs). Even if you are able to save this massive quantity of data, you will not be able to take advantage of it or extract value from it if you cannot manage or retrieve it on demand. Then the data are therefore of little value, especially when 80% of the data are an unstructured form. Demands for IT managers in the future can employ the data in an influential manner and to predict what will happen, for example, retailers can manage the price of goods based on the data from real-time supply and demand and equally banks could avoid fraud on the basis of business activities.

Data analysis ability will become the core competence of any organization to some degree if it wants success in a newer, smarter world. Building a set of smart systems that supports integration and innovation at all levels will be the foundation for these sorts of operations.

TECHNIQUES AND APPLICATIONS OF BIG DATA

Characteristics of Big Data

Big Data is not a definite concept and many people are confused about how to understand and define it. "BIG" is insufficient to accurately describe all the features of data mining. It has four main characteristics:

1. Vast volume. The data order of magnitude ranges from terabyte (TB) to PB even to EB; as the volume is so vast that it cannot be expressed in gigabytes or TB,

the starting measurement unit of Big Data is at least a PB (2^{40} bytes), EB (2^{50} bytes), or a zetabyte (2^{60} bytes).

2. Various types. Data from different applications and different equipment determine its diversity. There are three types:
   - Structured: data produced by a financial system, information management system, medical system, etc. These are characterized by a strong causal relationship between the data.
   - Unstructured: videos, images, audio, etc. These data are typified as exhibiting no causal relationship between the data.
   - Semistructured: HTML documents, posts, webpages. This type is distinguished by a weak causal relationship between the data. Multitype data have higher requirements for data processing ability.

3. Low-value density. The amount of irrelevant information is phenomenal which, in turn, requires us to mine deeper for useful information. The diverse application of the Internet in the modern world means that information acquisition is everywhere. The amount of information is massive but its value density is low. A pressing question which needs to be resolved in the era of Big Data is how to maximize value more quickly with a powerful machine algorithm.

4. Fast processing velocity. The cycle of processing data has evolved from weeks, days, and hours into the realm of minutes and seconds. The improvement in velocity is closely related to a reduction in cost and an increase in efficiency, helped along by cloud computing (the Internet of Things). Greater time efficiency is the most notable feature of Big Data and distinguishes it from traditional data mining.

Techniques of Big Data

Massive data processing includes obtaining useful data related to specific applications, aggregating these data and making them easy to store, analyzing data correlations, and identifying relevant properties; and allowing the results of the data analysis to be properly displayed (Jagadish et al., 2014). This manner of processing is similar to the traditional method. The core techniques that Big Data would solve are related to these corresponding steps:

- Data description: Because of data variety, the first step before processing is a uniform description for different formatted data. Unified data structures not only simplify the system's processing complexity but also reduce processing data overhead in upper application. In order to deal with large quantities of data, data descriptions based on ontology have become a research hotspot. This description mainly concentrates on the models of consistency, logical consistency, and relation consistency. The present study concentrates on small data sets, and thus far there is no case which can successfully describe data uniformly at PB or above.
- Data storage: Data in quantities of TB or PB are increasing at an incredible speed. In order to meet vast-volume storage, a distributed storage system is

needed, for example the Hadoop distributed platform. When the data amount increases, the data distribution balance and system extensibility are maintained by adding storage nodes. According to the variety of data structures, different storage strategies can be chosen according to the different data formats. Structured, semistructured, and unstructured data can adopt similar shared-nothing distributed and use the parallel database system, distributed storage system for document, and distributed storage system for files.

- Data mining: With the emergence of texts, images, and network data, new machine learning applications for dealing with large data are being put forward and have caused much concern. As the generalization ability is limited, traditional machine learning such as support vector machine, decision tree, Bayesian, and neural network, etc., are not able to adapt to the need for rapid analysis of a large-scale network. Recently, labeled or unlabeled semisupervised learning and ensemble learning with multiple models are new directions of the Big Data research.
- Data display. Data visualization is the process of converting data into graphs. Structured data can be represented through data tables and various statistical graphics; unstructured data are usually shown using a 3D (three dimensions) shape due to the variety and complex relationships of the data. The research hotspots of data visualization at present tend to focus on hierarchical visualization, multidimensional visualization, document visualization, web visualization, etc.

Application of Big Data

The White Paper on Big Data in China, published in 2013, suggests that large network, financial, health, enterprise, and government managing and security data are the six major application fields which promise to be the most advantageous for development. However, the possible applications of Big Data far exceed even these. It is possible to assert that any organization, individual, industry, or fields decision-making will rely on the analysis and study of Big Data at some time in the near future.

THE FRAMEWORK OF THE SMART SERVICE SYSTEM

The smart service industry is a type of system engineering based on the newest information technologies, such as Big Data, cloud computing, and Internet of Things, which will help to fully realize the possibilities of intelligence-based service. Its essence is the application of an information network to achieve the intelligence of traditional industry's comprehensive service and management (Zhu, 2014). The smart service industries primarily involve transportation, grid, water, environmental protection, medical treatment, pension, community, household, education, territory, etc., which are all considered to need to be much "smarter." The smart service industry's core is perception, interconnection, and intelligence, and its basis is in large data and providing a common platform.

Strong ability in data collection, storage, analysis, and use is needed for the smart service industry. Whatever the demand, it can therefore be satisfied in a short period of time. Pieces of information are joined into a single pool by the common platform of the smart service industry. The level of industry management and service can be effectively enhanced through comprehensive perception, integration, and sharing of service information.

The smart service system is composed of a smart service terminal, smart service network, and virtual information network, as well as software-defined service, as shown in Fig. 3. The system can realize these functions: unified server, unified indoor

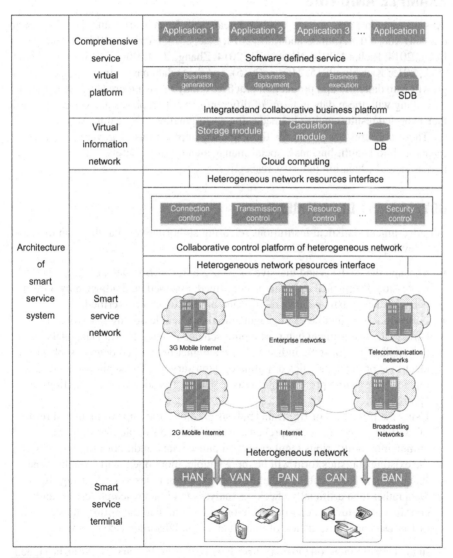

FIGURE 3

Composition of the smart service system.

service, unified terminal identity, and addressable, communicated, perceived, and controllable functions owned by all service terminals.

Pieces of single "rings" in traditional industry, subjects, and techniques are transformed into corresponding "chains" in the Internet of Things. By crossing and combining, these "chains" can be regarded as collaborative and innovative "chains."

EXAMPLE ANALYSIS

This massive data are various, involving nearly all the industries and deep into each domain (Xue, 2013; Andreas and Ralf., 2014; Cate, 2014; Fabricio, 2014; Ju et al., 2014; Levin, 2014; Richard, 2014; Wang et al., 2014; Zhang, 2014; Bhui, 2015; Gunasekaran et al., 2015; Kaushik, 2015; Martin, 2015), and those data have a trend of accelerated growth with daily life and production practice. It may make a more accurate judgment by dealing with these data in terms of different sorts of emphasis and different areas, then expected results can be obtained using corresponding practical measures.

These concepts are stated for the Big Data applications in government departments, public health, business, social management, public safety, intelligent transportation, and education industry, respectively.

GOVERNMENT DEPARTMENT

For government statistical institutions releasing authoritative data, they can increase their development by using Big Data.

- Through the analysis and massive relevance index of Big Data, exiting professional statistical data can be confirmed, assessed, and adjusted by a third party, so the statistical data's quality and credibility can be verified.
- Following the principle of improving efficiency and lessening grassroots burden, the government can start a pilot scheme relating to Big Data analysis and applications in some industries with a higher networked degree, such as electronic product statistics or public opinion surveys. These pilot schemes can replace the existing professional statistical survey as soon as the conditions are appropriate.
- Using the principles of Big Data analysis promotes the improvement and reform of existing government comprehensive statistics and sample investigations, eliminating multifarious regulations and unnecessary audit constraints, so that the existing statistics form will be more simple, more open, and more humane.
- Integrating and restructuring the present evaluation index system; using Big Data rather than artificially checking analyses to obtain research results, and coordinating relevant departments in order to formulate the norms and standards of Big Data analysis, in case of market chaos and disorderly competition.

In the United States, on Obama's first day in office on January 21, 2009, he signed his first memo: "Transparent and Open Government." This launched the data.gov, a data portal, as part of his commitment of "open government." The website is used to prevent private companies taking advantage of data that the government collected for business profit but not for public services.

PUBLIC HEALTH

Big Data's continuous expansion creates new challenges for the healthcare industry. A lot of information about patients' treatment services is produced. And as this information is progressively digitized hospitals are confronted with an urgent problem regarding how to manage and analyze this huge mass of disparate yet sensitive data in a gainful manner.

The concept of Big Data is, firstly, a cloud computing platform which can be constructed for discrete, vertical, and single information systems using the contemporary medical field; secondly, the discrete information can be integrated to promote effective coordination of the business; and thirdly, personal health information is extracted from various systems, institutions, and even medical equipment to build a complete personal health record.

Another example would be that health workstations built in the community and residents might expect to be inspected 16 times. The results can be sent to the cloud in real time and patients with chronic ailments would be able to keep track of their health records and not need to have follow-up appointments. This could save three billion Chinese Yuan for physical checkups if the health workstation is built in a city of 10 million people in the preliminary estimate. It could also be used to design a special work package for the family doctor, and this package might allow the doctor to send the results from measurements of blood glucose, blood pressure, blood oxygen, and other data to the pad as soon as they are available, while this pad can also be used to store information as part of a follow-up record, and the records could be uploaded to the cloud center. Finally, users could view real-time inspection records through the Internet.

Industry analysts have pointed out that a health management company in the age of Big Data would be able to send demic data collected by wearable devices to contribute to the electronic health records. If the record registers abnormal index it will sound a warning. Doctors could then provide immediate professional guidance, while the network care center could set up an algorithm according to the doctors' opinion and determine which patients require priority treatment.

BUSINESS

Big Data not only has the potential to change almost all aspects of business behavior—from research, sale, marketing, to supply chain management but also to provide new opportunities for development.

Areas using Big Data most widely at present are pushing advertisement, market segmentation, investment options, and product innovation. Almost all electronic commerce will have targeted marketing on their website, and this will be a result of the analysis of marketing data. With the change in business environment, great changes have already been taking place in marketing: whereas previously data were obtained through questionnaires and direct contact with users, now user information is recorded in each site, each webpage, each ad, along with the user's location, whether it is single visit or repeated visit to the site, how long the user spent on the site during each visit, whether it is a direct visit or via search engines, what the user views, what he is most concerned about, etc. The user's habits and hobbies are mined from the vast quantities of data, and products and services are identified which conform to the user's interests and search habits are then recommend to the user. Moreover, as consumers' purchasing behavior becomes more and more rational and they become more likely to shop around, a website is born in the right time to unify and comprehensively analyze massive data from many websites. Through comparison and analysis by the site, users can choose the highest cost-performance commodity.

Enterprises have become more astute, and this kind of intelligence is collected using Big Data analysis. Now almost all the world-class Internet companies have extended their businesses into Big Data. For example, on November 11, 2013, Alibaba's companies, Tmall and Taobao, created $35.019 billion daily trading records by capturing and summarizing the data of user usage and requirements; Google provided map function to developers in 2005 and launched the first mobile map application the next year providing every street's position in all important cities around the world. In order to establish a more accurate digital marketing value system, and ultimately achieve ascendancy in the era of Big Data, Tencent has started to build "the next generation of Tencent" and has created an environment where Tencent Website, Video, and Weibo can communicate with each other.

SOCIAL MANAGEMENT

Knowledge of human society is basically divided into two categories: natural science and social science. Natural science's object is the physical world, which requires precision in areas such as the launching of satellites or the driving of submarines, as a popular saying goes, "a miss is as good as a mile." Social science's object of study is social phenomena like economics, political science, and sociology. Although it demands precision, humans are the main research object, which inevitably leads to uncertainty, thus social science is often called a proto-science. Due to the progress of information technology, and the accumulation of data in recent years, private activities are recorded with unprecedented frequency. The records are thorough and constantly updated, which provides a tremendous wealth of resources for the quantitative analysis in social science. The analysis can be more accurate and calculation more precise. Some scientists believe that with the help of Big Data, social science won't remain a proto-science for long and may be able to make the transition into a proper science.

A wave of construction of Smart Cities both at home and abroad has been ever more visible in recent years. According to Guo Wei, the chairman of Digital China

Holding Limited and domestic leader of Smart City construction, there are more than 60 cities incorporating Smart City construction into the "12th five-year plan" in our country at present. One of the problems with the construction of a Smart City is how to integrate and manage the massive amounts of data produced by the city. Firstly, the data must be collected in areas where data have not previously been collected and the key is the Internet of Things. Secondly, the data from all the different systems must be able to dock effectively, which is the task of system integration, and finally, there must be scope to take advantage of data visualization to reveal and display information and patterns hidden within large data so that this knowledge can be used by city managers, policy makers, and the general public in an intuitive form.

The core of a Smart City is data collection, integration, analysis, and display. The future of the Smart City must be data-driven. Therefore, the construction of a Smart City must essentially use information technology to solve problems relating to social governance and improve gross national happiness.

PUBLIC SAFETY

The introduction of large-scale data analysis concerned with security management originated in New York.

New York is the world's financial and commercial center, and occupies an important position in the United States. New York was in the past known as the "City of Crime," because the population was so large that it contained a vast mix of both good and evil people. From the 1970s, the city became home to many gangs and there were many instances of issues with drug abuse. The city's public security situation gradually deteriorated. In 1994, the Police Department of New York started a CompStat (short for COMPlaint STATistics) system, which is a map-based statistical analysis system. At that time the Internet had not achieved the great popularity it enjoys today, and staff collected data from New York's 76 precincts by phone and fax every day, and then input data into "CompStat" uniformly to aggregate and analyze. A total of 1561 homicides in 1994 were down to 466 by 2009, which marked the lowest number in 50 years. This index helped to make New York amongst the safest big cities in the United States.

With this system's great success in New York, it was gradually utilized in other areas. In 1996, the system obtained the Innovations in American Government Award from Harvard. In 1998, Vice-President Al Gore announced the promotion of "Crime Mapping and Data-Driven Management" in all police departments throughout the country.

As time has gone by, the accumulation of more and more data has yielded many discoveries and demonstrated that this method can sometimes provoke unexpected discoveries. In 2006, by integrating and mapping the crimes data and traffic accident data from more than 20 years on one map, it was found that the area with a high incidence of traffic accidents also tended to have a high incidence of crime, even the time period of the highest frequency of traffic accidents was the same as for criminal incidents. In order to maintain traffic safety and strike against crime, the National Highway Traffic Safety Administration (NHTSA), Bureau of Justice Assistance (BJA), National Institute of Justice (NIJ), and other related departments which originally belonged to different federal agencies, jointly established a "new method of data driving: crime and traffic safety" based on this new discovery. A complete and rigorous system with data integration and analysis was set up for use by the police. Due to the system's fluctuations, it needed to accumulate 3 years' data for a big city and four or five years' data if the city's population was below 100,000, in order to function. In addition, the criminal activity and traffic accidents hardly ever took place in the exact same spot. In order to determine the common areas which most frequently witnessed these sorts of activities, the system needed not only to collect data, but also to use cluster-associated data display technology.

After determining the common trouble spots, the traffic police and police resources can be integrated, which will not only improve the efficiency in the using police, but also maximize the effect of patrols.

This kind of policing management model based on data has attracted much attention from academics, and this mode has been labeled "data-driven policing" by some scholars.

INTELLIGENT TRANSPORTATION

Intelligent transportation has been devoted to better traffic management and convenience of travel since its foundation. Historical data present in Big Data can be used to judge or forecast whether a transport policy and strategy is reasonable, for example in terms of what impact the odd-and-even license plate rule will have on the traffic or on congestion indexes in the future. According to the historical travel characteristics, it can be observed where the traffic flow is greatest and at what time the traffic is most congested. If this information is included in a taxi app, the customers can judge the best location for catching or alighting from a taxi based on their current location.

In the past, as the accuracy of cameras was not high, there was a problem with license plate recognition errors. Such errors can no longer occur thanks to Big Data techniques. Rules can be identified through access to billions of records and errors can be corrected by analyzing data on the basis of these rules.

By analyzing large data, we can see that some cameras' error rate is low during the daytime but high at night. There are two reasons for this, the luminance provided by lights may be not sufficient during the evening, or the recognition rate of some cameras may be low in some lanes because of low hanging branches hiding the camera. When similar recognition errors or deviations appear, we can take advantage of Big Data to support and increase efficiency.

Disputes caused by flight delays have been a hot topic of discussion in China. Similar delays also happen in the United States but boycotts or occupations of the plane rarely happen. After Data.gov was put into use, the US Department of Transportation collected data about takeoff, arrival, and delay times for all flights. Some programmers developed Flyontime.us, a system of analyzing flight delay time. This system is open to everyone, and anyone can inquire about the flight delay rates and waiting time at airports.

By entering the airport name and clicking on the system's homepage, users can access detailed data about whether or not an aircraft is on time and the average delay time in all sorts of conditions, such as weather condition, date, time, or airline.

These data and the analysis results have a positive effect on consumers and the economy:

- Help consumers find the best flight which most closely meets their needs. Without these data, consumers cannot get the same information as airlines when they are choosing between two airlines. Flight history data are an effective reference point for consumers.
- Minimize the uncertainty of waiting time as far as possible. Single delay can seem to be random and irregular; but when the data are aggregated over a period of time, the delay time can form patterns which are orderly and stable, Flyontime.us passes on this information to passengers and helps them make their own rational decisions and manage their time effectively.
- Promote healthy competition in the aviation market. Flyontime.us ranks all the relevant airlines for their average delay time, for example, the 4617th flight of American Eagle has a total of 182 services yearly, with an average delay of 7 min, whilst the 4614th flight of this company performs the same service but is an average of 8 min ahead of time. These public data can undoubtedly be used to promote market competition.

After Data.gov opened, the flight delay rate in the United States has been declining, from 27% in 2008 to 20.79% in 2009 and to 20.23% in 2010.

Airport delays in different weather conditions are shown in Fig. 4.

EDUCATION INDUSTRY

MIT Professor Brynjolfsson once said the influence of Big Data was similar to the invention of microscope centuries ago. The microscope promotes natural observation and measurement of the "cell," and has been proven to be revolutionary and important in our conception of historical progress. Big Data will become our microscope for observing human behavior. It will expand the scope of human science, promote the accumulation of human knowledge, and lead to a new economic prosperity (Xu, 2012).

	2003 (Jun-Dec)	2004	2005	2006	2007	2008	2009	2010	2011	2012	2013
	Percent of total delay minutes										
Air carrier delay	26.3%	25.8%	28.0%	27.8%	28.5%	27.8%	28.0%	30.4%	30.1%	31.9%	29.4%
Aircraft arriving late	30.9%	33.6%	34.2%	37.0%	37.7%	36.6%	36.2%	39.4%	40.8%	41.4%	42.1%
Security delay	0.3%	0.3%	0.2%	0.3%	0.2%	0.1%	0.1%	0.2%	0.1%	0.1%	0.1%
National aviation system delay	36.5%	33.5%	31.4%	29.4%	27.9%	30.2%	30.6%	25.7%	24.8%	22.5%	24.2%
Extreme weather	6.1%	6.9%	6.2%	5.6%	5.7%	5.4%	5.0%	4.4%	4.1%	4.0%	4.1%

FIGURE 4

Percent of total delay minutes of different airports.

Early in May 2012, Harvard and MIT announced that they would invest $60 million in the development of an online education platform. At the same time, they would make the teaching processes of the two schools free to the world and the platform would be accessible free of charge to other universities and educational institutions.

One of the reasons that it was designed to be free of charge was because of the technical background of Big Data. More learners around the world can study using the platform because it is openly available. Additionally, the platform designers can collect data from these learners and study their behavioral patterns in order to create an ever-improving online platform. For example, by recording mouse clicks, they can research learners' trajectory, observe and record the reactions of different people on to knowledge, examine which points might need to be repeated or stressed, and which information or learning tools are the most effective. In a manner similar to Flyontime.us, their behavior produces observable patterns and order which can be observed to a certain extent through the data accumulation. By analyzing these data, the online learning platform can make up for the lack of face-to-face with a teacher by improving the operation of the platform.

Moreover, learners' study behavior can be evaluated and guided via an online education platform. By tracking the learning process in real time through recording the video for each slide, tips and advice are given and mistakes can be pointed out to help them form a more customized and scientific learning method and habit. By judging whether the learner reviews the material or not and calculating the question number, the learner's behavior can be assessed. In addition, learners can also build supporting groups to correct and evaluate assignments and reports reciprocally.

Applications of Big Data in education build an effective environment without school for learners. It makes people step out of school and choose the learning method by themselves. Predictably, the responsibility for education will fall once more to the individual in the apprenticeship era from government in the school period, and the educational method goes back to being customized for each student. People will be able to enjoy more freedom and take more responsibility for their own learning and education, and at the same time this represents a huge liberation in the field of education.

CONCLUSIONS

In this chapter, we have presented the architecture of a smart service system based on Big Data. We have also included summaries of some examples of smart service systems based on Big Data.

X. Liu[1,3], W. Wei[2], X. Shang[1,3] and X. Dong[1,3]
[1]Chinese Academy of Sciences, Beijing, China [2]The Academy of Equipment, Beijing, China [3]Qingdao Academy of Intelligent Industries, Qingdao, China

REFERENCES

Andreas, G., Ralf, R., 2014. Big data—challenges for computer science education. Lecture Notes in Computer Science, vol. 873029–40., (including subseries Lecture Notes in Artificial Intelligence and Lecture Notes in Bioinformatics).

Bhui, K.S., 2015. Big data and meaning: methodological innovations. Epidemiol. Psychiatr. Sci. 24 (2), 144–145.

Cate, F.H., 2014. Privacy, big data, and the public good. Science 346 (6211), 818.

Fabricio, C., 2014. Big data in biomedicine. Drug Discov. Today 19 (4), 433–440.

Gunasekaran, A., Tiwari, M.K., Dubey, R., Wamba, S.F., 2015. Special issue on big data and predictive analytics application in supply chain management. Comput. Ind. Eng. 82, I–II.

Guo, H.D., Wang, L.Z., Chen, F., 2014. Scientific big data and digital earth. Chin. Sci. Bull. 59 (35), 5066–5073.

Jagadish, H.V., Johannes, G., Alexandros, L., 2014. Big Data and its technical challenges. Commun. ACM 57 (7), 86–94.

Ju, S.Y., Song, M.H., Ryu, G.A., Kim, M., Yoo, K.H., 2014. Design and implementation of a dynamic educational content viewer with Big Data analytics functionality. IJMUE 9 (12), 73–84.

Kaushik, D., 2015. Special issue on software architectures and systems for Big Data. J. Syst. Softw. 102, 145.

Levin, E.L., 2014. Economics in the age of Big Data. Science 346 (6210), 715–721.

Li, B., 2013. Research on development trend of Big Data. J. of Guangxi Education (35), 190–192.

Liu, Y., He, J., Guo, M.J., Yang, Q., Zhang, X.S., 2014. An overview of Big Data industry in China. China Commun. 11 (12), 1–10.

Martin, F., 2015. Big Data and it epistemology. J. Assoc. Inf. Sci. Technol. 66 (4), 651–661.

Ren, Y.M., 2014. Big Data are coming. China Public Science (4), 11–15.

Richard S.J., 2014. Governance strategies for the cloud, big data, and other technologies in education. In: IEEE/ACM 7th International Conference on Utility and Cloud Computing, pp. 630–635.

Wang, P., Ali, A., Kelly, W., Zhang, J., 2014. Invideo: a novel Big Data analytics tool for video data analytics and its use in enhancing interactions in cybersecurity online education. WIT Trans. Info. Commun. 60, 321–328.

Xu, Z.P., 2012. The Big Data Revolution. Guangxi Normal University Press, Guangxi, China.

Xue Y., 2013. Internet of Things, cloud computing, Big Data applications in healthcare. Age of Big Data.

Zhang Z.Q., 2014. Solving Traffic Problems by Big Data. Wisdom City.

Zhu, H.B., 2014. Coordination innovation architecture for iot and development strategy of smart service industry. J. Nanjing Univ. Posts Telecom. (Nat. Sci.) 34 (1), 1–9.

Vision-based vehicle queue length detection method and embedded platform

1

Y. Yao[1], K. Wang[1] and G. Xiong[1,2]

[1]The State Key Laboratory of Management and Control for Complex Systems, Institute of Automation, Chinese Academy of Sciences, Beijing, China
[2]Dongguan Research Institute of CASIA, Cloud Computing Center, Chinese Academy of Sciences, Dongguan, China

CHAPTER OUTLINE

1.1 INTRODUCTION

In recent years, more and more countries have made significant investments in the R&D (research and development) of intelligent transportation systems (ITS) and their practical application. In ITS, automatic detection of vehicle queue length and other parameters can provide a lot of important traffic information, and can be used for prosecutions related to traffic accidents and for traffic signal control. By using cameras mounted around the traffic road, a wealth of parameters can be measured, such as vehicle type, traffic volume, traffic density, vehicle speed, and so on. The data from the measurement of these parameters can be used for traffic adaptive management and vehicle dynamic guidance.

Big Data and Smart Service Systems. DOI: http://dx.doi.org/10.1016/B978-0-12-812013-2.00001-0

Scholars and practitioners globally have done research and conducted practical experiments related to vehicle queue length detection by using embedded video technologies, such as hardware technology, programming design, algorithms of length detection, image processing, pattern recognition, network technology, and many other fields. R&D areas of study tend to be mainly concerned with hardware design, software design, and algorithm analysis. Significant achievements have been made in video pattern processing and recognition areas with contributions from many scholars all over the world. For example, researchers from UMN (University of Minnesota) have developed the first video-based vehicle detection system by using the most advanced microprocessor available at the time of the study. The test results showed positive results in different environments, so the system can be put into practical use. Compared to the United States, Europe, and Japan, China's research on ITS began later than their American counterparts, as has video detection of vehicle queues. However, since the 1990s China has carried out a series of research projects and implementation projects based around intelligent traffic management. China has significantly accelerated the research and application steps on ITS, and achieved many research results from experiments related to urban traffic management, highway monitoring systems, toll systems, and security systems. Due to the breadth of existing technology fields, and the many enduring problems which are difficult to overcome, it is still hard to achieve full automation of ITS.

At present, the limitations when video-based queue length detection technology is put into practice include: (1) setting the thresholds is difficult, (2) the rate of false alarms is high, (3) the precision of acquired data is low and influenced by external environmental interference, (4) collecting large amounts of data causes many transmission and processing problems, and (5) commonality of data and algorithms is not high, and it is not easily portable or adaptable.

Many scholars have dedicated themselves to researching these issues, for example, Hoose (1989); Rouke, Bell (1991); Fathy and Siyal (1995a); Fathy, Siyal (1995b); Li and Zhang (2003); etc., and they have proposed a variety of methods and algorithm frameworks to address these limitations. These studies promote the development and progress of embedded vehicle queue length detection.

At the same time, it is obvious that large amounts of data are required when processing video images, which means the signal processor needs to balance complex computation and real-time satisfaction synchronization. The embedded video vehicle detection system can satisfy these requirements and proves advantageous in the following ways: (1) vision-based detection can detect many parameters in a large traffic scene area, e.g., different traffic parameters in multiple lanes, (2) compared with other methods, it can track and identify vehicles in motion within a certain range, (3) compared to other sensors, video sensors (such as cameras) can easily be installed, operated and maintained, without shutting down the roads or damaging surface facilities or features, and (4) the embedded platform can make sure the requirement for computing speed, computational complexity, and application performance in real-time images or videos processing are fulfilled. Here we make use of a DM642EVM DSP video board, together with a visual detection algorithm to obtain the on-road vehicle queue length.

Previous studies have shown that, in order to obtain vehicle queue length, the vehicle motion detection and presence detection should be conducted for incoming video images. In this chapter, we analyze the video sequence obtained from the fixed camera, and utilize the vehicle presence detection and vehicle motion detection to calculate the queue length of vehicles. Finally, the detection results are shown by the DM642 DSP video board embedded platform.

This chapter is organized as follows: In Section 1.2 we introduce the hardware structure for signal transduction of the vehicle queue detection system. Section 1.3 provides the algorithm for video-based vehicle queue length detection. Section 1.4 analyzes the data flow of the system. Section 1.5 presents the experimental results and our analysis of the system. Finally, the chapter draws its conclusions in Section 1.6.

1.2 EMBEDDED HARDWARE

The embedded video traffic information collection system of CASIA (Institute of Automation, Chinese Academy of Sciences) is shown in Fig. 1.1, including cameras, video boards, routers, laptops, and parameter configuration software. The cameras are installed on the eighth floor of the automation building, 100 m from the stop line, and at a vertical distance of approximately 30 m from Zhongguancun East Road. The control software can adjust the angle and focal length of the cameras, and parameter configuration software can be easily installed in notebooks, with visualized measurements recorded in real time. The video board processes the incoming signal, using detection algorithms to assess the vehicle queue length, and finally sends the results to the parameters configuration software. The video board is the principal part of the system, and we introduce this in the following.

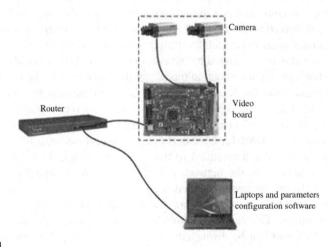

FIGURE 1.1

The whole embedded video traffic information collection system.

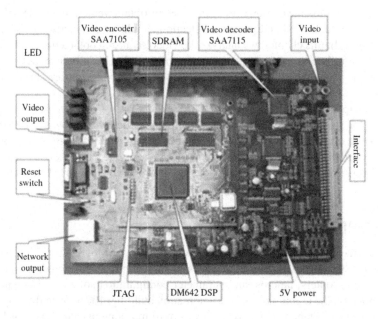

FIGURE 1.2

The video board.

As is shown in Fig. 1.2, the video board has four components: the video processing chip DM642, the video capture module, the video display module, and the network module, including two input ports and one output port. The analog video signal from the camera is converted to a digital signal by the decoder chip, and the digital signal is then delivered to the DSP. DSP processes each frame image, extracts and analyses the image data, and calculates the queue length. At last, the processed video signal is translated to analog signal by the encoder chip, and shown on the monitor.

Fig. 1.3 shows the input and output module of the video board. The whole system uses CCD cameras, and the decoder SAA7115 connects the cameras and the input ports of DM642. The analog signal from the camera is converted into digital signal which is in BT.656 by SAA7115, and is transported into the system by the ports VP0 and VP1 of DM642. In DM642, the video data are compressed into JPEG, and then the video stream data are transmitted to the Ethernet through RJ-45. At the same time, the PC connected to the network can receive the data using the parameters configuration software for queue length detection.

Based on the whole system we can use the network to realize surveillance and communications. The video data from port VP2 is converted into analog signal by SAA7115, and can be displayed on the monitor. The EMIF interface, two 48LC4M32B2 chips are used as the SDRAM memory to extend the available

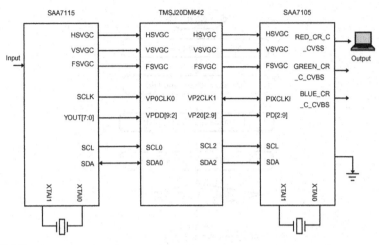

FIGURE 1.3

Input and output module.

memory-space, and FLASH is used to store the initialization code and configuration information for this system.

1.3 ALGORITHMS OF VIDEO-BASED VEHICLE QUEUE LENGTH DETECTION

The proposed algorithm of video-based vehicle queue length detection includes two major operations: the detection of a vehicle queue and the calculation of the queue length. Detection of a vehicle queue requires vehicle motion detection and presence detection. As we can see from Fig. 1.4, after setting the detection area and completing the initialization, the system begins to conduct a queue length detection. First, motion detection can eliminate those vehicles moving in a normal manner which maintain a certain distance from the queue. Subsequently, presence detection is used to filter the road background so we can identify the vehicle queue. Using the algorithm, a considerable amount of running time has b een saved. Next, we need to identify the measurements of the mini_region in order to calculate queue length as the length of each mini_region is settled.

1.3.1 VEHICLE MOTION DETECTION

Vehicle motion detection is based on applying the differencing technique to profiles of images taken along a road. At present, the most common technique for motion detection is interframe difference and background difference. The interframe difference

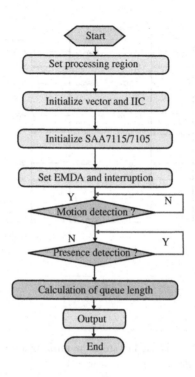

FIGURE 1.4

The whole detection of the system.

has utility but it cannot acquire a full object. Although the GSS background subtraction can acquire all the information relating to an object, it also needs time to adapt to the situation when a moving object becomes a part of the background. Therefore, we propose a combination approach utilizing interframe difference and background subtraction in order to confirm accuracy as well as to promote the effectiveness of the measurement. The GSS applied in this chapter is used for background setting and updating, and consists of three Gaussian distributions, and the rate of background learning is 5000.

In order to save computational time and reduce the huge amount of data which needs to be processed, the motion detection and presence detection for queues are not conducted along the entire road simultaneously. As in Fig. 1.5, motion detection is applied for both the head and tail of the queue, whilst presence detection is applied for only the tail of the queue during the detection. It continues to scan the queue head (stopped line), and the length of the queue clears to zero once the head moves. When no movement is detected in the head, and the tail is stationary at the same time, the queue length can be measured.

Fig. 1.6 shows the progress of the algorithm. First, the interframe difference is used for motion detection. When there is no obvious difference between the current

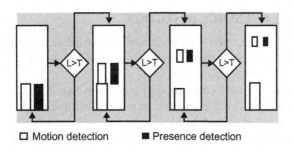

☐ Motion detection   ■ Presence detection

FIGURE 1.5

Algorithm diagram for queue detection.

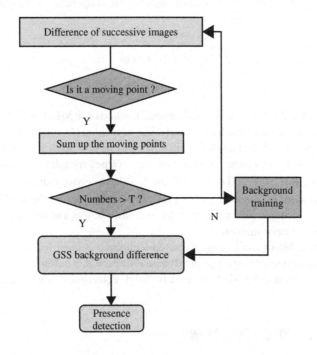

FIGURE 1.6

Combined algorithm flowchart of motion detection.

frame and former frame, the current frame is adopted as a part of background. Otherwise, the complete information of an object can be obtained using background subtraction. Through cooperation between the two methods, if a substance stops and becomes a part of the background, the background model will be updated and motion information can be detected immediately thereafter by interframe difference. Additionally, when an object starts to move, the system can respond appropriately due to its sensitivity to movement.

1.3.2 VEHICLE PRESENCE DETECTION

The vehicle presence detection is an important step for queue detection as it extracts vehicles from the surface of roads. Here, the approach is based on applying edge detection to these profiles.

Edges are less sensitive to the variation in ambient lighting and have been used for detecting objects in full frame applications. The method used here is based on applying morphological edge detector (MED) operators to a profile of the image. Basic operations consist of erosion, dilation, opening operation and closing operation. The definition is as follows: $F = f(x, y)$, $(x, y) \epsilon R^2$ is an image, and (x, y) is the pixel coordinate of each point. $f(x, y)$ denotes the gray level of each point (x, y), and $b(i, j)$ denotes a set of structural elements. In this chapter, the structural elements we selected are in a model of 3×3. Common basic MED operators are as follows:

$$D_r = (f \oplus b) - f \tag{1.1}$$

$$E_r = f - (f \odot b) \tag{1.2}$$

$$E_{de} = D_r - E_r = (f \oplus b) - (f \odot b) \tag{1.3}$$

Fathy and Siyal (1995a) presented several methods for MED. MED is based on the summation of erosion-residue (E_r) and dilation-residue (D_r) operators (E_{de}), which can detect edges at different angles, whilst the other morphological operators (except Open-Close) use E_r, D_r or the minimum of these values for edges are undetectable. As in the above Eqs. (1.1) and (1.2), D_r is the D-value of erosion dilation and E_- is the D-value of erosion. E_- is shown in Eq. (1.3). In addition, before the MED, the separable median filtering is performed in order to remove noises and reduce disturbances from the variable environment.

A combined MED and histogram-based technique is used for vehicle presence detection in this paper. An appropriate dynamic threshold is automatically generated to detect vehicles, and the MED is used for edge detection to ensure accuracy and precision.

1.3.3 THRESHOLD SELECTION

When the queue detection system is installed on roads, there is a necessity for a training phase to determine the proper threshold values of the histogram. Here, we show the example of Otsu method (1979). In Eq. (1.4), u is the average gray value of the whole image, and w_0 represents the proportion of points in foreground whilst w_1 is the proportion of points in the background, and u_0 and u_1 are the average gray values of the foreground and background, respectively.

$$u = w_0 * u_0 + w_1 * u_1 \tag{1.4}$$

Assuming a dark background image, in Eq. (1.4), $w_0 = \dfrac{n_0}{n}$, n_0 is the number of foreground pixels with a gray value below t, and $w_1 = 1 - \dfrac{n_0}{n} = 1 - w_0$.

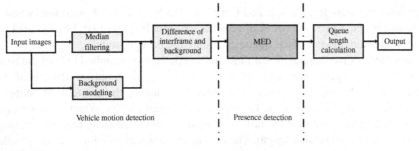

FIGURE 1.7

Algorithm diagram for vehicle queue length detection.

Proceeding through the gray value from the minimum to the maximum until a certain gray value t is found maximizing the following, Eq. (1.5):

$$g = w_0 \times (u_0 - u)^2 + w_1 \times (u_1 - u)^2 \qquad (1.5)$$

Thus, the value of t is the proper threshold value T. If the gray value f of a point is greater than $T(f \geq T)$, we surmise that it belongs to vehicle edges. Otherwise, if the gray value f is lower than $T(f < T)$, it belongs to the background.

To reduce computational time, the equivalent formula (1.6) can be used instead of (1.5) to find the greatest g.

$$g = w_0 \times w_1 \times (u_0 - u_1)^2 \qquad (1.6)$$

In this way, the threshold selected can be updated dynamically.

1.3.4 ALGORITHM SUMMARIZATION

In this chapter, the entire strategy for queue detection is based on the aforementioned vehicle motion detection and presence detection is as in Fig. 1.7. The proper T is definite by OTSU to differentiate the roads and vehicles. For motion detection, the combined approach of the interframe difference and background subtraction not only improves sensitivity but also promotes the effect of the detection results. The edges are identified using morphological gradient E_{de} and are clear and accurate enough for presence detection.

Before it is possible to perform the practical detection for a queue, separable median filtering is done to remove noise. The background is created in GSS with three Gaussian distributions which can update dynamically, and the rate of background learning is 5000. The combined motion detection algorithm eliminates the normal moving vehicles in order to identify the stopped cars. If a car does not run for a while and becomes a part of the background, its no-moving information can be easily detected using interframe difference. The background model is then reestablished and the stopped object is saved in the tracking modules. Thus even if the object runs again, it will be immediately identified. In order to decide the selection of the threshold, the histogram is scanned from 0 to 255 by gray level, until the largest g is gained by Eq. (1.6), and edges of vehicles will also be identified. Finally, MED is used to measure the tail of the queue excluding the background.

In order to save computational time, motion detection is applied to both the head and tail of the queue, whilst presence detection is applied only to the tail of the queue during the detection process. Continually scanning the queue head (stopped line), the length of queue clears to zero once the head moves. When no movement is detected in the head, and the tail is stationary at the same time, then the distance between them is the queue length. The next time the toll moves forward one profile, the mini_region_number will increase by one. Only when the value of the vehicle edges is greater than the threshold T, will the queue length increase (adding the mini_region_number). Conversely, the mini_region_number will subtract one.

In this chapter, the length of each mini_region responsible for calculating queue length is 5 m (about the average length of a vehicle). Using the formula $L = 5 \times$ mini_region_number, we can finally obtain the vehicle queue length.

1.4 PROGRAM PROCESS OF DM642

The software system encodes the input images transmitted by cameras, and produces JPEG images which the PC can debug. The encoding library and decoding library are integrated together in RF-5 (Reference Framework 5), and Fig. 1.6. shows the program flow chart of DM642.

First, initialize modules:

1. Initialize processor and system board. Initialize BIOS environment and CSL (Chip Support Library); set 128K cache, so as to map to the CE0 and CE1 space of EMIF, and request the highest priority; checking the maximum length of DMA priority sequence.
2. Initialize RF-5. Initialize the channel module of RF-5 and the module of I^2C and SCOM that works for the inner units' communication and transformation.
3. Establish the input and display channels. Build up an example of the input and display channels.

The system then runs the six task modules under the management of DSP/BIOS. These modules comprised two image capture tasks, one image compress task, one video output task, one network task, and one network initializing task. All of the tasks are integrated by RF-5, communicate with each other through SCOM module, and transport information about the data and control between the function modules. Through the cooperation of these tasks, the queue length can be calculated and shown on the software in real time.

We take advantage of TI CCS2.20.18 (Code Composer Studio) EDI to develop and debug the code. The DSP program first performs the initialization, then starts DSP/BIOS, controls the six tasks, processes data, then sends out the detection results.

1.5 **EVALUATION**

The results of the operations of the algorithms compared to the manual observations of the images confirm that the queues are detected and their parameters are accurately measured in real time.

The experimental station is installed on the eighth floor of the automation building, and the camera is mounted facing a northern intersection running from a south to north direction in front of the building. The results of the operations of the algorithms were observed over a period of 2 weeks and are shown in Fig. 1.8. In our experiment, images from the second camera, which is mounted on the stop line of the intersection, are processed by the parameters configuration software in real time. Considering the experimental environment, there is one left lane and two straight lanes which are to be detected without taking measurements for the right lane (see the blue lane sign in Fig. 1.8). As far as we can see in Fig. 1.8, the queue is marked in red and the results calculating the length can be read directly on the top left of the picture and in the right area of the software.

Fig. 1.9 illustrates the complete detection process of a queue length applied to the detection results of the left lane in Fig. 1.8. Firstly in Fig. 1.9A the queue starts to appear when there is no motion at the stop line as the traffic light is red, and the length is measured as 10 m. Then the length increases to 75 m in Fig. 1.9B. Next, Fig. 1.9C shows the maximum length (85 m) for this queue. Finally, Fig. 1.9D shows the end of the queue—the length data fall to zero immediately once the head of the vehicle queue moves.

FIGURE 1.8

Results of queue length.

The stare of queue   Queue added   The maximum queue   The end of queue

FIGURE 1.9

Detection process of a queue length.

Weather	Days	Weather	Days
Sunny	5	Clear	1
Rainy	2	Sunny and Windy	2
Cloudy	1	Cloudy and Sunny	2

FIGURE 1.10

Weather conditions during experiment.

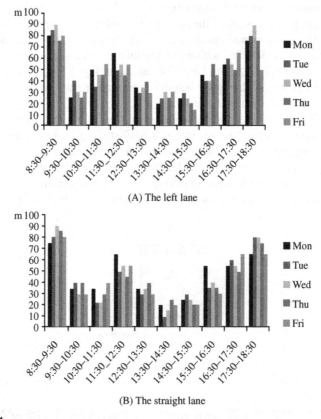

(A) The left lane

(B) The straight lane

FIGURE 1.11

Statistics showing average values for queue detection results.

The evaluation phase was performed over a 2-week period. In order to evaluate the accuracy of the algorithm, acquired images and the corresponding values of the queue length have been saved every 15 s in case of queue response, and every 20 min otherwise. The number of acquired images is about 120 frames during 08:30 am–6:30 pm every day in various weather conditions as shown in Fig. 1.10.

Fig. 1.11 describes the statistics of the average value for queue detection results for the lanes heading left and straight ahead. The most common period for a queue to appear and reach the longest is between 8:30–9:30 am and 4:30–6:30 pm every day, during the daily rush hours. At the same time, the average data for the left lane are greater than the straight lanes, as there are two straight lanes, which helps to relieve congestion while there is only one left lane. The time required for queue detection is about 0.5–5 s. This is the time when the queue is fully present and detected in the scene and the algorithm is executed for the entire scene. It meets the requirements for qualifying as a real-time system.

1.6 CONCLUSIONS

In this chapter we have presented a real system for traffic queue detection. It is able to detect queues in each of the monitored lanes, providing their duration along with a severity index. By means of an extensive testing phase, the system is shown to be robust with respect to weather conditions and illumination variations. As an important area of research for ITS, we still have a large amount of work to investigate in greater depth. In order to minimize false results, future works will include an analysis of the proposed improvements, the setting of an appropriate stop line, and steps to compensate for camera vibration and so on. Furthermore, other vehicle parameters such as the vehicle type, vehicle speed, and license plate are all important and interesting areas to be studied in the future.

ACKNOWLEDGMENT

This work was supported in part by the National Natural Science Foundation of China under Grants 71232006,61233001, 61304201, and 61174172; Finnish TEKES's project "SoMa2020: Social Manufacturing" (2015–2017); Chinese Guangdong's S&T project (2014B010118001, 2014A050503004), Chinese Dongguan's S&T project (2013508102018), and Dongguan 's Innovation Talents Project (Gang Xiong).

REFERENCES

Fathy, M., Siyal, M.Y., 1995a. An image detection technique based on morphological edge detection and background differencing for real-time traffic analysis. Pattern Recognition Letters 16, 1321–1330.

Fathy, M., Siyal, M.Y., 1995b. Real time image processing approach to measure traffic queue parameters. IEEE Proceedings-Vision Image and Signal Processing, Vol.142, 297–303.

Hoose, N., 1989. Queue detection using computer image processing. Road Traffic Monitoring, 94–98.

Li, Y., Zhang, X.G., 2003. Detecting the length of traffic queue by image processing. Computer Applications and Software, 47–49.

Otsu, N., 1979. A threshold selection method from gray-level histogram. IEEE Transactions on Systems, Man and Cybernetics 9, 62–66.

Rouke, A., Bell, M.G.H., 1991. Queue detection and congestion monitoring using image processing. Traffic Eng. Control 32, 412–421.

Improved information feedback in symmetric dual-channel traffic

Y. Duan[1], F. Zhu[1,2], G. Xiong[1,3], Y. Li[1] and Y. Lv[1,3]

[1]The State Key Laboratory of Management and Control for Complex Systems, Institute of Automation, Chinese Academy of Sciences, Beijing, China [2]Qingdao Academy of Intelligent Industries, Qingdao, China [3]Dongguan Research Institute of CASIA, Cloud Computing Center, Chinese Academy of Sciences, Dongguan, China

CHAPTER OUTLINE

2.1 INTRODUCTION

Traffic flow has triggered great interest in researchers in the past few decades because traffic problems have an obvious effect on society and have thus attracted the attention of people from almost all fields. The problem has grown progressively more serious and therefore needs to be solved as soon as possible. Research aiming to improving the ability of the existing traffic facilities has been undertaken by some universities and institutes. Real-time information feedback to guide vehicles' choices of routes has proven to be effective in improving the traffic situation. A paper authored by Wang et al. (2005) proposed an advanced real-time information feedback for intelligent traffic systems. They proved that the congestion coefficient feedback strategy (CCFS) is more effective than the travel time feedback strategy (TTFS) and the mean velocity feedback strategy (MVFS) in a two-route scenario with each single route following the cellular automaton model (CAM) proposed by Nagel and Schreckenberg (1992). CCFS takes the feedback time delay of TTFS into account and provides a better feedback strategy than MVFS. However, it has not considered the effect of space delay. Sun et al. (2009) have adopted CCFS in an asymmetric two-route scenario but they did not change the nature of CCFS. In this chapter, we present an improved information feedback called improved mean number feedback strategy (IMNFS) taking into account the effect of space delay. The simulation results adopting IMNFS and the other different feedback strategies, such as MVFS, CCFS, ICCFS, IICCFS, and MNFS, are also reported.

The outline of this chapter is as follows: in Section 2.2, the CAM and the two-route scenario will be briefly introduced, followed by CCFS together with its improved versions; finally we will outline in detail a completely new feedback strategy, IMNFS together with MNFS. In Section 2.3, the simulation results of the different feedback strategies will be presented and some related discussions will be presented based on the contrast of the results. In Section 2.4, conclusions will be drawn.

2.2 CAM AND INFORMATION FEEDBACK STRATEGIES

The CAM proposed by Nagel and Schreckenberg (1992) is a very useful and simple model for analyzing traffic flow. It was proposed as a one-dimensional model. It can be used to simulate the traffic flow providing proper boundary conditions. Here, the mechanism of CAM will be introduced as a base simulation platform.

The road is divided into L sites. Each site may be either occupied by one vehicle or be empty. Each vehicle has an integer velocity v with values between 0 sites and v_{max} sites. The distance between a vehicle and the nearest vehicle ahead of it is d. To contrast with the strategy previously proposed, the parameters in this chapter follow the values set in CCFS. Therefore, the length of a site is 7.5 m and $v_{max} = 3$.

One update of the system consists of the following four consecutive steps, which are performed in parallel for all vehicles:

1. Acceleration: If $v \leq v_{max}$, then $v = v+1$;
2. Slowing down (due to other cars): If $d < v$, then $v = d$;
3. Randomization: with probability p, $v = v - 1$;
4. Car motion: each vehicle is advanced by v sites.

The probability p takes account of the natural velocity fluctuations which result from human behavior or varying external conditions.

The two-route scenario (Wahle et al., 2000) comprises of a symmetric dual-channel between the starting point and the destination. The dual-channel consists of Route1 and Route 2, which are in the same direction and with the same length. At the entrance of the dual-channel is a board on which the feedback information is displayed. Vehicles arriving at the entrance can choose one of the routes to travel to the destination based on the real-time information feedback. Again, the parameters and boundary conditions of the two routes are identical to those in CCFS to provide a contrast between the results yielded by CCFS and the strategies proposed in this chapter. In the simulations, Route1 and Route2 L were the same length. At every time step, a new vehicle is generated at the entrance of the two routes. These vehicles can be divided into two types: dynamic and static. If a vehicle is dynamic, it will choose one of the two routes based on the information feedback. If a vehicle is static, it will randomly choose one route ignoring the information feedback. The proportion of dynamic vehicles is S_{dyn}. If a vehicle enters one route, it will update according to CAM. If a vehicle is not able to enter the desired route, it will wait for one time step and make a choice in the next time step. If a vehicle reaches the end of the two routes, it will be removed.

The simulations are performed using the following steps:

1. Initialization: set the routes and information feedback board empty;
2. Update: at every time step. The information feedback will be displayed on the information board. A vehicle will be generated in the entrance of the two routes and will choose one route either according to the board or at random. All vehicles in the routes update following the CAM mechanism.
3. Calculation: the information feedback will be calculated at every time step. The traffic statistics will also be calculated to evaluate the traffic conditions.

The traffic conditions are characterized by the flow of two routes. Adopting the definition of average flow F in one time step in CCFS,

$$F = V_{mean}\rho = V_{mean}\frac{N}{L} \tag{2.1}$$

where V_{mean} represents the mean velocity of all vehicles on one road, N represents the total number of vehicles on one road, and L is the length of the routes.

CCFS adopts the congestion coefficient C as feedback information.

$$C = \sum_{i=1}^{m} n_i^w \tag{2.2}$$

where n_i represents the vehicle number of the ith congestion cluster in which vehicles are close to each other without a gap between any two of them (Wang et al., 2005).

Although CCFS has been better than previous feedback strategies, it can be improved and made more effective. Fig. 2.1 shows a phenomenon when C of the two routes are the same but a rational vehicle will choose Route 2, which is less congested, instead of randomly choosing one of the routes as would happen in real traffic.

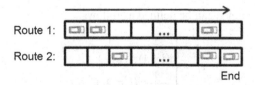

FIGURE 2.1

Two routes with the same C in CCFS.

The difference between CCFS and the real world indicates that CCFS has ignored the distance between the cluster and the entrance. The effect of a cluster varies according to the distance. To reflect the difference, this chapter proposed ICCFS in which the congestion coefficient C is defined as follows:

$$C = \sum_{i=1}^{m} \frac{1}{d_i} n_i^w \tag{2.3}$$

Another improved version IICCFS is also proposed and the congestion coefficient C is defined as follows,

$$C = \sum_{i=1}^{m} \frac{1}{d_i(d_i + 1)} n_i^w \tag{2.4}$$

where d_i is the distance between the entrance and the first site of the ith cluster, while the other parameters have definitions identical to those in CCFS.

In real-world traffic, most vehicles choose a route based on the number of cars or the level of congestion of vehicles on the roads. Therefore, this chapter gives a simple mean number feedback strategy, in which the information feedback is defined as follows:

$$NF = \sum_{i=1}^{L} \frac{1}{L} n_i \tag{2.5}$$

where NF is the mean number of roads, and L is the length of the route. $n_i = 1$ if site i is occupied by a vehicle otherwise, $n_i = 0$.

Obviously, MNFS has not considered the space delay which represents the different effects of sites from different distances. A method to improve MNFS, IMNFS, is proposed here. In IMNFS, NF is defined as follows;

$$NF = \sum_{i=1}^{L} e_i n_i \tag{2.6}$$

where e_i should satisfy two conditions as follows:

$$\begin{cases} \sum_{i=1}^{L} e_i = 1 \\ e_i > e_j (i < j) \end{cases} \tag{2.7}$$

Therefore, a kind of e_i can be defined as follows:

$$e_i = \begin{cases} \dfrac{1}{i(i+1)} + \dfrac{1}{L+1}(i = 1) \\ \dfrac{1}{i(i+1)}(i = 2,3,\cdots L) \end{cases} \tag{2.8}$$

Taking into account the space delay and problems arising in real-world situations, this chapter has offered ways of improving CCFS and has proposed ICCFS, IICCFS and MNFS, and IMNFS. In the next section, simulations adopting these feedback strategies together with MVFS will be presented.

2.3 SIMULATION RESULTS

All simulation results in this chapter are obtained using 10,000 time steps excluding the initial 5000 time steps on the basis that the routes have reached a relatively stable state after this initial period; $S_{dyn} = 0.5$, $L = 2000$. In the simulation results, the average flow, vehicle number, and average speed of the two routes in every time step will be calculated and shown in the figures. TTFS has been proved to be unstable and not as effective as CCFS, and therefore this chapter ignores TTFS. Firstly, the results of average flow F adopting CCFS, ICCFS, and IICCFS are shown in Fig. 2.2.

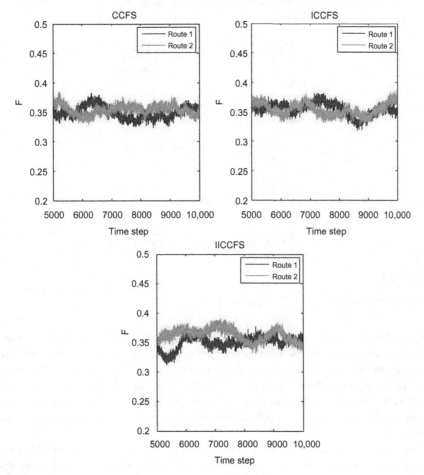

FIGURE 2.2

The average flow F of CCFS, ICCFS, and IICCFS.

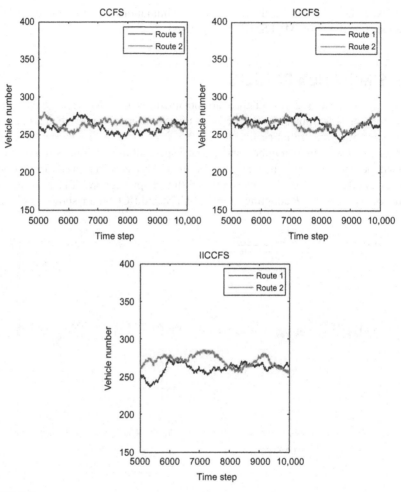

FIGURE 2.3

The vehicle numbers of CCFS, ICCFS, and IICCFS.

The results of the vehicle numbers are shown in Fig. 2.3, while the results of average speed are shown in Fig. 2.4. Comparing the three figures, we can see that there are some slight differences. To further elucidate this, Table 2.1 gives the total average flow of the three feedback strategies. Table 2.1 shows that IICCFS is slightly better than ICCFS and ICCFS and also marginally better than CCFS. The results have encouraged us to try another feedback strategy that can more obviously improve the traffic situation.

From the results shown above, we can see that the improved versions of CCFS are insufficient. Therefore, we have tried MNFS and IMNFS, and the simulation results shown in Figs. 2.5, 2.6, and 2.7. Fig. 2.5 shows that IMNFS is obviously better than

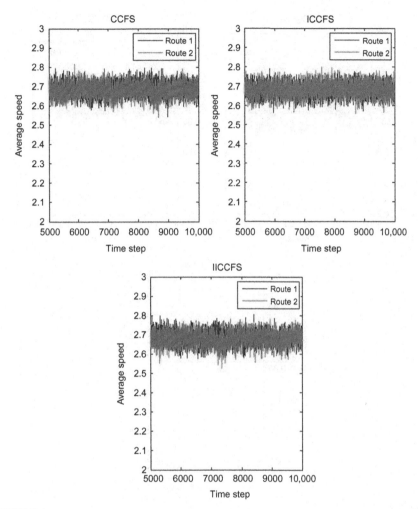

FIGURE 2.4

The average speed of CCFS, ICCFS, and IICCFS.

Table 2.1 Average flow *F* of CCFS, ICCFS, and IICCFS

	Average flow *F*		
Strategy	**Route 1**	**Route 2**	**Total**
CCFS	0.3493	0.3543	0.3518
ICCFS	0.3544	0.3538	0.3541
IICCFS	0.3503	0.3633	0.3568

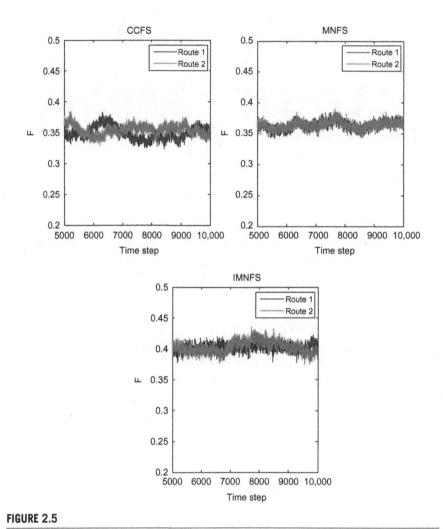

FIGURE 2.5

The average flow F of CCFS, MNFS, and IMNFS.

the other two strategies, while MNFS is a little better than CCFS. Figs. 2.6 and 2.7 show that the improvement of IMNFS is mainly due to the number of vehicles. Table 2.2 shows how great an improvement is evident.

From all the simulation results shown above, IMNFS seems to be the most effective strategy. To test whether IMNFS continues to be the best strategy if the proportion of dynamic vehicles changes or the length of the route changes, this chapter

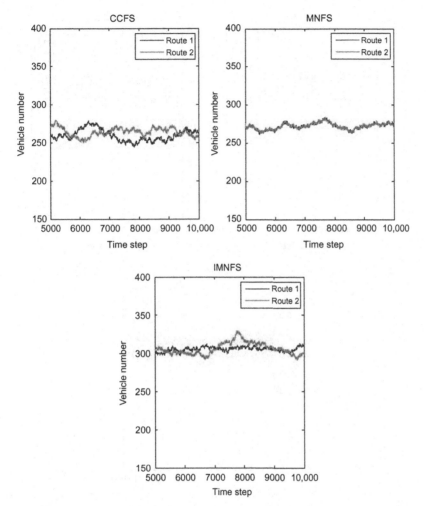

FIGURE 2.6

The vehicle numbers of CCFS, MNFS, and IMNFS.

offers the simulation results when S_{dyn} varies from 0 to 1 in Fig. 2.8 and when L varies from 100 to 5000 in Fig. 2.9. Fig. 2.8 shows that with the increase of S_{dyn}, IMNFS retains its position as best amongst these strategies. The average flow of IMNFS and MNFS increases along with S_{dyn}, while the other strategies keep the same level of average flow or even slightly reduce. Fig. 2.9 once again shows that IMNFS is the best strategy when L changes.

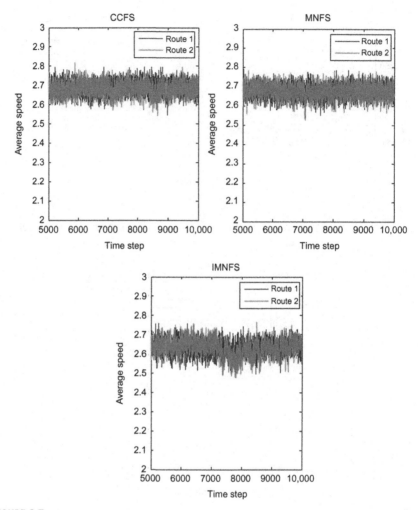

FIGURE 2.7

The average speed of CCFS, MNFS, and IMNFS.

Table 2.2 Average flow *F* of CCFS, MNFS, and IMNFS

	Average flow *F*		
Strategy	*Route 1*	*Route 2*	*Total*
CCFS	0.3493	0.3543	0.3518
MNFS	0.3644	0.3644	0.3644
IMNFS	0.4018	0.4029	0.4024

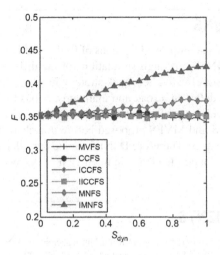

FIGURE 2.8

The average flow F by performing different strategies vs. S_{dyn}; $L = 2000$.

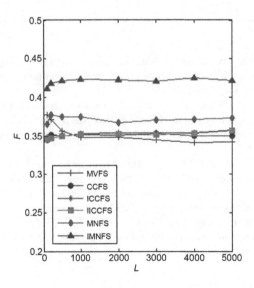

FIGURE 2.9

The average flow F by performing different strategies vs. L; $S_{dyn} = 0.9$.

2.4 CONCLUSIONS

This chapter proposes two improved versions of CCFS and two other feedback strategies: MNFS and IMNFS. Through simulations of the different strategies, IMNFS is proven to be the most effective feedback strategy in a two-route scenario. IMNFS has considered space delay on a road and maintains its position as the best strategy when the dynamic vehicles percentage changes or the length of the route changes. In contrast with CCFS and MVFS proposed before this chapter, IMNFS offers significantly more advantages. Therefore IMNFS can be considered to be a meaningful improvement for information feedback in intelligent traffic systems.

ACKNOWLEDGMENTS

This work was supported in part by the National Natural Science Foundation of China under Grants 71232006, 61233001, 61304201, and 61174172; Finnish TEKES's project "SoMa2020: Social Manufacturing" (2015–2017); Chinese Guangdong's S&T project (2014B010118001, 2014A050503004), Chinese Dongguan's S&T project (2013508102018), and Dongguan's Innovation Talents Project (Gang Xiong).

REFERENCES

Chen, B., Xie, Y., Tong, W., Dong, C., Shi, D., Wang, B., 2012. A comprehensive study of advanced information feedbacks in real-time intelligent traffic systems. Phys. A Statist. Mech. Appl. 391 (8), 2730–2739.

Fukui, M., Ishibashi, Y., Nishinari, K., 2013. Dynamics of traffic flows on crossing roads induced by real-time information. Phys. A Statist. Mech. Applicat. 392 (4), 902–909.

Nagel, K., Schreckenberg, M., 1992. A cellular automaton model for freeway traffic. J. Phys. I 2 (12), 2221–2229.

Sun, X.Y., Wang, B.H., Wang, Q.M., et al., 2009. Effects of information feedback on an asymmetrical two-route scenario. Chinese Sci Bull 54 (016), 2284–2288.

Wahle, J., Bazzan, A.L.C., Klügl, F., Schreckenberg, M., 2000. Decision dynamics in a traffic scenario. Phys. A Statist. Mech. Applicat. 287 (3), 669–681.

Wang, W.X., Wang, B.H., Zheng, W.C., Yin, C.Y., Zhou, T., 2005. Advanced information feedback in intelligent traffic systems. Phys. Rev. E 72 (6), 066702.

Yokoya, Y., 2004. Dynamics of traffic flow with real-time traffic information. Phys. Rev. E 69 (1), 016121.

Secure provable data possession for big data storage

3

Z. Zou[1] and Q. Kong[2,3]

[1]Dongguan Research Institute of CASIA, Cloud Computing Center, Chinese Academy of Sciences, Dongguan, China [2]The State Key Laboratory of Management and Control for Complex Systems, Institute of Automation, Chinese Academy of Sciences, Beijing, China [3]Qingdao Academy of Intelligent Industries, Qingdao, China

CHAPTER OUTLINE

3.1 INTRODUCTION

As information systems become less independent and more distributed, big data processing will also become increasingly commonplace. The various technologies involved in data storage and sharing will be industrialized, costs will fall, and eventually big data analysis and utilization will become mainstream (Barlow, 2013). Nowadays, a large number of data processes which used to require months, days, or hours have been reduced to minutes, seconds, or even fractions of seconds. But shorter processing time has led to higher-risk security issues.

The growth in data creation globally is estimated to reach 40% per year. That is roughly 35 zettabytes per year, while the overall size of global data for 2011 was 1.8 zettabytes. Effective utilization of big data for business growth has given rise to concern among organizations (Snijders et al., 2012). Big data analytics is an iterative process involving multiple tools and systems (Beryer, 2011). Verifying the authenticity of data has become a critical issue for those storing data on untrusted servers (Ateniese et al., 2007). It arises in peer-to-peer storage systems (Maniatis et al., 2005), network file systems, long-term archives, and database systems. Such systems prevent storage servers from misrepresenting or modifying data by providing authenticity checks when accessing big data application.

However, archival storage require guarantees about the authenticity of data in storage, namely that storage servers possess data. It is insufficient to detect that data have been modified or deleted when accessing the data, because it may be too late to recover lost or damaged data (Alexander and Wälde, 2011). Archival storage servers retain tremendous amounts of data, little of which is accessed. They also hold data for long periods of time during which there may be some instances of data loss from administrative errors as the physical implementation of storage evolves, e.g., backup and restore, data migration to new systems, and changing memberships in peer-to-peer systems (Chen and Lee, 2012).

Today, data storage security has become evermore essential for maintaining the trustworthiness of cloud computing platforms (Kubiatowicz et al., 2000). Although many systems provide convenient and efficient services on the network, the loss of critical data can bring unexpected disasters, or even push them into destruction. With the superiorities of high reliability, cross-platform (Wang et al., 2009) and safe data sharing structure (Wang et al., 2009), object storage system is the most popular and has become the focus of cloud storage. Meanwhile, increasing network bandwidth and stable yet flexible network connections make it increasingly possible for clients to subscribe to high-quality services from data and software that reside solely in remote data centers (Ateniese et al., 2007 and 2011). Therefore, a reliable and light-weight processing mechanism should be established in the object systems in order to ensure that applications can be operated on using reliable data. However, the applications never encounter the object data directly, so the new data storage model provides many challenging design issues that provoke potential uncertainty about the security and performance of the overall system. The model of remote computation makes it much more difficult to fulfill guarantees about the verification and correctness of the data on untrusted servers. What is more serious is that in order to save money and storage space, service providers might neglect to keep or, in some cases, deliberately delete rarely accessed data files which belong to an ordinary client. Considering the large amount of outsourced data and the client's constrained resource capability, the core of the problem is how the client can find an efficient way to perform periodical integrity verifications without the local copy of data files.

Provable data possession (PDP) transforms a distributed system's ability to efficiently verify massive data sets on distributed object storage (Ko et al., 2009). PDP allows a client application to verify data objects in remote stores without transferring data to the client and without having to ask the store to access the entire object. It obtains very small amounts of metadata and network bandwidth and, by using spot-checking, allows the server to access the entire file. Nevertheless, the existing PDP schemes (Zhu et al., 2010) are able to force the client to renormalize into partitions that can be queried from a single replica, but lack the ability to gather data from across the entire cluster. Previously proposed solutions are incapable of adequately coping with the problems posed by dynamic change and inherent data corruption. The work of Schwarz and Miller (2006) meets most of the requirements for proving data possession, but provides less formal security analysis.

In order to solve this problem, we have designed a novel scheme and made use of the hash table structure in the object storage system in order to cooperate with the dynamic data. Given the need for security, the new scheme structure will pay more attention to verification and data damage in both object storage devices and auditing protection. Moreover, the secure storage implement, which also supports dynamic data updating, can be of vital importance during practical use.

3.2 OBJECT STORAGE SYSTEM USING SPDP

3.2.1 OBJECT STORAGE SYSTEM

Object stores can preserve end-to-end management and provide a level of virtualization and aggregation, whilst also guaranteeing data path security. An object store allows secure nonmediated and shared access to resource storage management. Our research is based on the implement of the OpenStack Object Storage (OpenStack Security Guide, 2013), which is an open source project. The OpenStack Object Storage program is designed for many different types of storage application. The nodes (including host node, proxy node, storage node, and authorized node) in the system are connected by a ring, which maps the storage data to physical devices. The ring ensures that every replication is stored in a separate zone. In addition, data replication uses a push model, with records and files generally only being copied from local to remote replicas.

An object is the basic storage entity and any optional metadata that represent the files stored in the object storage system. In an object store, metadata are an integral part of the object which are managed, stored, and recoverable with the object's client data. This built-in mechanism at the storage level considerably reduces the effort required to manage and store metadata in a distributed application along with the client data.

When uploading data to an object storage system, the stored data consist of a location, the object's ID, and the metadata, consisting of key/value pairs. However, a store security based on an object provides increased protection at the objects level rather than for whole volumes, thus allowing nontrusted hosts to sit on the networks and allowing shared access to storage without giving hosts access to all data in the volume. Object storage provides a richer computational environment within the stores based on invoking object methods (Juels and Kaliski, 2007). Remote network computation makes it much more difficult to achieve guarantees about the security and correctness of the data. Thus, it cannot verify the data using standard techniques.

We describe techniques for remote data checking that allow clients and applications to provably verify the object storage security and correctness of data remotely, i.e., without transferring the data back to the client. Our design can tackle the constraints of distributed object storage networks and avoid the transfer of large amounts of data across networks, performing the mass of computation at the object store.

3.2.2 DEFINITION OF SPDP

Before establishing the structure of the Secure Provable Data Possession (SPDP), we propose two preparatory and pivotal definitions:

DEFINITION 3.1   *(Object Verifiable Tag).* The tag used for object Verification is m emerged when an object b is activated by a message, and stored on the server together with the object.

With the use of an Object Verifiable Tag, which acts as verification metadata for the object, the object server can produce a proof that allows the client to check whether the server possesses the correct object or not.

DEFINITION 3.2   *(Secure Provable Data Possession).* An SPDP scheme is a kind of collection system including two algorithms and an interactive protocol *(KeyGen, TagObject, and Proof).*

- *KeyGen(1^k)* takes a security parameter k as the input, and returns a pair of matching public and secret keys *(pk, sk).*
- *TagObject(pk, sk, F)* is run by the client to generate the verification metadata. It takes as inputs a public key *pk*, a secret key *sk*, and a file *F*, and returns the verification metadata T_b.
- *Proof(pk, C, P($H_0|m$))* is run by the object server in order to generate a proof of possession. It takes as inputs a public key *pk* and motivated by the challenge *C*. It returns a proof of possession *V* that is determined by the challenge *C* and the posterior probability $P(H_0|m)$ to accept/reject the modification or addition. $P(H_0|m)$ offers the probability of server misbehavior detection on the condition of having observed the history of time variable m.

3.2.3 SPDP VERIFICATION ALGORITHM

We construct SPDP verification algorithm in five phases.
SPDP verification algorithm.

SPDP VERIFICATION ALGORITHM

1. *Setup.*
   - generate *KeyGen(1^k)*→*(pk, sk).*
2. *Query.*
   - select a block *b* to the server;
   - compute the verification metadata *TagObject(pk, sk, F)*;
   - obtain the result T_b (Each value $T_{i,b}$ is a function of the index *i* of the block *b*, $T_{i,b}$ and the file *F* are stored on the server).
3. *Challenge.*
   - for $T = 1 \le j \le c, c \in C$:
   - compute the indices i_j that is chosen using a pseudo-random permutation keyed with a fresh randomly-chosen key for each challenge *c*;
   - compute $T = T_{i1, bi,1} \cdot \ldots \cdot T_{ij, bi,j} \cdot \ldots \cdot T_{ic, bi,c}$ (note that $T_{ij, bi,j}$ is the i_j-th value).
4. *Forge.*
   - compute $P(H_0|m) = P(H_0) P(m| H_0)$;
   - compute $V = (pk, T, P(H_0|m))$.
5. *Check.*
   - check the validity *V* of the server's proof, and output "accept" or "reject".

In the Setup and Query sections, the client computes a verifiable tag T_b for each file block. To maintain consecutive storage, the client generates the random values by concatenating the block index *i* to a secret value, which prevents the use of the tag to obtain a proof for a different block. In the Challenge section, the spot-checking technique prevents the server from anticipating which blocks will be queried in each challenge.

During the course of the verification of metadata in the SPDP scheme, we check the object stored in the server from the beginning to the end. However, this process will inevitably cause a significant increase in costs and is time-consuming with regards to some aspects of computation and communication. It is obviously inappropriate to adopt such a primitive approach which will diminish the advantages of object storage: scaling arbitrarily up and down on demand.

3.2.4 HIERARCHICAL STRUCTURE

When a large amount of data and a high frequency of requests try to access the storage system, the crucial issues change from focusing on accuracy to finding an efficient approach which can be used to locate the object data. Previously employed methods often tend to prove unsatisfactory, in that they are inclined to pursue a higher searching rate and higher reliability but at the expense of extra memory consumption, corresponding with a high level of conflict in object metadata request.

A Bloom filter is a multi-hash function mapping rapid search algorithms. Compared to other data structures, it performs well in space-efficient representation and rapid insert/query. Bloom filters have received a great deal of attention not only from the research community but are also put into practice. The huge space savings often outweigh the cost of false-positives if these are kept at a sufficiently low rate. According to Google's Bigtable, in order to determine whether a value was in the object data, it uses a Bloom filter algorithm for each data file to maintain a Bloom filter data object.

One problem with the Bloom filter is that over time it fills up when it has to deal with a large set or stream of data. This means that at some point the Bloom filter becomes unusable due to its high error rates (Ahmadi and Wong, 2007; Rottenstreich et al., 2012). There exist various scenarios in which one would like to phase out or erase old items which were added a long time ago.

A basic Bloom filter can only represent a set, but neither allows for querying the multiplicities of an item, nor does it support deleting entries. As such, we have redesigned our Bloom filter to have sliding window semantics, as illustrated by Fig. 3.1. This figure also shows k independent hash functions $h_1, \ldots h_k$.

In order to support a sliding window, we have added an underlying bit vector with a fixed width parameter w. A large w quickly diminishes the space savings from using a Bloom filter. There will also be a lot of unused space which manifests itself as unused zeros. A small w may quickly lead to maximum counter values. Therefore, choosing the right value is a difficult trade-off which depends on the distribution of the data.

For our object system, we have adopted hash index tables (Tamassia and Triandopoulos, 2005; Askitis, 2009) on the object data hierarchical structure which can promptly confirm the position of the value through the key. In addition, a new tag is appended to the active file. After the append completes, an in-memory structure is updated and the hash table maps every key to a fixed-size structure giving the file, offset, and size of the most recently written tag for that key. When a write occurs, the key directory is automatically updated with the location of the latest data. The old data are still present on disk, but any new read will use the latest version available in the new directory. Reading a value is simple, and does not require more than a

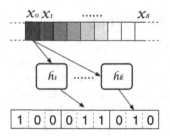

FIGURE 3.1

Sliding window of a Bloom filter.

single disk seek. We look up the key in our directory, and from there we are able to read the data using a value determined by the object ID, position, and size that are returned from that enquiry. Due to the necessity to speed up the hash-table rebuilding, the renewal process for compaction produces new data structures to preserve the location of the value.

The architecture for object storage (illustrated in Fig. 3.2) is based on a hierarchical structure with three layers representing the relationships between all objects for stored resources. The access layer offers a secret key throughout the course, and the processing layer manages verification and seeks for value, while the storage layer directly completes object storage on many physical devices.

By using this simple and understandable structure, our SPDP model can not only meet our speed goal but also support dynamic data operations, especially when writing an incoming stream of random items. In addition, the renew process can realize the object storage fast recovery and not lose data.

The benefits from the hash index tables of Bloom filters and huge space savings are that the object storage system can reduce 99% of disk access in practice and use a very small amount of memory space. So this approach greatly improves the performance of checking during the course of verification metadata.

3.2.5 THE ARCHITECTURE FOR SPDP MODEL

The architecture for SPDP model (illustrated in Fig. 3.3) shows two kinds of flows, real line and virtual line. The real line denotes the access from client to server; and the virtual line expresses the interaction between client and server.

An SPDP scheme checks that an outsourced storage site retains a file. The client preprocesses the file, generating a small piece of metadata which is locally stored, then transmits the file to the server and may delete its local copy. The server stores

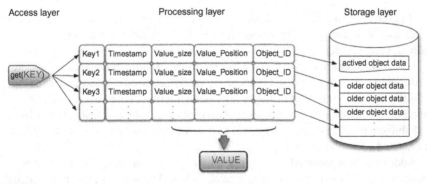

FIGURE 3.2

Hierarchical structure for object storage.

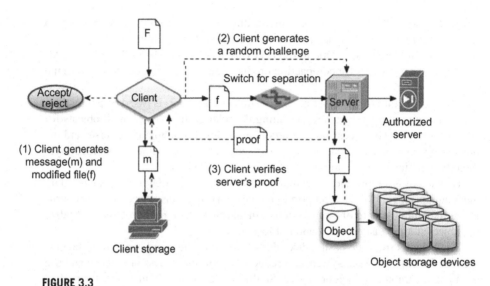

FIGURE 3.3

The architecture for SPDP model.

the file and responds to challenges issued by the client. The details of the process can be described as follows:

1. The client changes the content or property of the file and stores it at the server;
2. Before deleting the local copy of the file, the client executes a data possession challenge to make sure the server has successfully stored the file;
3. The server then asks to compute a function of the stored file, which it sends back to the client. Using its local metadata, the client verifies the response.

The server must answer challenges from the client and failure to do so represents a data loss. However, the server is not trusted. Even though the file is totally or partially missing, the server may try to convince the client that it possesses the file. The server's motivations for misbehavior can be diverse and include reclaiming storage by discarding data that have not been or are rarely accessed (for monetary reasons), or hiding a data loss incident (due to management errors, hardware failure, or compromise by outside or inside attacks). The goal of an SPDP scheme that achieves probabilistic proof of data possession is to detect server misbehavior when the server has deleted a fraction of the file.

Additionally, authorized servers run an authentication service to receive object connection parameters and an authentication token. The server's response to a challenge consists of a small, constant value, and notably the server does not send back to the client any of the file blocks. Therefore, by using a hash table hierarchy, the object data can be easily and quickly positioned in the object storage devices.

3.3 SECURITY ANALYSIS AND IMPLEMENTATION

3.3.1 SPDP PERFORMANCE ANALYSIS

The important performance parameters of an SPDP scheme include:

- Computation complexity: The computational cost to preprocess a file at Client (C), to generate a proof of possession at Server (S), and to verify such a proof (at C);
- Object access complexity: The number of files accessed to generate a proof of possession (at S);
- Communication complexity: The amount of data transferred (between C and S).

For a scalable data store solution, the amount of computation and files accessed at the server should be minimized, as the server may be involved in concurrent interactions with many clients. We stress that an efficient SPDP scheme cannot consist of retrieving entire object data without considering minimizing network communication bandwidth. Whilst relevant, the computational complexity of the client is not of great importance, even though our schemes also seek to minimize this complexity.

In order to meet these performance goals, our SPDP schemes sample the server's storage by accessing a random subset of files. In doing so, the PDP schemes provide a probabilistic guarantee of possession, as a deterministic guarantee cannot be provided without accessing every file. In fact, uniquely in our SPDP scheme, the client may ask for a proof for all the files, making the data possession guarantee deterministic. Sampling proves that data possession with high probability is based on accessing a limited amount of data in the file, which radically alters the performance of proving data possession.

The server and client computation is expressed as the total cost of performing modular exponentiation operations. In order to maintain a level of simplicity, the security parameter is not included as a factor when estimating the relevant costs. However, in the creation of a security strategy, the checking result can be a critical factor in the detection of misbehavior.

3.3.2 APPROVED DIRECTORIES OPTIMIZATION

Our object storage system can store, retrieve, and delete objects stored on local devices. Each object is stored using a path derived from the object name's hash and the operation's timestamp. Any deletion or modification would be treated as a version of the file. This ensures that deleted or modified files are replicated correctly and older versions do not magically reappear in failure scenarios. With dynamic verifiable SPDP, a distributed replicated object store will create multiple versions of data and update currency information every time an object changes, and all of these objects will be remotely verifiable, which makes it a tremendously complex task.

Approved directories that associate current versions of objects in hash files have been addressed in order to reduce the scale of the information (Yamamoto et al., 2007; Goodrich et al., 2008). The object replication process reads these hash files, validating objects without consulting the index. It then transmits the hashes to each remote server that should hold the partition, and only approved directories with differing hashes on the remote server are updated. After pushing files to the remote server, the replication process prompts it to recalculate hashes for the updated secure directories. This optimization improves the performance of approved directories by reducing the average query time, and guarantees the updated path security at the same time.

3.3.3 SECURE PROTECTION STRATEGY

In our security strategy, the checking of a server's proof is connected with knowledge of misbehavior detection. If the output is "accept," the Check section will execute a proof generation repeatedly until it extracts the selected blocks. On the other hand, if the Check section cannot extract blocks, then a "reject" response will issue forth with more than negligible probability.

Protection against the corruption of a small portion of the data is necessary in order to handle servers that try to hide data loss incidents. This applies to servers that wish to preserve their reputation. Data loss incidents may be accidental. A practical and robust security mechanism should be taken into sufficient consideration for detecting data corruption and be impervious to data corruption.

In the SPDP model, $P(H_0|m)$ (using $P(detect)$ to replace) has been presented to denote the probability of server misbehavior detection. We continue to analyze $P(damage)$ and $P(attack)$ which depend on the deletion strategy of attackers and the auditing strategy of clients, respectively. $P(damage)$ denotes the probability of original data damage; $P(attack)$ denotes the probability of successful attack. Thus:

$P(attack) = P(damage)(1-P(detect))$

An attack is successful if the attacker causes damage to the original data or the attacker is not detected by the auditing mechanism. When data corruption is detected, the auditor must handle the problem in time. Even when data corruption is not detected, a secure protection strategy should ensure that no data are lost. We offer a secure protection strategy as follows:

1. The auditor will be detected with a high probability if the server corruptions exceed the maximum likelihood estimator of $P(detect)$;
2. The auditor will recover the data with high probability if the server corrupts at the maximum likelihood estimator of $P(damage)$ for statistical samples.

The second probability option for the state of object storage system seems a more reasonable choice as it makes full use of prior knowledge and observation of historical information.

3.4 ROBUST AUDITING WITH AUTHENTICATION SYSTEM

In this section, we propose event auditing and log analyzing to make any object storage data-checking scheme based on an authentication system of OpenStack Object

Storage more robust. In order to ensure this robustness, we integrate the auditor unit with data checking and verification to strengthen the guarantee achieved.

3.4.1 ROBUST AUDITING

The auditor unit in an authorized server will repeatedly crawl on the local server to test the integrity of the object, file, and account information. Once incomplete data (e.g., if there is bit rot that might alter the code) are found, the file will be isolated. Then a replicator would replace the problem file using other copies of the file. The replicator here is used to compare the local data with each remote copy which has been subject to the replication process to ensure that they all contain the latest version. Object replication uses a hash list to quickly compare each child of a virtual section. If other errors occur, for example a failure in finding the desired object list in a server, the error information will be recorded in the log.

3.4.2 AUTHORIZED SERVER

The authentication/authorization (auth) part of an authorized server can be an external system or a subsystem run within our object storage system. The clients can pass each request using an auth token (a string which can be sent back to the auth system for validation), and the server validates each token and caches the result. The token does not change from request to request. When presented with a valid token, the auth system responds with an overall expiration within seconds. The server will cache the token up to the expiration time.

3.4.3 LARGE OBJECT PROCESSING

Our SPDP schemes put no restriction on the format of the data, and do not have to be encrypted in particular files stored at the server. This feature is of great utility since we anticipate that SPDP schemes will have the biggest impact when used for large public repositories (e.g., digital libraries, astronomy/medical/legal repositories, archives, etc.).

Large object processing has gone through various iterations before settling on implementation. In order to maintain an even dispersion of disk usage throughout the cluster, the obvious storage pattern is to simply split larger objects into smaller segments, which can then be glued together during a read. However, the eventual consistency window of the container listings could theoretically cause a GET method on the manifest object to return a whole invalid object for that short term, and can potentially affect this manifest approach based on the path prefix. In reality this is an unlikely scenario, unless you are running very high concurrent uploads in a limited testing environment, which isn't running object-updaters or container-replicators. Large object processing is a living feature which will continue to be improved and may evolve over time.

3.5 **EXPERIMENTAL RESULTS**

Through security analysis and implementation, we have demonstrated the secure protection strategy for object storage. The Monte-Carlo simulation has been used to determine the probability of damage, through modeling an attacker that corrupts object data randomly. Our experimental results use specific parameters for encoding and data checking. As illustrated in Fig. 3.4, the corruptions are divided into two varieties: content corruption and index corruption. The simulation then runs different numbers of object data corruptions in order to analyze the probability of data damage.

We conducted experiments on an Intel Core 2 processor with 2.2 GHz. The maximum allowable size for a storage object upon upload is 5 GB but it also supports the segmentation of large objects. For metadata, the total byte length of any key/value pair cannot exceed 4 kB. The experimental results indicate that the probability of damage will increase with the augmentation of corrupted object data, but the loss of data content will more easily cause damage to stored resources. Hence, it is necessary to establish specific original data protection or seek a hidden isolation strategy to achieve specific secure storage goals. Subsequently, we evaluated the performance of our SPDP scheme at the time of checking proof for different sizes of object metadata (shown in Fig. 3.5). Compared to the original PDP scheme, our SPDP scheme can achieve efficiency of verification and simultaneously ensure storage security.

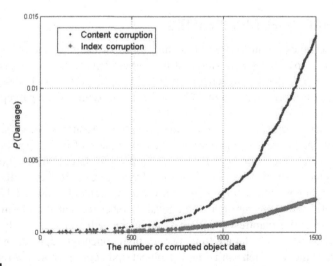

FIGURE 3.4

The results of damage for two types of data corruptions.

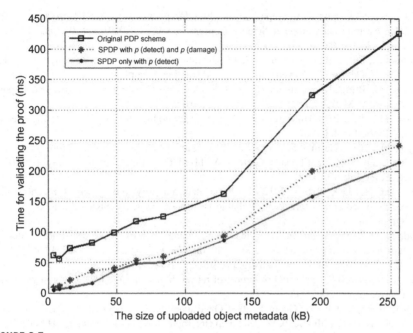

FIGURE 3.5

Verification time for different object metadata.

3.6 CONCLUSIONS

In this chapter, we have presented the architecture of the SPDP scheme for use in an object storage system. Based on the SPDP algorithm and the hierarchical structure, we have established data authorization between clients and servers. Our design works well with object storage networks and avoids the transfer of large amounts of data across networks, performing bulk computation at the data store. The results of our experiments show that our scheme can guarantee object storage security but still needs further improvement when dealing with original data protection under the approved directories optimization and protection strategy.

REFERENCES

Ahmadi, M., Wong, S., 2007. A cache architecture for counting bloom filters. In: 15th International Conference on Networks (ICON-2007), p. 218, doi:10.1109/ICON.2007.4444089, ISBN 978-1-4244-1229-7.

Alexander, K., Wälde, J., 2011. Efficient denial of service attacks on web application platforms, 28th Chaos Communication Congress, Berlin, Germany.

Askitis, N., 2009. Fast and compact hash tables for integer keys. In: Proceedings of the 32nd Australasian Computer Science Conference (ACSC 2009), vol. 91, pp. 113–122. ISBN 978-1-920682-72-9.

Ateniese, G., Burns, R., Curtmola, R., 2007. Provable data possession at untrusted stores. In: CCS'07, October 29–November 2, 2007, Alexandria, Virginia.

Ateniese, G., Burns, R., Curtmola, R., 2011. Remote data checking using provable data possession. ACM Trans. Info. Syst. Sec. 14 (1), Article 12.

Barlow, M., 2013. Real-Time Big Data Analytics: Emerging Architecture. O'Reilly Media, Inc., Sebastopol, CA.

Beryer, M., 2011. Gartner Says Solving 'Big Data' Challenge Involves More Than Just Managing Volumes of Data. Gartner. Archived from the original on July 10, 2011. Retrieved July 13, 2011.

Chen, H.C.H., Lee, P.P.C., 2012. Enabling data integrity protection in regenerating-coding-based cloud storage. In: Reliable Distributed Systems (SRDS), 2012 IEEE 31st Symposium.

Goodrich, M.T., Papamanthou, C., Tamassia, R., Triandopoulos, N., 2008. Athos: Efficient authentication of outsourced file systems. In: Wu, T.-C. (Ed.), ISC 2008, LNCS 5222. Springer-Verlag, Berlin, Heidelberg, pp. 80–96.

Juels, A., Kaliski, B.S., 2007. PORs: proofs of retrievability for large files. Cryptology ePrint archive, Report 2007/243.

Ko, S.Y., Hoque, I., Cho, B., Gupta, I., 2009. On availability of intermediate data in cloud computations. Proc. 12th Usenix Workshop on Hot Topics in Operating Systems (HotOS XII).

Kubiatowicz, J., Bindel, D., Czerwinski, Y., Geels, S., Eaton, D., Gummadi, R., et al., 2000. Oceanstore: An Architecture for Global-Scale Persistent Storage. ACM SIGPLAN Notices, USA.190–201.

Maniatis, P., Roussopoulos, M., Giuli, T., Rosenthal, D., Baker, M., Muliadi, Y., 2005. The LOCKSS peer-to-peer digital preservation system. ACM Transactions on Computing Systems 23 (1), 2–50.

OpenStack Security Guide, 2013. OpenStack Foundation, Havana. Copyright 1. Some rights reserved.

Rottenstreich, O., Kanizo, Y., Keslassy, I., 2012. The variable-increment counting bloom filter. In: 31st Annual IEEE International Conference on Computer Communications, Infocom 2012, pp. 1880–1888, doi:10.1109/INFCOM.2012.6195563, ISBN 978-1-4673-0773-4.

Schwarz, T.S.J., Miller, E.L., 2006. Store, forget, and check: using algebraic signatures to check remotely administered storage Proceedings of the 26th IEEE International Conference on Distributed Computing Systems (ICDCS'06). IEEE, Los Alamitos, CA.

Snijders, C., Matzat, U., Reips, U.-D., 2012. 'Big Data': big gaps of knowledge in the field of Internet. International Journal of Internet Science 7, 1–5.

Tamassia, R., Triandopoulos, N., 2005. Computational Bounds on Hierarchical Data Processing With Applications to Information Security. ICALP.

Wang, C., Wang, Q., Ren, K., Lou, W., 2009. Ensuring data storage security in cloud computing Proceedings of 17th International Workshop on Quality of Service (IWQoS). IEEE, Los Alamitos, CA.1–9.

Wang, Q., Wang, C., Lim, J., Ren, K., Lou, W., 2009. Enabling public verifiability and data dynamics for storage security in cloud computing. Computer Science Volume 5789, 355–370.

Yamamoto, G., Oda, S., Aoki, K., 2007. Fast integrity for large data. Proceedings of SPEED '07. European Network of Excellence (ECRYPT), Amsterdam, Netherlands.

Yumerefendi, A.Y., Chase, J., 2007. Strong accountability for network storage. Proceedings of FAST. China Ship Scientific Research Center (CSSRC), Shanghai, China.

Zhu, Y., Wang, H., Hu, Z., Ahn, G-J., Hu, H., Yau, S.S., 2010. Efficient provable data possession for hybird clouds. In: CCS'10, October 4–8, 2010, Chicago, Illinois, USA.

The responsive tourism logistics from local public transport domain: the case of Pattaya city

4

W. Ngamsirijit

National Institute of Development Administration, Bangkok, Thailand

CHAPTER OUTLINE

4.1 INTRODUCTION

Due to the dynamic nature of tourism demand and supply, tourism logistics management can be challenging, especially in designing and implementing a logistics system for the public transport domain (Naim et al., 2006). Faced with various unexpected changes, logistics system requirements and constraints can quickly evolve. As such, most public transportation development projects conducted in tourist cities are often unsuccessful. Pattaya city, one of the most popular tourist cities in Thailand, is facing these dynamic and complex challenges both in terms of supply and demand. Accompanying Pattaya's rapid development and population explosion, particularly

Big Data and Smart Service Systems. DOI: http://dx.doi.org/10.1016/B978-0-12-812013-2.00004-6

evident after the year 2000, have been many attempts to improve the tourism infrastructure through revamping and upgrading the transportation grid, with the public transport often being assigned a central role. There are periodic episodes of intense focus on Pattaya's main mode of public transport, the so-called *baht bus*, as a proposed major element in such plans, but most of the attempted projects have ended up as mere appendages to other transportation models which have been proposed and pursued simultaneously. Furthermore, with such diversity in views about the role of the baht bus in the overall makeup of available transportation (i.e., with some suggesting that it be discarded, while others argued for its improvement), implementation of earlier visions of the baht bus' role have become increasingly fraught and diluted. Consequently, only minor improvements in the sections of the proposals which addressed the baht bus were ever implemented. Moreover, key proposals for improvements to the operation of the baht bus; such as schemes to limit traffic volume, streamline baht bus routes, and implement bus service substitutes, fell by the wayside from their inception, as they encountered resistance from entrenched forces who opposed the reordering.

With attempts to promote the logistics supporting creative tourism initiative in 2011, the National Research Council of Thailand (NCRT) and the Thailand Research Fund (TRF) had provided funding for a research project concerning tourist logistics entitled "The study of Demand Responsive Transportation (DRT) for Pattaya tourism service." This was designed to enhance the baht bus' public transport capability, particularly in relation to tourism. This chapter illustrates the framework and methodology for the design and implementation of these sorts of responsive tourism logistics in Pattaya. In doing so, the framework for the local public transport tourism domain has been once again resurrected and discussed, along with what many viewed as a promising new approach to urban transport design.

4.2 PREVIOUS RESEARCH

In general, tourism logistics should be considered in the context of logistics management. The design of the flow of goods, people, information, and knowledge must harmonize with the characteristics of the city in order to promote a high-quality and high-performing support for tourism. When considering economic implications, it is logical that if transport is limited or ineffective, visitors are likely to respond by altering their itinerary or opting to travel to other destinations. Consequently, this affects a city's ability to compete on the macrolevel (Predeaux, 2000). Unlike the traditional system of public transportation, the contemporary system has evolved from focusing solely on the efficiency aspects of logistics and building system capabilities to responding to distinct situations arising within industry. Modern concepts of responsiveness have been overwhelmingly concerned with supply chain and logistics fields. This manifests itself in the ability to meet customer needs and to react to market changes within a reasonable time in order to secure a competitive advantage (Kritchanchai and MacCarthy, 1999; Koffman, 2004; Holweg, 2005). Transport can achieve this sort of responsiveness by having various forms of transport available in particular areas, by establishing a variety of routes services, and by forming integrated transport networks so that the customer service level can be enhanced. In addition, transportation should have the flexibility to be able to adapt to a variety of transportation purposes. Information pertaining to the transport system must therefore be accurate and precise. Demand for information must be well understood, taking into account the change in the nature of the demand for transport including longer and more specialized transport links, greater sensitivity to the timing of connections, arrivals, and departures, an expanded reliance on communication and computer networks, greater speed of movement and transactions, and the provision standard equipment and procedures (Janelle and Beuthe, 1997). In the tourism industry, one of the situations that has emerged is a focus on extracting new value from the attractions and destinations by means of creative tourism. This has been promoted as means of adding value to both services and the city in many countries (Lindroth et al., 2007; Richards, 2013). In most cases, creative tourism does not involve a major transformation of the destination but merely the addition of value to existing sites and cultural activities, i.e., offering activities and workshops at local places or the opportunity to visit and live with local people. As such, logistics infrastructure development is considered an important mechanism by which travel satisfaction can be promoted and foster interest in new attractions. The main objective has radically altered so that performance is now measured by travel responsiveness rather than travel capacity, as with the more traditional logistics solutions in which new transport modes are used predominantly as a means to increase capacity.

4.3 PROBLEMS AND CHALLENGES

The system of tourism logistics has not yet been widely used to develop economic potential in Thailand because of limitations in communication and coordination between organizations involved in the tourism industry. There is also a lack of support for enhancing tourism infrastructure and instead greater attention is paid to marketing. This is one of the reasons for the low growth rate of the tourism industry. In order to support the growth of the tourism industry on the basis of value and experience creation for the tourists, the transportation system must be improved and developed in an attempt to respond to the transportation needs of the tourists. This responsiveness is here considered to be a key operational performance target for logistics in Pattaya's creative tourism market. Creative tourism is delivered through scheduled activities and workshops. In addition, tourists may choose to travel with a package tour program with prescribed activities and visits not limited to, but often inclusive of, creative tourism elements. Transportation must be adequately responsive for successive scheduled groups of tourists and in order to accommodate their preferences for visiting many attractions within a planned period of time. Of course, in order to meet the needs of creative tourism travelers, especially when they could change their itinerary, route, and even mode of transportation at short notice, the system must be able to estimate the travel demands of different types of tourists, receive travel requirements from the passengers, be able to schedule vehicles in a more dynamic and flexible way by applying postponement strategies, adjusting for unforeseen eventualities, and centralizing transit/transfer points as well as building collaboration among the different players.

The main challenge for tourism logistics is that public transportation vehicles in Pattaya currently utilize nonfixed rather than fixed routes. The most popular modes of transport are taxis, private vehicle rent, and motorcycles. Even the baht bus designated to operate on the basis of a fixed route has evolved to operate a nonfixed route in reaction to behavioral and social aspects of Pattaya tourists and residents. Baht bus drivers will adjust the routes when they believe there are too many vehicles on a particular route, resulting in many unoccupied passenger seats. People are used to hopping on and off the bus freely along the route and they do not seem to wait in line at prescribed bus stops. Furthermore, baht bus drivers often pull over and park their vehicles in a way that blocks the designated bus lane.

The traffic congestion issue is also challenging for responsive tourism logistics because of the results which come from temporarily adjusting routes to serve changing demand. This is because when a new route is formed to meet passenger needs, old routes are not terminated but remain in operation. This is deemed to be one of the contributing factors to situations in which, outside peak hours, most baht buses run empty or nearly empty. In order to be sensitive to such concerns, careful designing and planning for tourism logistics in Pattaya must be taken into account during decision-making when considering whether a baht bus should operate nonfixed routes, fixed routes, or an integrated semifixed route.

4.4 TOURISM DEMAND AND SUPPLY CHARACTERISTICS

Pattaya city is a tourist destination. Most of the local communities have been transformed into commercial communities providing tourist services and facilities due to the successful nurturing of tourism in the area. Ninety percent of the total labor market has an occupation related to the tourist industry. These communities are facing population migration from all regions of the country and from foreign countries as people flock to the area to work and live in the city. Consequently, the social conditions are complex and varied. There are 38 tourist attractions within Pattaya city itself and 12 on the periphery of the city (Table 4.1).

The initial development of guidelines for sustainable tourism development in Pattaya city starts with describing the vision for the new city image as "New Pattaya: The World Class Greenovative Tourism City." This concept also involves applying the so-called "3Rs" in order to fully realize this vision. These consist of: (1) rebrand, (2) revitalize and develop facilities, and (3) raising capacity and capability. To promote tourism development based on such a plan, four development areas have been outlined as follows:

- Eco-tourism: to preserve marine nature areas with beautiful coral reefs around the island from the beach area of Pattaya city and Jomtien Beach to the Koh Larn and surrounding islands.

Table 4.1 List of tourist attractions of Pattaya city

Tourist attractions in the city				Tourist attractions outside the city	
1	Pattaya water park	20	Pattaya Pirom Submarine	39	Khao Cheechan Buddha Image
2	Bottle museum	21	Wong Prachan beach	40	Wat Yan Sang Wararam
3	The Sanctuary of Truth	22	Elephant Garden	41	Nong Nooch Garden and Resort
4	Mini Siam	23	Superkart Racing	42	The Million Years Stone Park & Pattaya Crocodile Farm
5	Pattaya Beach	24	Monster World	43	Elephant Village Pattaya
6	Wongamat beach	25	Tuxedo Magic Castle	44	Three Kingdoms Park
7	Jomtien beach	26	Siriphon Orchid Farm	45	The Horseshoe Point Resort Pattaya
8	Koh Larn	27	Paintball Park and Bungee Jump	46	Sriracha Tiger Zoo
9	Mabprachan reservior	28	Snake Show	47	Khao Kheow Open Zoo
10	Point of View Pattaya	29	NS P Snake Show	48	Bira International Circuit
11	Suan Chaloemphrakiat	30	Pattaya Airpark	49	Pattaya Flying Club
12	Pattaya Kart Speedway	31	Lakeland Water Cable Ski	50	Silver Lake Vineyard
13	Wang Sam Sien	32	S K Pattaya Ranch		
14	Krom Luang Chumphon Khet Udomsak monument	33	Chang Siam		
15	Viharna Sien	34	Elephants Trekking		
16	Underwater World	35	Wonderland Pattaya		
17	Ripley's Believe It or Not! museum	36	EasyKart		
18	Sukhawadee	37	Pattaya Floating Market		
19	Khao Phra Tamnak	38	Pattaya Circus		

- The wide range of tourism: all areas of Pattaya municipality and some parts of Jomtien municipality (from urban areas of south Pattaya to Jomtien and railroad east) have plans to organize and improve the tourism capacity.
- Culture and tourism in the designated area of special interest include the city's east side, from the eastern boundary of the railway line to National Highway No. 7, to the southern stretch of Highway 36 and Na-Jomtien area. To promote various cultural tourism activities, the city center is linked to this area by developing four routes for the bus transportation network covering Huai Yai, Pattaya, and Jomtien.
- The natural resources and tourism in the rest of the areas must preserve such natural resources as water and forest, promoting local agricultural products, and developing areas with low density and large plots of land.

In spite of the strong focus of the government on providing an efficient public transport system to connect to other places with the city, there is also the need to improve the transport system within the city itself. The routes and road networks in the city have their own constraints and cannot be increased or expanded due to the limitation of space within the city. It is imperative for logistics planning that the issues facing the city be resolved by providing, for instance, a city-central transportation center which can bring together all transport networks to facilitate a more straight-forward travel, the city park buildings and related services, a monorail transportation system to link the network to various destinations for the convenience and benefit of tourists in the future. Pattaya is a city that has potential in terms of the growing numbers of tourists, a more diverse variety of tourists, and certain geographical advantages. Nevertheless, at present the city's public transportation system has no regular bus services but only baht buses and motorcycle services. Improving baht bus services could provide a great number of possibilities for the city in accordance with the city's expansion plan to increase tourist attractions and to enhance the capability of existing infrastructures including roads and establishments.

Key input information for responsive transportation planning is data relating to the travel behavior of tourists. It is a fact that the travel behavior of tourists in each city is different. In order to design a responsive transportation system, there is a requisite need for a clear understanding of the behavioral patterns of tourists traveling around the city. Studies on travel behavior are regularly conducted as new tourism areas and cities are developed. The models used in this research include residential location choice, auto availability choice, and trip-making behavior. They provide understanding of the relationships between factors like traveling distance, household characteristics, and the number of vehicles used whilst traveling.

Travel behavior can be affected by passengers' decision-making. When looking at the behavior of tourists, they often tend to make last-minute, or short-term, decisions when selecting destination modes of transportation and the extent of travel frequency, rather than making these decisions in a more measured manner. The influencing factors for short-term decisions include the distance to the destination, service level of available transportation, the attraction of the places, and so on. In contrast, those who are resident in the city tend to make more premeditated, medium-term decisions, which are influenced by factors such as vehicle ownership. Long-term decisions consist of the selection of a workplace, types of residences, and residential location. When considering in the context of a tourism city, tourists not only travel but may also stay longer or even turn out to be residents. Thus, a common set of decision-making factors are summarized below:

- Residential location includes the number of attractions, tourist density, number of establishments, accommodation rates, type of accommodation, and vehicle accessibility.
- Tourist characteristics include travel objectives, lifestyles, travel companions, and time allotted for travel.
- Travel characteristics include travel distances, type of transport vehicles, number of places visited, frequency of visits to the same places, departure time for travel, arrival time to accommodation, travel time spent, and travel plan changes.

A Pattaya tourist questionnaire survey of 500 respondents was conducted during October–November 2010. In the study, the samples consist only of tourists who stay overnight in Pattaya, traveled by public transport, and spent more than one night in areas of North Pattaya, Central Pattaya, South Pattaya, and Jomtien Beach. It did not survey citizens and tourist groups that visited the city through traditional tour agency services. The statistical analysis and cluster analysis show that the nature of tourism demand in each area varies in many aspects. Based on the results, the characteristics of public transportation consistent with Pattaya tourism demand are described as follows:

- Tourist demand can be divided into two groups based on the location: (1) North Pattaya and (2) Central Pattaya, South Pattaya, Jomtien Beach.
- Public transport routes covering Central Pattaya, South Pattaya, and Jomtien Beach should have a connection to more remote Pattaya areas, while routes around North Pattaya should cover areas within the Pattaya and around the city.
- Public transport routes from Central Pattaya, South Pattaya, and Jomtien Beach have greater flexibility than the one from North Pattaya, due to factors such as the large number of places tourists visit and the adjustment of travel plans during a day trip.
- A bus from North Pattaya area should be more frequent than those serving the other areas. This is because tourists have to make frequent vehicle connections and they tend to travel within the city and around Pattaya.
- Departure and return times to accommodation for most tourists are relatively similar. Services must be provided for these travel times and do not have to extend into less busy periods.

Overall, the results illustrate that areas of Central Pattaya, South Pattaya, and Jomtien Beach are likely to be more appropriate for DRT than the North Pattaya area which has a high density of tourist traffic operating within the city.

4.5 PUBLIC TRANSPORTATIONS

The types of public transport vehicles used by tourists are nonfixed route types of conveyance including baht bus, van, and taxi. The baht bus is a typical and cheap mode of transportation for traveling in the city. Currently, the city has a total of five baht bus lines: Chareonratpattana village–Na Jomtien line, City Circle line, Naklua–Siam Country Club line, North Pattaya–Central Pattaya, and Bali Hai Pier–Bang Lamung District Office. To add or adjust baht bus lines requires the permission of the Ministry of Transport. The committee will conduct a meeting to discuss and consider the appropriateness of the new proposed route. In terms of transport regulation, it is required that baht buses operating on designated routes run from at least 0830–1630 hours.

However, due to the high volume of tourists and independent operation of the baht buses, drivers are free to drive around and pick up passengers at will. In other words, an adjustment of vehicle routes informally takes place during the journey. Drivers adjust their route when they consider there are too many vehicles on the route and unoccupied seats on the vehicle. Another reason for adjusting the route is that a cooperative has been concerned about the service level in certain areas and that the number of passengers has recently increased. Some routes are therefore temporarily established to serve these passengers. The majority of baht buses operate in the vicinity of the beach due to the high travel demand from tourists. In order to receive more fares and serve the greatest possible number of passengers, transfer points are located around the intersections of major roads. In doing so, drivers can alter their intended destination when the initial route has few or no passengers. Transfer points can reduce the risk from any uncertainty in demand. However, it could be argued that this approach can cause traffic congestion on main streets, especially during peak periods. Transportation routes overlap and vehicles are often overcrowded on the main routes. Responding to the needs of passengers and increasing flexibility on existing routes are currently achieved by allocating a large proportion of vehicles to areas with a high density of tourists and attractions. Few vehicles operate around the perimeters of the city; and these tend to pick up passengers and charge fares as a group. This shows that the baht bus service is responsive only to passenger volumes, not actual travel needs. It is not operated by clearly defining passenger needs and then allocating the vehicles.

4.6 PROXIMITY OF TOURIST ATTRACTIONS

In order to diversify Pattaya tourism beyond the traditional attractions of nightlife entertainment and to promote local features such as sport, nature and culture, and tourism development, it would be necessary to develop additional clusters of tourism facilities. These would need to be located outside the entertainment-based businesses of central Pattaya, which themselves form only a part of the 38 available tourist attractions in and close to the municipal center. There are another 12 places with development potential outside the city center.

Assessing the responsiveness of the baht bus is achieved by first assessing the distances between the current bus routes and attractions. This can illustrate how current baht bus operations can respond to tourist needs when they want to use the services to visit attractions. The calculation of the distances from the attraction to the road, i.e., bus route and attraction location are specified by using their Universal Transverse Mercator coordinate system. In a tourism context, responsive transportation is about the ability to provide services that have coverage which extends to major attractions, bus routes which operate between a variety of possible attractions to give the tourists greater choice, and proximity of the bus stop to the attractions. Based on the analysis of four bus routes, i.e., Chareonratpattana village–Na Jomtien, Pattaya Circle, North Pattaya–Central Pattaya, and Bali Hai pier–Bang Lamung district office, a number of different tourist attractions can be reached by each of the bus routes. The service is considered responsive when baht bus routes directly pass the attractions and passengers are able to select from a variety of routes and do not have to walk great distances to and from the attractions. However, only 14 (i.e., 36.8%) of the 38 primary attractions are covered by current baht bus routes.

4.7 CAPACITY FLEXIBILITY MODEL FOR RESPONSIVE TRANSPORTATIONS

Responsiveness within the transportation system can also be enhanced by the way it is operated as well as the construction of its infrastructure. To achieve responsiveness, the transportation system must improve the dimension of flexibility in particular. By means of flexibility, the system will have additional capacity to support greater passenger volumes. Once it is well equipped, responsiveness can be enhanced by managing operations to support the travel needs of those passengers in specific volumes. In assessing the transportation performance in supply perspectives, Morlok and Chang (2004) studied the ability of the transportation system to respond to demand uncertainty by using the principle of "base capacity flexibility." The calculation of capacity flexibility starts by assessing the maximum capacity of transporting containers or passengers (MAXCAP model) and this capacity, the so-called "base pattern capacity" is employed as baseline to reflect the flexibility of the system. The MAXCAP model contains objective function and constraints.

$$\max z_M = \sum_{r=1}^{R} x_r \qquad (4.1)$$

where

x_r = loaded passenger volume on traffic lane r (passengers/month)
r = lane, referring to origin and destination node (OD) pair

constrained by:

$$x_r = \alpha_r \cdot \left[\sum_{r=1}^{R} x_r \right] \forall r \qquad (4.2)$$

where

α_r = traffic pattern factors for each path p

$$\sum_{p \in P_r} \phi_p \cdot f_p = x_r \ \forall r \tag{4.3}$$

$$\sum_{p \in B_a} (f_p + e_p) \leq \gamma \cdot w_a \ \forall a \tag{4.4}$$

where

f_p = loaded passenger volume on path p (passengers/month)
ϕ_p = average passenger–load factor on each path p
P_r = set of paths that service the same OD pair
e_p = empty passenger volume on path p (passengers/month)
B_a = set of paths sharing arc a
w_a = vehicle volume on each arc a
γ = passenger capacity of vehicle (passengers/vehicle).

$$\sum_{a=1}^{A} [T_a \cdot w_a] \leq H_{\text{car}} \tag{4.5}$$

$$\sum_{a \in E_n} w_a = \sum_{a \in V_n} w_a \ \forall n \tag{4.6}$$

$$\sum_{p \in F_n} (f_p + e_p) = \sum_{p \in M_n} (f_p + e_p) \forall n \tag{4.7}$$

where

T_a = vehicle travel time on arc a (hour),
H_{car} = vehicle hours available (vehicle-hour/month),
E_n, V_n = set of arcs entering, leaving terminal n, and
F_n, M_n = set of paths entering, leaving terminal n.

Fig. 4.1 shows the locations of transportation (C, G, H, K, L, O, S) and paths between locations (1–12) to determine the capacity flexibility. These paths are the shortest route (Option 1) and it is referred to the base case for comparing alternative routes for Options 2 and 3. The capacity flexibility for each option is different due to the selected routes for transportation. The study examines the maximum container-loading capacities of the route within the network with the minimum operating costs. This flexibility is created by considering three routing options as follows:

- Route Option 1: Shortest route (may have transition between the start and the destination);
- Route Option 2: Shortest route and second shortest route with no transition;
- Route Option 3: Route satisfying service level.

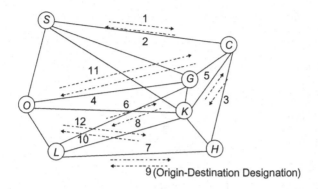

FIGURE 4.1

Model of locations and paths selected in transportation.

Table 4.2 List of parameters and values for base pattern capacity calculation in the Pattaya Circle route

	Pattaya Circle route	
Variable	**First path (1–4)**	**Second path (5–9)**
α_r	0.65	0.35
f_p	1600	370
Φ_p	0.7	0.5
e_p	2300	790
w_a	380	115
γ	10	10
T_a	Shown below	Shown below
H_{car}	1980	1980

4.8 CAPACITY CONSIDERATIONS OF BAHT BUS ROUTE

According to the capacity flexibility model, the parameters and values used to determine the base pattern capacity of the Pattaya Circle route, which mainly covers areas of Central Pattaya and South Pattaya, are shown in Table 4.2. The optimization method employed in the capacity flexibility model is based on linear programming to derive the maximum capacity under various constraints mentioned above. On the Pattaya Circle route (see Fig. 4.2), there are nine points illustrating the bus routes represented by x_{11}, x_{12}, x_{13}, x_{14}, x_{21}, x_{22}, x_{23}, x_{24}, and x_{25}.

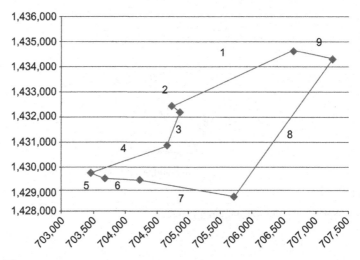

FIGURE 4.2

Simple illustration of the Pattaya Circle route.

The capacity flexibility of the Pattaya Circle route can be calculated as follows:

Objective function

Maximize capacity $= x_{11} + x_{12} + x_{13} + x_{14} + x_{21} + x_{22} + x_{23} + x_{24} + x_{25}.$

Constraints:

Constraint 1: Number of passengers in the jth arc of the ith path must be equal to the travel factor of each arc of total passengers in the ith path.

$$x_{11} = x_{12} = x_{13} = x_{14} = 0.65(\textstyle\sum x_1)$$

$$x_{21} = x_{22} = x_{23} = x_{24} = x_{25} = 0.35(\textstyle\sum x_2)$$

Constraint 2: Number of passengers in the jth arc of the ith path must be equal to the loading factor of each arc of the passenger in the jth arc of the ith path. The number of passengers in the first and second paths is 1600 and 370 passengers per day, respectively.

$$x_{11} = x_{12} = x_{13} = x_{14} = 0.7(1600)$$

$$x_{21} = x_{22} = x_{23} = x_{24} = x_{25} = 0.5(370)$$

Constraint 3: Overall the number of passengers in vehicles and amount of unoccupied capacity in the jth arc of the ith path must not exceed the total loading capacity in the jth arc of the ith path.

$$e_{11} = e_{12} = e_{13} = e_{14} = 2300 \, passengers \, a \, day$$
$$e_{21} = e_{22} = e_{23} = e_{24} = e_{25} = 790 \, passengers \, a \, day$$
$$w_{11} = w_{12} = w_{13} = w_{14} = 380 \, passengers \, a \, day$$
$$w_{21} = w_{22} = w_{23} = w_{24} = w_{25} = 115 \, passengers \, a \, day$$
$$\gamma_{11} = \gamma_{12} = \gamma_{13} = \gamma_{14} = 10 \, passengers \, per \, vehicle$$
$$\gamma_{21} = \gamma_{22} = \gamma_{23} = \gamma_{24} = \gamma_{25} = 10 \, passengers \, per \, vehicle$$

Constraint 4: Overall vehicle travel time in the jth arc of the ith path must not exceed the total vehicle operating time.

$$T_{11} = 0.8/40 = 0.02 \, h$$
$$T_{12} = (0.9 + 0.73 + 0.73 + 0.9 + 0.5)/40 = 0.094 \, h$$
$$T_{13} = 3.95/40 = 0.09875 \, h$$
$$T_{14} = 3/40 = 0.075 \, h$$
$$T_{21} = (1.71 + 0.93 + 0.93)/40 = 0.12275 \, h$$
$$T_{22} = 1.34/40 = 0.0335 \, h$$
$$T_{23} = (0.93 + 0.93)/40 = 0.0465 \, h$$
$$T_{24} = 3.65/40 = 0.09125 \, h$$
$$T_{25} = 1/40 = 0.025 \, h$$
$$\sum wT = 141.2173 \, vehicle - hour/day$$
$$H_{car} = 1980 \, vehicle - h/day$$

The results from analysis of linear programming show that the maximum capacity of the first path under specified constraints is 1050 passengers per day. Arc 1–4 has a capacity of 263 passengers per day. In the second path, there are capacities of 180 passengers a day with 36 passengers per day in Arc 1–5. The total loading capacity of the Pattaya Circle route equals 1230 passengers a day under total vehicle operating time of 1980 vehicle-hours per day. When operating in fixed route mode, 380 vehicles are traveling from the start to the end of the route. The analysis results show that the maximum capacity is 1302 passengers a day with a maximum capacity of 1050 and 252 passengers a day for the first and second paths, respectively. It shows that the fixed route mode provides more capacity flexibility than the semifixed route, equaling 5.85% more.

4.9 ROUTING FOR DRT

Faced with the initial limited success and outright failure of many of the projects, solving Pattaya's traffic problems, especially in its main streets, has been a lengthy process. With new requirements and constraints continuously emerging, the design and development of the Pattaya transportation system is getting harder to accomplish with each passing year, and there is no obvious resolution yet in sight. The mayor, contending with constraints such as limitations of city space, the mix of residents and tourists, and residential lifestyle, has to select an appropriate system among several options for the city's transportation. This has to be accomplished through a more responsive inbound transportation system within the city. Without proper analysis, operating Pattaya's baht bus in semifixed route mode seems to respond to the travel needs of tourists as passengers who hop on and off at any location along the route. The drivers can use other paths to pick up passengers where they can see them wait- ing for vehicles. Nevertheless, based on the results of the capacity flexibility model, operating a fixed route mode can offer the system additional capacity in terms of pas- senger volume. Baht buses making the transition from driving in a semifixed route pattern, which can respond to the immediacy of tourist waiting time, to the fixed route pattern will not only yield higher capacity flexibility for the system but it will reduce traffic congestion in the closely packed Pattaya tourism area as vehicles will be spread throughout the Pattaya area and drive longer distances along the designated routes in both directions.

In a renewed and earnest attempt to find a solution to Pattaya's inbound transpor- tation logistics issue, working groups have been formed to maximize the prospect of finding a solution which would be acceptable to all stakeholders in the city's trans- portation equation. Four principal entities are entitled to input on related rerouting decisions taken concerning the role of the baht bus in Pattaya's future transportation system. First is the Pattaya Police Department, which is in charge of managing traffic flow, implementing traffic regulations, and securing civilians and tourists when they are traveling in the city. Second is the Chonburi Transportation Authority Office, which is responsible for vehicle route design and arrangement, vehicle registration, and national transportation policy implementation. Third is Pattaya City Hall, which has the authority to initiate, develop, and improve the transportation infrastructure of the city. The final entity is the Pattaya Transport Cooperative, which operates the baht buses in designated routes around the city. Out of necessity, this effort has not only to involve the four organizations mentioned above, but also requires changing attitudes towards the planning and implementation of expected transport solutions in a more collaborative and integrative manner.

Finally, DRT is not something that can be designed by only considering the big- ger picture. If the city is to move in the direction of pursuing a DRT approach to public transportation, it would need to do so with a foundation of clear information about both the macro and micro sides, and a clear understanding of both supply and demand.

REFERENCES

Holweg, M., 2005. The three dimensions of responsiveness.. International Journal of Operations & Production Management 25 (7), 603–622.

Janelle, D.G., Beuthe, M., 1997. Globalization and research issues in transportation.. Journal of Transport Geography 5 (3), 199–206.

Koffman, D., 2004. Operational Experiences With Flexible Transit Services: A Synthesis of Transit Practice.. TCRP Synthesis-Transportation Research Board, Washington D.C.

Kritchanchai, D., MacCarthy, B.L., 1999. Responsiveness of the order fulfillment process.. International Journal of Production & Operations Management 19 (8), 812–833.

Lindroth, K., Ritalahti, J., Soisalon-Soininen, T., 2007. Creative tourism in destination development. Tourism Review 62 (3/4), 53–58.

Morlok, E.K., Chang, D.J., 2004. Measuring capacity flexibility of a transportation system.. Transportation Research Part A 38, 405–420.

Naim, M.M., Potter, A.T., Mason, R.J., Bateman, N., 2006. The role of transport flexibility in logistics provision.. The International Journal of Logistics Management 17 (3), 297–311.

Predeaux, B., 2000. The role of transport system in tourism development. Tourism Management 21 (1), 53–63.

Richard, G. 2013, Creative tourism: development, trends, and opportunities. Available online at: http://www.academia.edu/4940996/Creative_tourism_lecture [accessed 9.20.2013].

Smart cities, urban sensing, and big data: mining geo-location in social networks

5

D. Sacco, G. Motta, L.-I. You, N. Bertolazzo, F. Carini and T.-y. Ma
University of Pavia, Pavia, Italy

CHAPTER OUTLINE

5.1 INTRODUCTION

The advent of smartphones with GPS sensors enables users to geo-locate themselves. Such a feature can precipitate a shift from the social and collaborative Web 2.0 to a local and mobile Web 3.0. A key step has been the integration of geographic information systems (GISs) and social networks in location-based social networks (LBSNs). LBSNs offer space-temporal information that can be accessed through public application programming interfaces (APIs). So, LBSNs not only provide geo-located information for urban sensing, but also do not require any infrastructure and, therefore, are a low-cost and readily available source.

Conversely, urban sensing typically requires real-time analysis. Such a requirement, combined with the huge amounts of information which need to be processed, implies the necessity for a Big Data approach. This chapter surveys existing research on using the social network as an information source and on data-mining techniques to analyze such information, and proffers an illustrative case study whereby social network information is processed into a Big Data framework, in order to analyze mobility in an urban area. Specifically:

1. Section 5.2 analyzes the quantitative aspects of the research related to LBSNs from various perspectives, e.g., country, year, and publishing channel, it also proposes the use of a survey method, called systematic literature review (SLR).
2. Section 5.3 discusses the research results from various viewpoints, namely data sources, technologies, and visualization, and also proposes a reference model for use scenarios.
3. Section 5.4 illustrates a case study, based on the Big Data approach to urban sensing which validates our reference model.
4. Section 5.5 reports the conclusions.

5.2 SYSTEMATIC LITERATURE REVIEW

An SLR is an "explicitly formulated, reproducible and up-to-date summary" (Egger et al., 2008), which is based on a structured and explicit method. Our SLR template (Pai et al., 2004) implies the following steps:

1. Question formulation: the research focus is determined.
2. Source selection and inclusion: we select sources and identify the origins of the studies and describe related criteria.
3. Quality assessment and data extraction: defines criteria and models for the extraction of relevant information from studies.
4. Synthesis and summary of study results: illustrates key points which have emerged from selected studies.
5. Result interpretation: results are interpreted and limits of the review are discussed.

Below, we illustrate each step.

5.2.1 QUESTION FORMULATION

Our objective is to identify initiatives, experiences, and viewpoints on location and mobility mining of social network data. Thus, our research question (RQ) is "How do we exploit geo-located data from social networks and what level of maturity has been reached in its application?" This question includes the following more specific RQs:

RQ1: What aspects do the various applications of location and mobility mining of social network data have in common?

RQ2: Which topics are most discussed in this trending research area?

Therefore, the expected outcomes of our SLR are: (1) to provide an overview of the "state of the art," (2) the identification of gaps in current research, solutions, trends, and future research, and (3) recommendations about the best practices for use in location and mobility mining of social network data.

5.2.2 SOURCE SELECTION

SLR has been performed on English-based web search engines and has only been taken into account in documents written in English (as only a small number of relevant documents are written in other languages):

1. IEEE Computer Society (www.computer.org)
2. ISI Web of Knowledge (apps.isiknowledge.com)
3. ACM Digital Library (portal.acm.org)
4. Google Scholar (scholar.google.com)
5. Science Direct (www.sciencedirect.com)
6. SCOPUS Database (info.scopus.com)

Documents have been selected using criteria stemming from the RQ. We have included only the following "study types":

1. Case study: an exhaustive investigation of a single individual, group, incident, community, or enterprise.
2. Theory: a study of guidelines, an introduction to a particular subject or, finally, a theoretical analysis of the research issue.
3. Survey: a study with a statistical treatment of collected data.
4. Simulation: a study on simulation methods and related results.
5. Position paper: an opinion about a specific issue.
6. Instrument development: a new methodology or modeling language.
7. Literature review: collecting information about a particular topic through the analysis of the literature.

According to the above criteria, studies have been selected using the following steps:

1. The search string runs on selected sources. An initial set of studies is obtained by reading the title, abstract, and introduction. Studies that were unrelated to any aspect of the RQ are discarded.
2. Short papers, non-English papers, non-International Conference papers, and non-International Workshop papers are not considered.
3. Studies unrelated to the RQs are discarded.

We did not consider the publication of keywords as the same topic that may be referenced using different terms or acronyms. For each publication we have defined our own specific tags to classify the topics discussed. Our classification framework refers to publications on (1) location mining and (2) mobility mining. Publications dealing with mobility patterns are considered a subset as they are already location aware, as shown in Fig. 5.1.

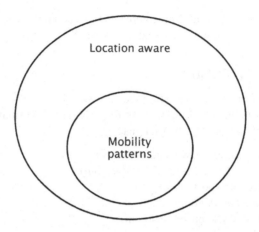

FIGURE 5.1

Analysis framework definition.

5.2.3 **INFORMATION EXTRACTION AND RESULT SUMMARIZATION**

Eighty-seven (out of 109) articles have been selected and classified by year of publication, geographical area, research method, and publication channel. We have classified selected documents into two main groups, namely "location aware and "mobility patterns." The articles range from 2009 to the second quarter of 2013. Fifty-one publications consider only location, while 36 publications also consider mobility patterns. No significant articles were published before 2009 as LBSNs only appeared in that year. Fig. 5.2 shows the distribution of articles by year. Considering that the records from 2013 show only the early months, the authoring of publications on this subject seems to be experiencing an exponential period of growth.

In the geographic distribution, the shares of America, Europe, and Asia are surprisingly close (35.6%, 32.2%, 25.3%, respectively). Twelve out of 28 publications in Europe come from the United Kingdom (see Tables 5.1 and 5.2).

Most articles are the product of conference proceedings (67.4%), as in Table 5.3. Many have been published in books that collect all kinds of research on geo-located data, based on social networks as well as other sources.

The number of reports (9.3%) reaffirms the interest of companies and universities in this subject. However, the lack of white papers may indicate that a structured approach does not yet exist within enterprises.

Case studies represent the majority of the study types, as shown in Table 5.4. The number of case studies and instrument development publications (87.3% in total) reflects the experimental approach being taken towards the issue. It is also motivated by the low number of theoretical papers (5.7%) and by the lack of position papers.

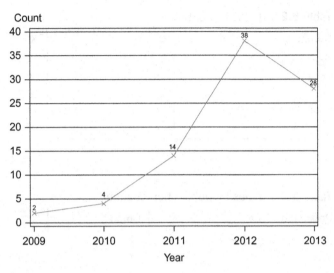

FIGURE 5.2

Distribution of articles by year.

Table 5.1 Articles by country

Country	Count	%
United States	30	34.5
United Kingdom	12	13.8
Japan	8	9.2
Taiwan	7	8.0
Brazil	4	4.6
China	4	4.6
Germany	3	3.4
Spain	3	3.4
Ireland	3	3.4
Switzerland	2	2.3
South Korea	2	2.3
Australia	2	2.3
Belgium	2	2.3
Italy	2	2.3
Singapore	1	1.1
France	1	1.1
Portugal	1	1.1

Table 5.2 Articles by continent

Continent	Count	%
North America	31	35.6
Europe	28	32.2
Asia	22	25.3
South America	4	4.6
Oceania	2	2.3

Table 5.3 Articles by publication channel

Publication type	Count	%
Conference proceedings	58	67.4
Journal article	14	16.3
Report	8	9.3
Book	6	7.0

Table 5.4 Articles by study type

Study type	Count	%
Case study	61	70.1
Instrument development	15	17.2
Theoretical	5	5.7
Simulation	3	3.4
Survey	2	2.3
Literature review	1	1.1

5.3 DISCUSSION

The tag cloud in Fig. 5.3 identifies the main topics discussed in the available literature. Thanks to the tag-based framework for categorizing topics, we can highlight the most active research areas. We have identified three main areas:

1. Data sources;
2. Mining techniques;
3. Use scenarios.

Let us consider the main contributions to each domain.

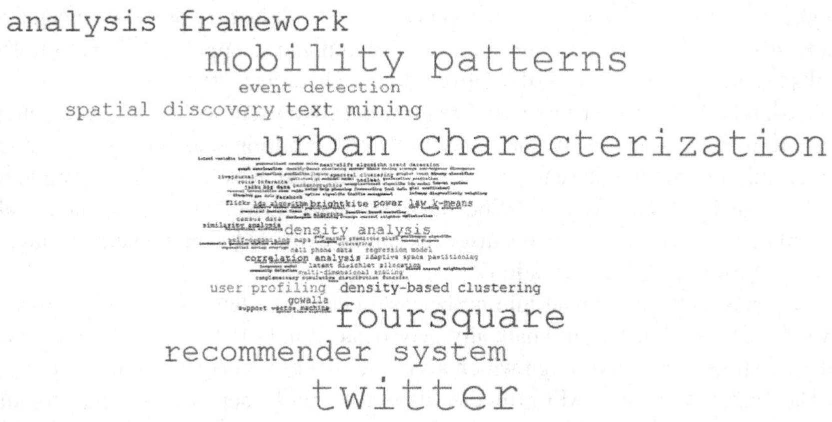

FIGURE 5.3

Major topics discussed in literature.

5.3.1 DATA SOURCES

The potential data sources for urban sensing are heterogeneous. They include: (1) mobile sensor data about the individual devices, (2) infrastructure sensor data about the context, and (3) social network data and other internet data (Zhang et al., 2011). Data sources can be used independently, but their combination enables the formation of a more comprehensive understanding. McArdle et al. (2012) present a traffic modeling framework based on data from Twitter, Foursquare, and cell phones; such an approach intends to replace the more traditional approach which is based on population census data and dedicated road surveys.

Cho et al. (2011) developed a model of human mobility that uses social network and cell phone data. It shows that social relationships can explain 10–30% of human movement, while periodic behavior explains 50–70%. The model reliably predicts location and dynamics of future human movement.

Finally, Noulas et al. (2013) combine data sourced from a Spanish telecommunication provider with a database of millions of geo-tagged venues from Foursquare, to infer the types of activities within neighborhoods in urban centers.

In the subsequent sections we focus on this social network data, namely data obtained from Twitter, Foursquare, and others.

5.3.1.1 Twitter

Twitter is a popular platform for real-time social sharing of short text-based messages, called "tweets." Users can choose to broadcast their tweets publically or keep them private, and can interact socially by following other users. Twitter's character limit for tweets (140-character posts) encourages the service to be used for frequent exchanges of information. Twitter and smartphone usage reflect the same growth, since Twitter users frequently interact through mobile devices. As Twitter is easy to use and interactions are short, many users post tweets while they are also engaged in other activities. This gives Twitter data good spatial and temporal coverage, and the results accurately reflect users' daily lives (Mai and Hranac, 2013).

In March 2012, Twitter reported 500 million active users worldwide, generating over 340 million tweets daily and handling over 1.6 billion search queries. Twitter delivers all of its content in real-time. Thus, a tweet written by a user can be immediately accessed by their followers. When large volumes of tweets are aggregated, real-time information about current occurrences can be extracted, which makes Twitter a valuable source for live information.

Twitter is suitable for data mining because (1) only a few Twitter accounts are private, (2) tweets can be automatically geo-located, and (3) Twitter provides a free real-time streaming API through which a sample of all tweets can be retrieved.

The Twitter streaming API provides filters that can be set on these data streams to only capture tweets within a specified geographic area or only those containing certain terms. When accessing data from Twitter's public real-time streaming feed, data are limited to 1% of the total tweet volume at any given time. Therefore, only a subset of the total tweets can be used (Gerlitz and Rieder, 2013).

5.3.1.2 Foursquare

Foursquare was created in 2009 and currently is the most popular location-based service, with over 15 million users reported in January 2012.

Foursquare is an LBSN where users can "check in" to different locations and share them with friends on Foursquare itself and also on other social networks. Users can upload pictures at a venue or leave "tips" on the venue page (e.g., a user may "check-in" to a hotel and leave a "tip" about how bad the service is). Foursquare also uses "gamification" techniques to encourage check-ins, including rewarding users with badges and points (Cheng et al., 2011).

Foursquare check-in data are not directly accessible; however, users can decide to share their check-ins on Twitter so check-ins can be retrieved via Twitter streaming API (Noulas et al., 2012). Therefore, Foursquare is a less valuable source for data mining than Twitter, even if the contents of Foursquare are more structured and precise (i.e., information about location-based activities).

5.3.1.3 Others

Several other papers refer to data sources for research purposes, because no API is available or the social network has terminated its service.

Gowalla was an LBSN created in 2009, which stopped its service after its acquisition by Facebook at the end of 2011. The service concept was to advertise in real-time your exact location to all your friends. Users could check-in to places and share this information with other friends on Gowalla itself, and on Twitter and Facebook (Scellato et al., 2010). Currently, only some check-in data are still available for research purposes.

Momo, started in 2011, provides two main functions: (1) "social discovery" allows a user to find people based on the geographical distance between them and

(2) instant messaging, that enables users to communicate. The application keeps updating user location onto the server by default. Thus, a rich set of spatio-temporal information about user position is available in public data sets (Chen et al., 2013).

BrightKite, launched in 2007, was a social networking website which allowed users to share their location, post notes, and upload photos. By "checking-in" at places, users could see people who are or were nearby. Furthermore, users could send public and private messages to friends. It offered a public API which provided geographic coordinates of user locations and lists of friends. At the present time, only previously collected data sets are available (Li and Chen, 2009).

Flickr is a social network for sharing pictures and other information. Users often associate their photos with tags and geographical information. Over 150 million photos are on Flickr with geographical coordinates (Van Canneyt et al., 2011). Images with GPS records can be easily trawled by using Flickr API.

The obvious question "why not use Facebook?" has an equally obvious answer. The Facebook API can be used to retrieve data from those users who agree to publish their posts to your application or system, so therefore it is not publicly available.

5.3.2 MINING TECHNIQUES

Machine learning and text mining are the main techniques for location and mobility mining. The objective of data inference goes from recognizing individual activities and contexts to extracting higher level human behavioral information (Guo et al., 2012). We here focus on the core techniques used in literature.

5.3.2.1 k-Means

k-Means can be used to reveal clusters of common behaviors across land segments. The land use of each cluster can be derived by analyzing the activity vectors of the regions within the cluster. k-Means depends on the initial randomly selected seeds and it needs to specify the number of clusters k (land uses) to identify (Frias-Martinex et al., 2012).

Fujisaka et al. (2010) first generated k clusters using an entire week of geo-located data retrieved from Twitter. Each k cluster is slightly different, since the algorithm starts with randomly selected k seeds. Such clusters can be used in mobility pattern investigations by using (1) an aggregation model to identify clusters where users tend to aggregate because an event is happening, and (2) a dispersion model, i.e., a reverse aggregation. In addition, Lee and Sumiya (2010) and Lee et al. (2011) use a similar approach, where they build a Voronoi diagram using the centerpoints (latitude and longitude) of the k-means results and regarding the regions as a set of regions of interests, in order to identify the occurrence of local events.

Preotiuc-Pietro and Cohn cluster Foursquare users on their movements across venues. By using k-means they identify groups and illustrate their centroid. These centroids or "typical behaviors" can then be interpreted and assigned to different human categories (e.g., student, stay-at-home, etc.). Finally, this information is utilized in domain-independent methods for location prediction. Son et al. (2013) use

k-means to classify similar geo-located tweets as a similar cluster. Some units may be incorrectly classified, due to their unusual characteristics. They consider these units as outliers where an event would happen.

Finally, in order to study mobility patterns, Li and Chen (2009) propose x-means, an extended k-means algorithm, which targets the cluster whose a priori number of location clusters is unknown, as it happens when users move from one location to another. x-Means uses several parameters, such as minimum and maximum cluster number, maximum number of overall iterations, and maximum number of iterations in the k-means loop.

5.3.2.2 Self-organizing map

A self-organizing map (SOM) is an unsupervised neural network that reduces the input dimensionality in order to represent its distribution as a map. Therefore, SOM forms a map where similar samples are mapped closely together. Specifically, Frias-Martinex et al. (2012) use an SOM to build a map that segments the urban land into geographic areas with different concentrations of tweets in the time period under study.

In turn, Behnisch and Ultsch (2009) use an emergent self-organizing map (ESOM) (an extension of SOM) for clustering and classification. ESOM preserves the neighborhood relationships of the high-dimensional data, as the finite grid has a disadvantage because the neurons at the edges of the map have very different mapping qualities compared to neurons in the center versus the border.

5.3.2.3 Density-based clustering

Density-Based Spatial Clustering of Applications with Noise (DBSCAN) is a density-based clustering algorithm that: (1) is based on density reachability and produces satisfying results in arbitrarily shaped clusters, (2) targets a number of dynamic clusters (i.e., the number of clusters is not given a priori), and (3) tolerates noise, thus taking into consideration that some data points are not assigned to any cluster.

Density-based clustering algorithms have an advantage in that clusters are defined by the density of data points and not by the spatial size and form of the cluster. Therefore, the DBSCAN needs the parameters ε and MinPts to determine the clusters. Specifically, Bawa-Cavia (2011) uses DBSCAN to examine activities in Foursquare with reference to a threshold distance that defines spatial fragmentation. This is pursued in order to test the hypothesis that the postmodern metropolis works as a social "archipelago," a fragmented set of islands characterized by high-density social activity.

Due to the high number of geo-located tweet occurrences, Wakamiya et al. (2012a) decided to reduce the data size with a minor loss of the original distribution. They adopt the NNClean (Nearest Neighbor Clutter Removal) algorithm, which filters high-frequency locational points. Then, in order to locate urban clusters with the ideally reduced dataset, they use DBSCAN. In turn, Pianese et al. (2013) introduced a set of criteria to automatically classify active users of Foursquare into categories based on spatial (S), temporal (T), and venue (V) features in their event traces. In this way they propose the extension of DBSCAN into three dimensions.

Lee (2012) uses incremental DBSCAN, an extension of DBSCAN, with the support of a sliding window of tweets by which new messages are reserved in memory until they are out of the time window. Thanks to incremental DBSCAN, the shape of clusters will change over time when a message is entered or deleted from the sliding window. Thus, incremental DBSCAN works as an online clustering algorithm. Qu and Zhang (2013) choose OPTICS because it identifies clusters of varying shape, size, and density, and does not require the presence of global parameters (such as the number of clusters and cutting thresholds). In order to identify spatial structures, it sorts the points by closeness. Like DBSCAN, OPTICS requires only two parameters; a given area with radius ε, and the presence of at least MinPts data points within it. It is used to cluster Foursquare check-ins.

5.3.2.4 Spectral clustering

Spectral methods are popular thanks to the quality of the clusters they produce and their easy implementation. Spectral clustering finds arbitrarily shaped clusters and does not pose any constraints upon them (conversely k-means, e.g., assumes the cluster to be convex). It also requires that the parameter k is used to define the number of desired clusters (Roslrer and Liebig, 2013).

Cranshaw et al. (2012) designed an affinity matrix between check-in venues in Foursquare that effectively blends spatial affinity and social affinity. They have also developed a way of comparing different clusters in terms of the similarity of the distribution of the users who visit them. In this way, they are able to discover distinct geographic areas of the city, reflecting the collective movement patterns of its people.

As it is not easy to estimate the right value for the parameter k, Roslrer and Liebig (2013) adopt the idea of evidence accumulation clustering, to combine different runs of the spectral clustering, where k is sampled from the interval k_{min} to k_{max} in every single run. The notion behind this method is to build clusters with different algorithms and parameterizations and then to aggregate all solutions into one final partition using every single partition to decide if instances should be placed together. If two venues are placed together in most solutions, it is reasonable to assign them to the same cluster in the final partition. In this context, this method could also be understood as a tool to enhance the validity of the resulting partition by reducing the impact resulting from a single nonoptimal clustering (such as clusters which are not well separated).

5.3.2.5 Mean-shift

Mean-shift is a nonparametric clustering technique that detects the modes of an underlying probability distribution from a set of discrete samples. Thus, a mean-shift can be used both as an algorithm to detect local maxima (modes) as well as a clustering technique (areas associated with the modes). Frias-Martinex et al. (2012) assume that there exists an unobservable underlying probability distribution related to locations from which people tweet. The modes of that distribution are determined to represent urban landmarks or points of interest in the city.

Van Canneyt et al. (2011) start from a large collection of geo-referenced photos on Flickr, and use mean-shift clustering to determine points of interest within a city. They then estimate the probability that a random user would visit a given place within a given temporal context. Yin et al. (2011) consider the location of a photo on Flickr as a data point. If one user takes multiple photos at the same place, it is only counted as one point. By applying mean-shift, they rank the trajectory patterns of Flickr users in 12 different cities.

5.3.2.6 Others

Joseph et al. (2012) apply the idea of topic modeling to cluster Foursquare users into meaningful groups that are representative of the different factors which drive check-in behavior. Specifically, they apply a topic model known as latent Dirichlet allocation (LDA). LDA is a latent space model commonly used to represent a large collection of documents in a compact set of hidden topics. Thus, each document can be described by considering how readily the words within it relate to the various hidden topics, and each hidden topic can be described by the words which are most readily associated with it (Hong et al., 2012; Long et al., 2012).

Ho et al. (2012) use not only LDA but also support vector machine (SVM) in event sentiment classification. SVM (a discriminative classifier) has a strong theoretical justification and competitive practical performance. SVMs have been successfully used in many machine learning tasks and operated by maximizing the margin between the nearest data points of two classes and the hyperplane that separates them (Karamshuk et al., 2013; Noulas et al., 2013).

Xu et al. (2013) use text-mining methods, including natural language processing (NLP) techniques, to identify place names mentioned in the tweets and geocode them. First, named entities (NE) are recognized and extracted from each individual tweet entry using the fundamentals of the NLP methods. All NEs are processed through geocoding and disambiguation processes and only those legitimate place names (e.g., New York City or Bryant Park) were geo-referenced using a GeoNames-based geocoder. A similar approach is used by other practitioners (Cheng et al., 2011; Watanabe et al., 2011; Baldwin et al., 2012; Boettcher and Lee, 2012; Lee, 2012; Oussalah et al., 2012; Colombo et al., 2013; Hu et al., 2013; Liang et al., 2013), but it does not allow accurate geo-location of users, only a probabilistic area of their actual or hypothetical future position.

5.3.3 USE SCENARIOS

The identification of use scenarios opens new perspectives at societal level, e.g., community healthcare, public safety, city resource management, and transportation management.

We here propose a classification of visualization objectives in urban sensing, that is an evolution of business intelligence (BI) solutions towards GIS's and Big Data visualization (Stodder, 2013). For each objective class, we will recall similarities to BI in Table 5.5.

Table 5.5 Visualization objectives classification

Class	Description	BI similarities	Objectives
Urban characterization	The results can be stored for users as a "snapshot" of a certain point in time. Users examine snapshots to identify changes in data over time, so they must be provisioned and presented consistently so that trends and comparisons are valid	It recalls dashboards. The view is static and it is previously defined by data analysts	To visualize and predict social ties and urban structure
Spatial discovery	It enables users to interact with data through analytical processes. Visual functionality for filtering, comparing, slicing and dicing, drilling down, and correlating data can then be integrated with the users' analytical application functions for forecasting, modeling, and statistical, what-if, and predictive analytics	It recalls on-line analytical processing. The view is dynamic and it allows users to navigate data	To analyze behaviors "on-line," in space and time
Exception alerting	It notifies users of particularly important changes in data or when situations arise that demand immediate attention. Alerts mean that something important in real-time data or event streams is happening	It recalls event processing in modern business activity monitoring solutions that detect and warn of problems or exceptions in real-time	To detect events or exceptions to standard behaviors, e.g., disasters, diseases, unexpected crowds

The three visualization classes reflect the papers analyzed in our SLR. In total, 30 papers deal with urban characterization, 18 with spatial discovery, 12 with exception alerting. Other papers use geo-located data from social networks for recommender systems or user profiling. We do not subject them to further scrutiny since they do not target the city but the individual user.

5.3.3.1 Urban characterization

Rosler and Liebig (2013) provide insights on the activity profiles in urban environments. Clusters identified by Foursquare check-ins help to describe the socio-dynamics of urban districts at different times of the day.

Ferrari et al. (2011) extend the work on activity profiles to the mobility patterns that occur in an urban environment and to the analysis of social commonalities which occur between people.

Traditional municipal organizational units such as neighborhoods are studied by the Livelihoods project (Cranshaw et al., 2012), that shows their boundaries do not always reflect the living character of each area.

By processing Twitter data, Wakamiya et al. (2011) examine the relation between regions of common crowd activity patterns and major categories of local facilities. In a subsequent study, Wakamiya et al. (2012b) relate psychological and geospatial proximity of urban areas by borrowing crowd experiences from geo-tagged tweets, in order to demonstrate that people often rely on geospatial cognition rather than the real physical distance.

Joseph et al. (2012) mine check-ins to identify aggregations (i.e., groups, for example tourists, communities, for example, users tightly clustered in space, and interests, for example people who enjoy athletics) and how they use urban space.

Lawlor et al. (2012) explore the community structure of a network of significant locations in cities as observed from LBSN data. Their findings are useful in the study of social exclusion and segregation processes in cities, and are also of interest for geo-marketing analysts developing fidelity schemes and promotional programs.

McArdle et al. (2012) observe that given the distribution of population, workplace locations, a comprehensive set of urban facilities, and a list of typical activity sequences of city dwellers collected by using a national road survey, social network analysis reproduces not only the journey statistics but also the traffic volumes at main road segments.

Villatoro et al. (2012) propose a new system named the Social Sensing Platform, which collects tweets relating to a city and retrieves information such as their origin. Furthermore this system, through a DBScan algorithm, creates clusters that detect hotspots and day-to-day movement patterns.

Scellato et al. (2010) illustrate a graph-based approach that is aimed at studying social networks with geographic information and new metrics, with the purpose of characterizing how geographic distances affect social structure.

Silva et al. (2013) compare two participatory sensor networks, respectively derived from Instagram and from Foursquare. These datasets are analyzed to establish whether the same user movement and the popularity of regions in cities and the activities of users who use those social networks can be observed, and how users share their content during an allotted time span.

Frias-Martinez (2012) evaluates the use of geo-located tweets as a complementary source of information for urban planning applications. Contributions are focused on two urban planning areas: a technique to automatically determine land uses in a specific urban area based on tweeting patterns, and a technique to automatically identify urban points of interest as places with a high volume of tweets.

Yin et al. (2011) investigate how to rank the trajectory patterns mined from uploaded photos with geo-tags and timestamps. Instead of focusing on mining frequent trajectory patterns from geo-tagged social media, more effort is put into ranking the mined trajectory patterns and diversifying the ranking results.

5.3.3.2 Spatial discovery

Silva et al. (2012) study social behaviors by monitoring check-ins on Foursquare (Sagl et al., 2012) through Twitter and Flickr data. They analyze city dynamics spatially and temporally and identify seasonality involved in influencing human behaviors.

Oussalah et al. (2012) propose a system that identifies spatial patterns within geo-located Twitter and provides elements in terms of location, mobility, and topics discussed in tweets.

Cheng et al. (2011) investigate 22 million check-ins across 220,000 users and report a quantitative assessment of human mobility patterns by analyzing spatial, temporal, social, and textual aspects.

By analyzing topics in tweets, Hong et al. (2012) discover how information is created and shared across different locations and different linguistic characteristics. Again, Kling and Pozdnoukhov (2012) use word clouds, heat maps, and timelines to describe topic dissemination within the city. Conversely, Kamath et al. (2013) focus on Twitter hashtags and study their space-temporal dynamics through a sample of 2 billion geo-tagged tweets.

Qu and Zhang (2013) provide an analytic framework based on the traditional trade area analysis. They apply this framework to mobile location data in order to model customer mobility, create customer profiles and preferences, and examine interactions between customers and stores.

Whoo.ly, developed by Hu et al. (2013), provides neighborhood-specific information based on tweets. It automatically extracts and summarizes hyper-local information about events, topics, people, and places, and it can be used to explore neighborhoods.

Long et al. (2012) introduce the concept of location based social networking services, such as Foursquare. This paper, by LDA, explores local geographic topics through Foursquare check-ins in the Pittsburgh area. Also, Wakamiya et al. (2012b) explore urban complexity from crowd-sourced life logs, with the purpose of generating a socio-cognitive map of the urban space.

Bawa-Cavia (2011) perform a spatial analysis of the aggregate activity of social networks and show the distribution of social activity in a city, revealing refined data about spatial patterns.

5.3.3.3 Exception alerting

Boettcher and Lee (2012) introduce Event Radar, a detection system that finds local events such as parties, musicians performing in a park, or art exhibitions. Watanabe et al. (2011) provide a similar system to detect events. Finally, Baldwin et al. (2012) try to predict the impact of these sorts of events.

Mai and Hranac (2013) assert that tweets can be matched to traffic incidents by examining the content of the tweets for key words and comparing the timestamps and locations of the tweets and incidents. Results are confirmed for areas with sufficient density of Twitter usage.

Lee and Chien (2013) have developed an online text-stream clustering that combines three technical components, namely (1) a dynamic term-weighting scheme, (2) a neighborhood generation algorithm, and (3) an online density-based clustering technique. After acquiring detected event topics on microblogging websites, their system assists people in identifying the impact of events, enhancing event awareness, and organizing information upcoming events close to the analyzed location.

Van Canneyt et al. (2011) propose a system that recommends tourist attractions targeting the period when the user visits a city. The probability that a user could visit a given place within a given time context is also estimated.

Brown et al. (2012) propose a way to extract place-focused communities from the social graph by annotating its edges with check-in information. Using traces from two online social networks with location sharing, it is possible to extract groups of friends who meet face-to-face, with many possible benefits for online social services.

5.4 BIG DATA APPROACH: A CASE STUDY

Big Data is a popular term. However, as Gartner remarks (http://www.gartner.com/it-glossary/big-data/), Big Data implies not only "quantity" but also "velocity," which involves real-time processing, and "variety," which involves multiple information types, e.g., social media, context aware data, documents, images, videos, audio, etc.

We here illustrate a Big Data approach for mining the geo-located data of social networks. To the best of our knowledge, no paper has thus far dealt with Big Data architectures in terms of their ability to process "variety," "velocity," and "volume" of social network data. Our literature review found only two papers that discuss a Big Data approach to mine location-based data of social networks. Specifically: According to Crampton et al. (2013), in geographic Big Data processing one must consider: (1) social media data that are not explicitly geographic, e.g., tweets without geo-tags, (2) spatialities beyond the "here and now," e.g., scale-jumping and temporality, (3) methodologies that are not focused on the explicitly proximate, e.g., social network analysis, (4) social media data that are not produced by humans, e.g., Twitter robots, and (5) geographic data from nonuser-generated sources, e.g., census data. However, no architecture has so far been proposed.

Lee and Chien (2013) have developed a method for online event clustering and topic ranking in real-time event monitoring that uses message streams collected from Twitter data sets. They give a comprehensive description of their data-mining techniques to exploit Big Data and on system performances, but provide no detailed system architecture.

An overview of our roadmap can be found in Fig. 5.4. The left side depicts analysis activities and proceeds top down. First, in order to address urban sensing, one needs to define the appropriate data-mining techniques and related technologies. Finally, one must assess the availability of appropriate real-time sources.

The right side identifies the system design steps and proceeds from the bottom-up. After the identification of appropriate sources one can define access to real-time

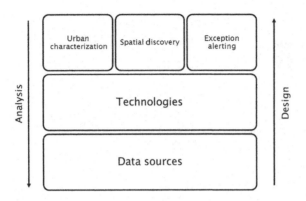

FIGURE 5.4

Reference model for urban sensing realization.

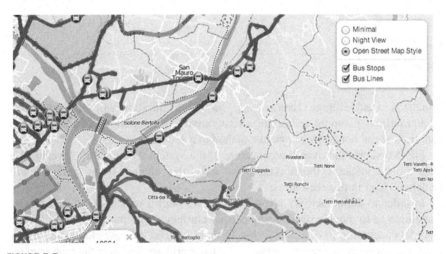

FIGURE 5.5

Public transport simulator.

streaming of data and design agents able to handle it. Next, systems and platforms to process data can be defined. They must be able to process and store large volumes of unstructured data and their performances must be in near real-time. Finally, objectives can be fulfilled by implementing the front-end system which shows results from the previous phase.

The above approach has been validated by means of its use in a real project. Firstly, we developed a simulator that transforms timetables from open transport data in Torino (Italy) to a visualization tool which shows the planned positions of each bus at a specific time (each moving point in Fig. 5.5). We decided to enrich this

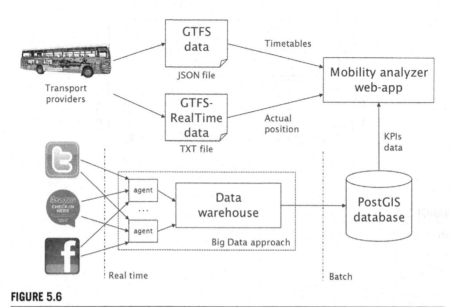

FIGURE 5.6

Overall architecture.

visualization and leverage urban sensing. Our specific question was: "how do we correlate transport planning and urban activity areas?" Exploitation of location-based data from social networks is a viable method to achieve it.

Fig. 5.6 shows the overall architecture of the system we intend to develop. Big Data implementation is the most unknown and critical element of the system. It will be defined later in this section.

In order to define activity areas in a city we built a tool for spatial discovery that allows us to model crowds using density clusters within the city and drill down their data according to different scales. In order to keep the case study simple, our approach has been to compute density on a fixed grid applied over the map (rectangles with identical dimension). To define the data which are to be used, we exploited Twitter streaming API, collected geo-located data in the Torino area in real-time and aggregated them on the map for each specific time range (1 h).

To retrieve Twitter data, we implemented FluenTD agents by Node.js on a virtual machine in Amazon Elastic BeanStalk. FluenTD (http://fluentd.org/) is an open-source log collector that enables a logging architecture with 125+ types of systems, by treating logs as JSON files. Node.js (http://nodejs.org/) is a platform built on JavaScript which facilitates the construction of fast, scalable network applications. It uses an event-driven, nonblocking I/O model that makes it lightweight, efficient, and oriented to data-intensive real-time applications which run across distributed devices. FluenTD and Node.js integration allows the building of real-time collection and filtering of geo-located tweets, and their storage in TreasureData (http://www.treasure-data.com/).

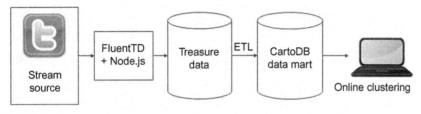

FIGURE 5.7

A service-oriented architecture for Big Data management.

TreasureData is a "Big Data as a Service" cloud solution that offers a time series, columnar, Hadoop-based, schema-free data warehouse stored on Amazon S3. It allows you to access data using Hive query language (http://hive.apache.org/) by JDBC. An extraction-transformation-loading (ETL) process accesses data in TreasureData, processes it and uploads it in CartoDB every 5 min. CartoDB is a "database as a service" cloud solution, based on a PostgreSQL database with GIS extension. As PostgreSQL databases can use extensions to run data-mining algorithms, we decided to apply density-based clustering online, whenever the map is opened or the zoom scale changes. Fig. 5.7 shows the final architecture for our prototype.

As this solution intends to implement a service-oriented architecture (SOA), it has two main advantages: (1) it can be easily extended and (2) a component can be replaced by others by process of decoupling. For example, the data stored in the data mart can be used to perform different analytics or to build an alerting system. As SAP Hana has a Predictive Analysis Library that offers native support to DBSCAN, we could use SAP Hana to implement it as a supplementary layer between TreasureData and CartoDB. If we want to easily implement LDA, we could replace TreasureData with Mahout on a Hadoop cluster. The ETL process, that may represent a bottleneck in terms of performance, can be replaced by ad hoc solutions, e.g., interfaces developed in Node.js to provide data filtering and storage in the data mart.

Fig. 5.8 shows the early results of our prototype. It considers tweets collected from 8:00 am to 9:00 am on July 10, 2013. The color density of rectangles changes according to tweet density in the same area.

Final integration between the crowd modeling tool and the public transport simulator allows spatial discovery of urban areas not covered by transport services during peak time when there is a high volume of people who may need to move from one place to another within the city.

Fig. 5.9 shows tweet density in San Francisco, from 8:00 am to 9:00 am on July 13, 2013.

The final system intends to construct a Big Data-oriented territorial intelligence solution that integrates the GIS, BI, and Big Data provided by social networks. Our mobility analyzer will be structured using a layered architecture. In this way the analyst will be able to select and combine only the information in which they are interested.

FIGURE 5.8

Tweet density in Torino.

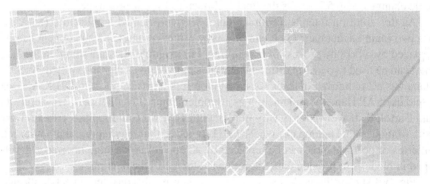

FIGURE 5.9

Tweet density in San Francisco.

Fig. 5.10 shows the mobility analyzer architecture.

The first layer is the core layer, it consists of a static map of an urban area showing geographic information. This layer is always shown in the mobility analyzer.

The second layer shows the routes and stops of the available public transport services.

The third layer shows a scheduled position for vehicles according to their timetables. The user, through this layer, can access a preliminary assessment of the ideal performance of the mobility. Each type of vehicle is represented by a specific icon for the sake of clarity.

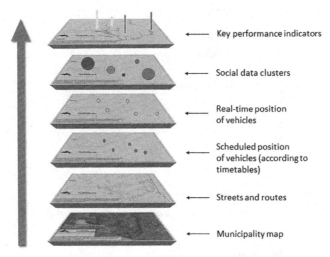

Key performance indicators

Social data clusters

Real-time position of vehicles

Scheduled position of vehicles (according to timetables)

Streets and routes

Municipality map

FIGURE 5.10

Mobility analyzer layers.

The fourth layer shows the position of vehicles in real time in order that it can be compared with the schedules. Real-time vehicle icons are drawn with a different color.

The fifth layer adds information about crowds of people. Social data are organized into clusters, according to specific algorithms. Circles with a different color and radius indicate the dimension of each cluster, in terms of data density and spread in a particular area. The purpose of this layer is to show areas of overcrowding and correlate them with the potential capture rate of the public transport provider.

The final layer calculates and shows key performance indicators about mobility performances.

5.5 **CONCLUSION**

Our SLR demonstrates the exponential growth of papers relating to urban sensing and social networks. The many publications including case studies and instrument development reflect the fact that these approaches are still in an experimental and early stage of development.

We have assessed the maturity of the new location-based capabilities of social networks which offer space-temporal information that can be accessed through public APIs. Maturity can be defined in terms of availability, integrability, and dependability (as shown in Fig. 5.11). LBSNs are an innovative source of large volumes of unstructured data that can be easily reused by applying Big Data approaches. However, most works focus solely on the validation of data-mining techniques,

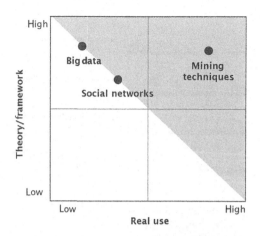

FIGURE 5.11

Maturity (availability, integrability, and dependability).

rather than on their application in real scenarios. Our prototype shows practical uses and the integration of urban sensing and open data has the potential to help municipalities gain insight into their provision of service for citizens.

In recent years we have seen a paradigm shift in the role of the user, from consumer to producer of information. Due to recent technological developments and their worldwide dissemination, Web 2.0 has changed users' approach to information creation and exploitation. Further evolution of the web has introduced new location-based capabilities and it represents a prime requirement for an Internet of things where connections between the physical and virtual world can be enhanced.

The paradigm we propose is infrastructure-less. Urban sensing can really benefit from social data and its implementation requires low capital expenditure. Thus, future research should move from focusing on the validation of mining techniques to real applications in smart cities using Big Data technologies, thus providing real-time analytics to municipalities and users.

Our future work intends to integrate different data sources, such as sensors, and more social media sources, to provide deeper insights for urban sensing. Furthermore, our system needs must increase in scale and validate performances against user needs. The next steps will include the development of a service orchestration layer to provide complete validation of our SOA.

REFERENCES

Baldwin, T., Cook, P., Han, B., Harwood, A., Karunasekera, S., Moshtaghi, M., 2012. A support platform for event detection using social intelligence. In: Proceedings of the Demonstrations at the 13th Conference of the European Chapter of the Association for Computational Linguistics. p. 69–72.

Bawa-Cavia, A., 2011. Sensing the urban: using location-based social network data in urban analysis. In: Pervasive PURBA Workshop.

Behnisch, M., Ultsch, A., 2009. Urban data-mining: spatiotemporal exploration of multidimensional data. Building Research & Information 37 (5-6), 520–532.

Boettcher, A., Lee, D., 2012. EventRadar: a real-time local event detection scheme using Twitter stream. In: Green Computing and Communications (GreenCom), 2012 IEEE International Conference, pp. 358–367.

Brown, C., Nicosia, V., Scellato, S., Noulas, A., Mascolo, C., 2012. The importance of being placefriends: discovering location-focused online communities. In: Proceedings of the 2012 ACM Workshop on Online Social Networks, pp. 31–36.

Chen, T., Kaafar, M.A., Boreli, R., 2013. The where and when of finding new friends: analysis of a location-based social discovery network. In: International Conference on Weblogs and Social Media.

Cheng, Z., Caverlee, J., Lee, K., Sui, D.Z., 2011. Exploring millions of footprints in location sharing services. In: Proceedings of the Fifth International AAAI Conference on Weblogs and Social Media, p. 81–88.

Cho, E., Myers, S.A., Leskovec, J., 2011. Friendship and mobility: user movement in location-based social networks. In: Proceedings of the 17th ACM SIGKDD International Conference on Knowledge Discovery and Data Mining, pp. 1082–1090.

Colombo, G.B., Chorley, M.J., Tanasescu, V., Allen, S.M., Jones, C.B., Whitaker, R.M., 2013 Will you like this place? A tag-based place representation approach. In: 2013 IEEE International Conference on Pervasive Computing and Communications Workshops (PERCOM Workshops), San Diego, CA, pp. 224–229.

Crampton, J.W., Graham, M., Poorthuis, A., Shelton, T., Stephens, M., Wilson, M.W., et al., 2013. Beyond the geotag: situating 'big data' and leveraging the potential of the geoweb. Cartography and Geographic Information Science 40 (2), 130–139.

Cranshaw, J., Schwartz, R., Hong, J.I., Sadeh, N.M., 2012. The livelihoods project: utilizing social media to understand the dynamics of a city. In: Proceedings of the Sixth International AAAI Conference on Weblogs and Social Media.

Egger, M., Smith, G.D., Altman, D. (Eds.), 2008. Systematic Reviews in Health Care: Meta-Analysis in Context. Wiley. BGM publishing group, London.

Ferrari, L., Rosi, A., Mamei, M., Zambonelli, F., 2011. Extracting urban patterns from location-based social networks. In: Proceedings of the 3rd ACM SIGSPATIAL International Workshop on Location-Based Social Networks, pp. 9–16.

Frias-Martinez, V., Soto, V., Hohwald, H., Frias-Martinez, E., 2012. Characterizing urban landscapes using geolocated tweets. in privacy, security, risk and trust (PASSAT). In: 2012 International Conference on Social Computing (SocialCom), pp. 239–248.

Fujisaka, T., Lee, R., Sumiya, K., 2010. Discovery of user behavior patterns from geotagged micro-blogs. In: Proceedings of the 4th International Conference on Uniquitous Information Management and Communication, p. 36.

Gerlitz, C., Rieder, B., 2013. Mining one percent of titter: collections, baselines, sampling. M/C Journal, [S.l.] 16 (2). ISSN 14412616. Available at: <http://journal.media-culture.org.au/index.php/mcjournal/article/view/620Rieder>. Date accessed: 18 oct. 2016.

Guo, B., Zhang, D., Yu, Z., Calabrese, F., 2012. Extracting social and community intelligence from digital footprints. Journal of Ambient Intelligence and Humanized Computing 5, 1–2.

Ho, S.S., Lieberman, M., Wang, P., Samet, H., 2012. Mining future spatiotemporal events and their sentiment from online news articles for location-aware recommendation system. In: Proceedings of the First ACM SIGSPATIAL International Workshop on Mobile Geographic Information Systems, pp. 25–32.

Hong, L., et al., 2012. Discovering geographical topics in the twitter stream. In: Proceedings of the 21st International Conference on World Wide Web.

Hu, Y., Farnham, S.D., Monroy-Hernández, A., 2013. Whoo.ly: facilitating information seeking for hyperlocal communities using social media. In: Proceedings of the 2013 ACM Annual Conference on Human Factors in Computing Systems, p. 3481–3490.

Joseph, K., Tan, C.H., Carley, K.M., 2012. Beyond local, categories and friends: clustering foursquare users with latent topics. In: Proceedings of the 2012 ACM Conference on Ubiquitous Computing, pp. 919–926.

Kamath, K.Y., Caverlee, J., Lee, K., Cheng, Z., 2013. Spatio-temporal dynamics of online memes: a study of geo-tagged tweets. In: Proceedings of the 22nd International Conference on World Wide Web, pp. 667–678.

Karamshuk, D., Noulas, A., Scellato, S., Nicosia, V., Mascolo, C., 2013. Geo-spotting: mining online location-based services for optimal retail store placement. arXiv preprint arXiv:1306.1704.

Kling, F., Pozdnoukhov, A., 2012. When a city tells a story: urban topic analysis. In: Proceedings of the 20th International Conference on Advances in Geographic Information Systems, p. 482-485.

Lawlor, A., Coffey, C., McGrath, R., Pozdnoukhov, A., 2012. Stratification structure of urban habitats. In: Workshop on Pervasive Urban Applications.

Lee, C.H., 2012. Mining spatio-temporal information on microblogging streams using a density-based online clustering method. Expert Systems with Applications 39 (10), 9623–9641.

Lee, C.H., Chien, T.F., 2013. Leveraging microblogging big data with a modified density-based clustering approach for event awareness and topic ranking. Journal of Information Science 39 (4), 523–543.

Lee, R., Sumiya, K., 2010. Measuring geographical regularities of crowd behaviors for Twitter-based geo-social event detection. In: Proceedings of the 2nd ACM SIGSPATIAL International Workshop on Location Based Social Networks, p. 1–10.

Lee, R., Wakamiya, S., Sumiya, K., 2011. Discovery of unusual regional social activities using geo-tagged microblogs. World Wide Web 14 (4), 321–349.

Li, N., & Chen, G., 2009. Analysis of a location-based social network. In: Computational Science and Engineering. CSE'09. International Conference, 4, pp. 263–270.

Liang, Y., Caverlee, J., Cheng, Z., Kamath, K.Y., 2013. How big is the crowd? Event and location based population modeling in social media. In: Proceedings of the 24th ACM Conference on Hypertext and Social Media, ACM, New York, pp. 99–108.

Long, X., Jin, L., Joshi, J., 2012. Exploring trajectory-driven local geographic topics in Foursquare. In: Proceedings of the 2012 ACM Conference on Ubiquitous Computing, Acm, New York, NY, pp. 927–934.

Mai, E., Hranac, R., 2013. Twitter interactions as a data source for transportation incidents. In: Transportation Research Board 92nd Annual Meeting (No. 13-1636).

McArdle, G., Lawlor, A., Furey, E., Pozdnoukhov, A., 2012. City-scale traffic simulation from digital footprints. In: Proceedings of the ACM SIGKDD International Workshop on Urban Computing, pp. 47–54.

Noulas, A., Mascolo, C., Frias-Martinez, E., 2013. Exploiting Foursquare and cellular data to infer user activity in urban environments. In: IEEE International Conference on Mobile Data Management, Vol. 1, pp. 167–176.

Noulas, A., Scellato, S., Lathia, N., Mascolo, C., 2012. A random walk around the city: New venue recommendation in location-based social networks. In: Privacy, Security, Risk and Trust (PASSAT), 2012 International Conference on Social Computing (SocialCom), pp. 144–153.

Noulas, A., Scellato, S., Mascolo, C., Pontil, M., 2011. An empirical study of geographic user activity patterns in Foursquare. Fifth International AAAI Conference on Weblogs and Social Media, pp. 70–573.

Oussalah, M., Bhat, F., Challis, K., Schnier, T., 2012. A software architecture for Twitter collection, search and geolocation services. Knowledge-Based Systems 37, 105–120.

Pai, M., McCulloch, M., Gorman, J.D., Pai, N., Enanoria, W., Kennedy, G., et al., 2004. Systematic reviews and meta-analyses: an illustrated, step-by-step guide. The National Medical Journal of India 17 (2), 86.

Pianese, F., An, X., Kawsar, F., Ishizuka, H., 2013. Discovering and predicting user routines by differential analysis of social network traces. In: IEEE International Symposium on A World of Wireless, Mobile and Multimedia Networks, pp. 1–9.

Qu, Y., Zhang, J., 2013. Regularly visited patches in human mobility. In: Proceedings of the SIGCHI Conference on Human Factors in Computing Systems, pp. 395–398.

Rösler, R., Liebig, T., 2013. Using data from location based social networks for urban activity clustering. In: Geographic Information Science at the Heart of Europe, pp. 55–72.

Sagl, G., Resch, B., Hawelka, B., Beinat, E., 2012. From social sensor data to collective human behaviour patterns: analysing and visualising spatio-temporal dynamics in urban environments. In: Proceedings of the GI-Forum 2012: Geovisualization, Society and Learning, pp. 54–63.

Scellato, S., Mascolo, C., Musolesi, M., Latora, V., 2010. Distance matters: geo-social metrics for online social networks. In: Proceedings of the 3rd Conference on Online Social Networks, p. 8.

Silva, T.H., Melo, P.O., Almeida, J.M., Salles, J., Loureiro, A.A., 2012. Visualizing the invisible image of cities. In: Green Computing and Communications (GreenCom), 2012 IEEE International Conference, pp. 382–389.

Silva, T.H., Vaz de Melo, P.O., Almeida, J.M., Salles, J., Loureiro, A.A., 2013. A comparison of Foursquare and Instagram to the study of city dynamics and urban social behavior. In: Proceedings of the 2nd ACM SIGKDD International Workshop on Urban Computing, p. 4.

Son, H., Lee, J., Rho, G., Cho, S., Yu, K., 2013. Event detection using geo-tagged contents of microblog. In: WSEAS International Conference Proceedings on Recent Advances in Computer Engineering Series (No. 9). WSEAS.

Stodder, D., 2013. Data Visualization and Discovery for Better Business Decisions. TDWI Best Practices Report. Renton, WA: The Data Warehouse Institute.

Van Canneyt, S., Schockaert, S., Van Laere, O., Dhoedt, B., 2011. Time-dependent recommendation of tourist attractions using Flickr. In: Belgian/Netherlands Artificial Intelligence Conference.

Villatoro, D., Serna, J., Rodríguez, V., Torrent-Moreno, M., 2013. The TweetBeat of the city: microblogging used for discovering behavioural patterns during the MWC2012. In: Citizen in Sensor Networks, pp. 43–56.

Wakamiya, S., Lee, R., Sumiya, K., 2011. Crowd-based urban characterization: extracting crowd behavioral patterns in urban areas from twitter. In: Proceedings of the 3rd ACM SIGSPATIAL International Workshop on Location-Based Social Networks, pp. 77–84.

Wakamiya, S., Lee, R., Sumiya, K., 2012a. Looking into socio-cognitive relations between urban areas based on crowd movements monitoring with Twitter. Information and Media Technologies 7 (4), 1571–1576.

Wakamiya, S., Lee, R., Sumiya, K., 2012b. Measuring crowd-sourced cognitive distance between urban clusters with Twitter for socio-cognitive map generation. In Proceedings of the Fourth International Conference on Emerging Databases-Technologies, Applications, and Theory, EDB, Vol. 12, pp. 5–12.

Watanabe, K., Ochi, M., Okabe, M., Onai, R., 2011. Jasmine: a real-time local-event detection system based on geolocation information propagated to microblogs. In: Proceedings of the 20th ACM International Conference on Information and knowledge management, p. 2541–2544.

Xu, C., Wong, D.W., Yang, C., 2013. Evaluating the "geographical awareness" of individuals: an exploratory analysis of twitter data. Cartography and Geographic Information Science 40 (2), 103–115.

Yin, Z., Cao, L., Han, J., Luo, J., Huang, T.S., 2011. Diversified trajectory pattern ranking in geo-tagged social media. In: SDM, pp. 980–991.

Zhang, D., Guo, B., Yu, Z., 2011. The emergence of social and community intelligence. Computer 44 (7), 21–28.

Parallel public transportation system and its application in evaluating evacuation plans for large-scale activities

F. Zhu[1], S. Chen[1], Y. Lv[1,2], X. Dong[1,3] and G. Xiong[1,2]

[1]*The State Key Laboratory of Management and Control for Complex Systems, Institute of Automation, Chinese Academy of Sciences, Beijing, China*
[2]*Dongguan Research Institute of CASIA, Cloud Computing Center, Chinese Academy of Sciences, Dongguan, China*
[3]*Qingdao Academy of Intelligent Industries, Qingdao, China*

CHAPTER OUTLINE

6.1 INTRODUCTION

With the rapid development of the economies globally, more and more large-scale activities like sport games, concerts, and exhibitions are held all over the world, especially in big cities. China, for example, has hosted a series of big events in recent years; the 2008 Beijing Summer Olympic Games, the 2010 Shanghai World Exhibition, the 2010 Guangzhou Asian Games, etc. In order to guarantee the success of these activities, public transportation management for effective emergency evacuation is one of the priority problems which it is necessary to address.

Public transportation management not only serves people's ability to perform their daily activities, such as traveling to work or school, but also plays an important role during special events. Large-scale activities often lead to massive pedestrian and vehicle flow within a limited space and within a short period of time. These traffic flows exhibit notably different characteristics when compared to normal daily activity. For example, the traffic flows usually become congested in the periods immediately before and after a large-scale activity. The categories and attributes of participants can normally be predicted according to the nature of the activity and private vehicles which may be prohibited from entering the area surrounding the location in which the activity is taking place. In case of emergency most attendees may need to be evacuated using public transportation within a short period of time.

Generally, the public transportation management for a large-scale activity must satisfy two types of demand; the demands resulting from the activity itself and those relating to people's normal daily activities. The latter has been studied intensively (Alfa and Chen, 1995; Carey, 1999; Rietveld et al., 2001; Horn, 2004; Roumboutsos and Kapros, 2008; Ding and Huang, 2010; Salicru et al., 2011), while the former attracts little research attention. This chapter focuses on the former demand, i.e., the demands brought about by a large-scale event. In a large-scale activity, there are various different types of participants requiring different traffic services. To keep the evacuation process quick, safe, orderly, and friendly must be the main goal of public transportation scheduling for the large-scale activity. Further considerations include balancing the interests of passengers, transportation companies, and the social environment, while maximizing the integrated benefit.

Most existing studies on traffic management and control still rely on the traditional theories and tools of transportation engineering, based on description of phenomena rather than analysis of principles and have tended to focus on control and traffic rather than service and people. All this leads to three main deficiencies in current transportation management and service; the lack of efficient coordination and management for the planning and operation of different modes of travel, the lack of sufficient supervision and control of traffic elements, and the lack of optimal design and execution of traffic services utilizing intelligent transportation systems. There is therefore an urgent need to study people-oriented management and service of intelligent transportation, which will benefit from a more in-depth understanding of travelers' behavior.

Recent advances in complex systems and computational intelligence have brought new perspectives and insights into the study of intelligent traffic control and management and provided us with new tools and integrated approaches at the system level. The ACP (artificial societies, computational experiments, and parallel execution) approach was originally proposed in Wang (2007, 2010) as a coordinated research and systematic effort utilizing emerging methods and techniques to model, analyze, and control complex systems. This approach consists of three steps: representation with artificial society models, analysis and evaluation using computational experiments, and control and management through parallel execution of real and artificial systems.

The ACP approach differs from traditional methods in that it integrates theoretical analyses, scientific experiments, and computational technologies. The ACP approach can efficiently utilize traffic information, taking into consideration both control and service functions, and promoting people-oriented management of transportation. By adding the control and management functions of social elements, the ACP-based parallel transportation systems are able not only to improve our cognitive competence of the dynamic formation and evolution mechanism of transportation systems but also to optimize the control and management process of the system in both normal and abnormal conditions.

Pioneering works have, up to now, been accomplished in many areas related to the parallel transportation system's theory and verification, e.g., traffic signal control, public transportation management, etc. The focus of this chapter is to present our work relating to the application of the ACP approach in public transportation management for large-scale activities, i.e., modeling and analysis of the parallel public transport systems (PPTS).

6.2 FRAMEWORK OF THE PPTS

In addition to the scheduling and monitoring functions used in daily operation, public transportation management faces many complex demands. These demands include evaluating evacuation plans before any actual operation and preparing emergency plans for possible incidents, etc., in order to address these demands, many experiments need to be conducted which often prove costly and the results are sometimes even impossible to implement in a real public transportation system. An artificial public transportation system (APTS) can "grow" live traffic processes in a bottom-up fashion and provide alternative versions of actual traffic activities, thus offering us a platform or a "living traffic lab" for public transportation analysis and evaluation (Wang and Tang, 2004a; Wang, 2007; Wang et al., 2007; Xiong et al., 2010). Based on APTS, we can conduct computational experiments relating to the traffic signal priority plan and the vehicle schedule plan. Furthermore, by integrating environmental factors, such as economic development and adverse weather, etc., these experiments can be designed and implemented from a holistic perspective, so reasonable results can be guaranteed (Wang and Tang, 2004b). This is the basic idea of the parallel public transportation system (PPTS).

As there is no accurate mathematical model for a transportation system, the PPTS (consisting of both real and artificial transportation systems) uses agent-based technologies to establish the APTS, which models the actual public transportation system. With the APTS, we can explore evolution rules and interactions which occur between various elements in an actual public transportation system through computational experiments. Then, by connecting the actual and artificial systems, we can compare and analyze the behaviors of the two systems under both normal and abnormal conditions, predict the future status of the systems, and adjust control and management methods (Miao et al., 2011; Zhu et al., 2011). Finally, parallel execution can be achieved using previously explored rules. On one hand, the operation of the public transportation system can be optimized and incidents can be reduced in normal conditions, but on the other hand, under abnormal conditions, the system can be corrected to return to normal conditions with minimal transition time loss. Fig. 6.1 summarizes the framework of the proposed PPTS.

The architecture of PPTS is composed of four layers (Wang, 2008; Zhang et al., 2008); the basic components layer, the data and knowledge layer, the computational

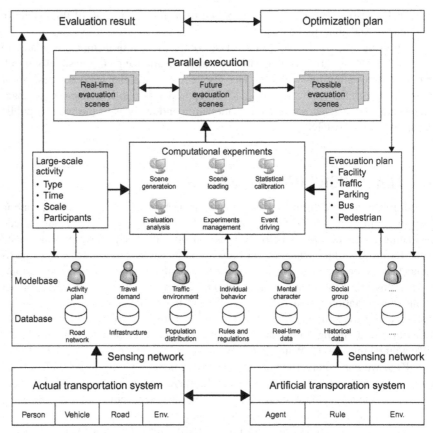

FIGURE 6.1

The framework of a PPTS.

experiment layer, and the parallel execution layer. In the basic components layer, distributed storage and computation of massive data is implemented on a cloud computing platform. This layer also establishes a multiagent environment, which includes an agent management system, a distributed directory server, an agent communication channel, etc. The data and knowledge layer sets up the participants' models, environment, rules, and the mechanism of the public transportation system using agent-based technologies, and creates a dynamic or "living" ontology to represent and organize transportation knowledge such as methods, algorithms, regulations, and case studies.

In the computational experiment layer, a scene generator is designed to support both real and virtual experiments, and an event driving engine is implemented based on discrete event simulation technology. The interaction of agents is simulated dynamically, and algorithm analysis tools are developed on the computational experiment platform. Thus, the experimental processes and results can be analyzed, evaluated, and optimized, and the knowledge base is renewed in real time accordingly. Two types of experiments are carried out in our implementation, one of which is traffic signal control optimization. By collecting public vehicle, social vehicle information and passenger information around the intersection using intelligent perception technologies, the optimized traffic control signal plan can be verified in real time and the maximum traffic efficiency can be achieved. The other type of experiment relates to intelligent scheduling of public transportation vehicles. Based on the perceived and predicted positions of public vehicles, the passengers in vehicles, and the passengers waiting at bus stations, the departure frequency and schedule plan can be optimized on a GIS (geographic information system) operating platform, and is thus able to achieve an intelligent management of public transportation.

In the parallel execution layer an experimental scene is generated based on real-time detected data. The software base and application protocols in the higher level are designed and these protocols serve as the interface between the experimental platform and the terminal users and enable the users to conveniently manage and configure experimental conditions. By monitoring and estimating potentially dangerous elements in the experiment, the event security can be passively queried and the risk can be actively evaluated. Finally, the graphical visualization human–computer interface is used, which can demonstrate the evolution process of both actual and artificial systems and the interactions between the two systems.

6.3 MODELING PARTICIPANTS USING AGENT MODEL

Public transportation systems are becoming increasingly complex, influenced by and influencing nearly all aspects of our society. As more and more facilities and activities are involved in transportation, the connections between the transportation system and the urban environment are also becoming ever more intertwined (Hranac et al., 2006; Koetse and Rietveld, 2009). All this makes the top-down reductionism method of traditional simulation ineffective, and there are still no effective methods which are capable of modeling and analyzing public transportation systems. However, since more simplistic objects or relationships are easier to model and justify, it is useful to build agent models based on tried and tested simple objects or relationships, and then develop a bottom-up approach to "grow" artificial systems and observe their behaviors through the interaction of simple but autonomous agents according to specified rules in given environments. In this context, the ACP approach is proposed to grow holistic APTS from the bottom up (Zhao et al., 2009).

The main idea of APTS is to obtain insights into traffic flow generation and evolution by modeling individual vehicles and local traffic behaviors using basic rules and observing the complex phenomena that emerge from interactions between individuals. In the process of growing ACP-based APTS from the bottom up, agent programming and object-oriented techniques are used extensively for social and behavioral modeling. Fig. 6.2 presents the structure of an agent that represents a person in

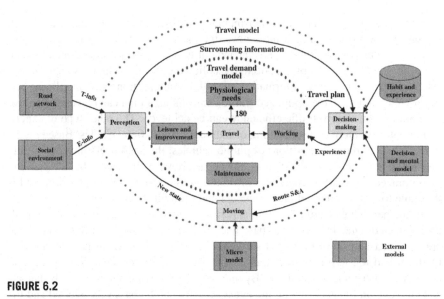

FIGURE 6.2

The structure of an agent in APTS.

APTS. Although now no single definition of agent is universally accepted, it is still widely accepted that an agent can be regarded as a computer system that is situated in an environment and capable of autonomous action in this environment in order to meet its design objectives.

Generally, travel is not undertaken for its own sake but in order to facilitate participation in an activity at a place that is separated from the original location. After constructing activity plans for each member of a population, travel demand can be surmised on the assumption that consecutive activities at different locations need to be connected by travel. Whilst one agent is carrying out its 24-h activity plan, its autonomy is mainly reflected in two ways; one is its habit and experience, and the other is through the decision-making process that is based on its decision and mental model. All these features form the foundation of our activity-based travel demand generation method, which fits well into the paradigm of multiagent simulation and provides us with a feasible approach for generating an individual's travel demand.

The travel demand of agent i can be expressed as:

$$(\mathbf{A}_i, \mathbf{D}_i, \mathbf{P}_i, \mathbf{M}_i, \mathbf{ST}_i, \mathbf{DT}_i) = (A_{i1}, A_{i2}, \ldots, A_{in}; D_{i1}, D_{i2}, \ldots, D_{in}; P_{i1}, P_{i2}, \ldots, P_{in};$$
$$M_{i1}, M_{i2}, \ldots, M_{in}; ST_{i1}, ST_{i2}, \ldots, ST_{in}; DT_{i1}, DT_{i2}, \ldots, DT_{in})$$

where $\mathbf{A}_i, \mathbf{D}_i, \mathbf{P}_i, \mathbf{M}_i, \mathbf{ST}_i, \mathbf{DT}_i$ are vectors for activity, destination, travel path, travel mode, start time, and end time, respectively. Each agent optimizes their activity plan by maximizing the utility of all activities in one day. For one activity, the utility is determined by start time, duration, destination, and so on, and can be expressed as the sum of the utility of the activity itself and the utility of the induced travel, as shown in the following:

$$F = \sum_{j=1}^{n} U_{act}(A_{ij}, ST_{ij}, DT_{ij}) + \sum_{j=1}^{n-1} U_{trav}(P_{ij}, P_{ij+1})$$

Based on the concepts and methods of artificial societies and complex systems, APTS differs from other computer traffic simulation programs in two main aspects. Firstly, the objective of traditional traffic simulation programs is to represent or reflect the true state of the actual systems, whilst the primary goal of APTS is to "grow" live traffic processes in a bottom-up fashion and envisage alternative versions of actual traffic activities. Secondly, APTS must deal with a wide range of information and activities. Most current traffic simulation programs focus on direct traffic-related activities alone, while APTS generates its traffic processes from various indirect facilities and activities, such as the weather and aspects of social interactions. More details about modeling transportation-related systems which use the ACP approach can be found in Wang (2008, 2010), Wang et al. (2007), and Zhang et al. (2008).

It is worth pointing out that, as well as providing feasible ways for the modeling decision processes of one agent, there are many other advantages of modeling transportation systems from the bottom up. For example, both cyber-physical systems (CPS) and cloud computing are naturally embedded into this approach. In fact, CPS, as well as cyber-physical-social systems, are special cases of intelligent spaces and can be considered as an extension of our intelligent transportation spaces (ITSp)—both intelligent spaces and ITSp were developed in our previous studies (Qu et al., 2010). As for cloud computing, it has been in use since the late 1990s in our work on agent-based control and management for networked traffic systems and other applications under the design principle of "local simple, remote complex" for high-intelligence but low-cost smart systems.

6.4 IMPLEMENTATION ON INTELLIGENT TRAFFIC CLOUDS

Agent-based PPTS are able to take advantage of the autonomy, mobility, and adaptability of mobile agents in handling dynamic traffic environments. However, a large number of mobile agents will lead to a complex organization layer that requires enormous computing and power resources. To overcome this challenge, we propose a prototype of a public transportation system using intelligent traffic clouds (Youseff et al., 2008; Armbrust et al., 2009; Buyya et al., 2009).

Using intelligent traffic cloud, complex computing and massive data storage can be implemented on cloud sites in a way that yields high performance at a low cost. The prototype system is shown in Fig. 6.3, and all services are put into intelligent traffic clouds. As well as transforming public vehicle schedule algorithms into schedule agents, the services also include agent performance evaluation and traffic detector

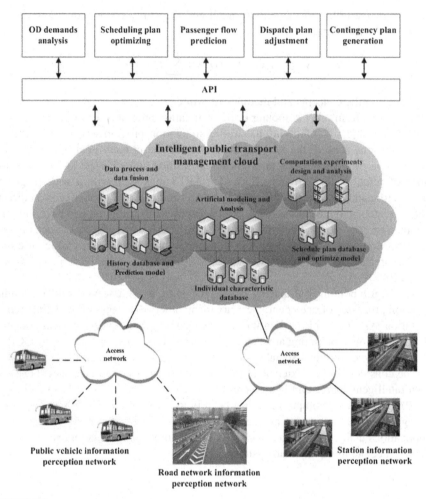

FIGURE 6.3

Parallel transportation management system based on intelligent traffic clouds.

data collection. Service consumers of intelligent traffic clouds include transportation managers, control algorithm developers, and the transportation control center. According to the demands of service consumers, intelligent traffic clouds can provide the following services (Li et al., 2011):

- Management services;
- Transform services from public vehicle schedule algorithms to schedule agents. The services use a standard transform mechanism and a universal API for traffic control algorithm developers;

- Performance test and evaluation services for vehicle schedule agents. This is based on the APTS, the operation results and performance of vehicle schedule agents which can be tested and evaluated in various traffic flow statuses, using typical intersections and networks;
- Storage management services for vehicle schedule agents. This service includes vehicle schedule agent naming, redundancy, encryption, storage, etc., and keeps the load of the whole storage system balanced;
- Storage services for operation data and detector data. These services record the running process of vehicle schedule agents and traffic flow data collected by various detectors.

With the support of cloud computing technologies, our agent-based parallel public transportation system will go far beyond other multiagent traffic management systems, addressing issues such as infinite system scalability, an appropriate agent management scheme, reducing the upfront investment and risk for users, and minimizing the total cost of ownership.

6.5 CASE STUDY

The prototype of parallel transportation management was employed for the 16th Asian Games in Guangzhou, China. This activity, which was unprecedented in both size and scale in the 59-year history of the quadrennial event, is the largest international event held in Guangzhou and provides an important chance to promote Guangzhou's international reputation and regional economic development.

More than 10,000 athletes from 45 countries and regions participated in 42 sports ranging from archery to chess. A large number of contestants, spectators, and visitors made the congested traffic in Guangzhou even worse. Safe and effective public transportation was essential to assure the success of the games. The specific PPTS for the 2010 Guangzhou Asian Games was developed to model the area surrounding the Guangzhou Tianhe sport center (Fig. 6.4). The Tianhe sport center is one of the main venue clusters for the Asian Games. It includes six venues, Tianhe stadium, Tianhe gymnasium, Tianhe natatorium, Tianhe softball field, Tianhe tennis school, and Tianhe bowling hall. The central business district, currently under construction is very near and several shopping centers are located in the surrounding area. The public transportation facilities in this area include two subway lines, 30 bus lines, and 28 bus rapid transit (BRT) lines. Although many measures are taken to relieve traffic pressures in this area, traffic flow is very high and congestion often occurs.

The Guangzhou municipal government was closely concerned with traffic evacuation for the competitions held in the Tianhe sport center and regarded it as one of the most important tasks in the preparation for the Asian Games. Hundreds of evacuation plans were drawn up by the transportation management government of Guangzhou. These plans were predominantly based on the individual managers' experiences, and their efficiency and reliability is very difficult, if not impossible, to evaluate. PPTS

FIGURE 6.4

The modeling area of PPTS.

provide us with one feasible way to evaluate these plans by carrying out computational experiments on artificial systems.

Here we use two evacuation plans for the 8th day (November 19, 2010) to demonstrate the evaluation. Table 6.1 shows the competition schedule for Tianhe sport center for this day. Fig. 6.5 shows the BRT schedule plans for four lines (B1, B2, B3, and B4) used in the two schedule plans. The schedule plans are similar to the normal plan apart from for the period between 7:00 pm and 9:00 pm. The buses that depart between 7:00 pm and 9:00 pm have been specially adjusted for the demands of evacuation and the vehicles are estimated to be in greater numbers than would occur in the normal plan.

Computational experiments are designed and executed in order to grow artificial transportation scenarios for November 19, 2010. Plenty of traffic parameters are collected in these experiments, and they are analyzed to generate quantitative evaluation results. Fig. 6.6 shows some of the results of the evaluation. Fig. 6.6(A) is the curve of traffic flow. It differs from the M curve of a normal day and has an additional peak period from 8:00 pm to 9:00 pm, which is caused by the two matches, football and badminton, ending around 8:00 pm. Fig. 6.6(C) shows the curve of average speed during the course of the day. It also has an additional valley from 8:00 pm to 9:00 pm. Fig. 6.6(B) and (D) are 4-h rooms of Fig. 6.6(A) and (C), and they show the traffic parameters more clearly.

Table 6.1 Competition schedule for Tianhe sport center in November 19, 2010

Sport	Time	Stage	Attendance	Venue
Football	6:30pm–8:30pm	M/QF	30,000–50,000	Tianhe stadium
Badminton	7:30pm–9:30pm	M/W/F	5000–7000	Tianhe gymnasium
Water polo	9:00am–11:10am 2:30pm–5:10pm 7:30pm–10:10pm	M/P	3000–5000	Tianhe natatorium
Softball	1:00pm–3:00pm 3:30pm–5:30pm 6:00pm–8:00pm	W/P	3000–5000	Tianhe softball field
Soft tennis	9:30am–5:00pm	M/W/SF/F	2000–3000	Tianhe tennis school
Bowling	9:00am–12:00pm	M/W/F	<1000	Tianhe bowling hall

M: men; W: women; P: preliminary; QF: quarterfinal; SF: semifinal; F: final.

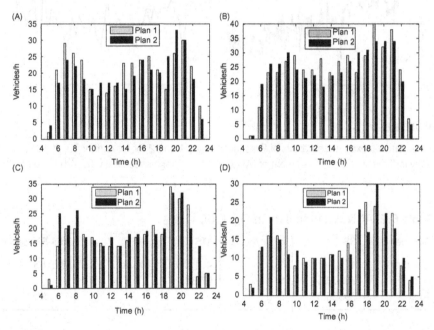

FIGURE 6.5

BRT vehicle schedule plans for November 19, 2010: (A)–(D) are schedule plans for lines B1, B2, B3, and B4, respectively.

Based on these data, quantitative analysis can be conducted for the two evacuation plans. For example, the mean values of the average speed in Fig. 6.6(C) are 28.5 and 26.38, and the analysis of variance (ANNOV) is shown in Table 6.2. The result shows that we cannot reject the hypothesis $H_0 : AV_{plan1} = AV_{plan2}$ at a confidence

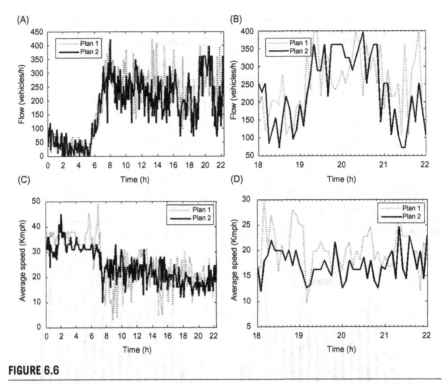

FIGURE 6.6

Computational experiment results of Evacuation Plans 1 and 2 for November 19, 2010: (A) 1-day traffic flow data; (B) 4-h room of (A); (C) 1-day average speed data; (D) 4-h room of (C).

Table 6.2 ANNOV of the data in Fig. 6.6C

Source	SS	df	MS	F	p > F
Columns	401.7	1	401.668	5.92	0.0153
Error	38963.9	574	67.881		
Total	39365.6	575			

level of 0.99, i.e., the differences between the two plans are not statistically significant. Next, we narrow down the comparison period to between 6:00 pm to 10:00 pm. The mean values of the average speed during this period are 20.16 and 17.23. Table 6.3 shows the ANNOV of this period. The results show that we can reject the hypothesis $H_0 : AV_{plan1} = AV_{plan2}$ at a confidence level of 0.9999, i.e., the differences of the two plans are statistically significant.

Table 6.3 ANNOV of the data in Fig. 6.6D

Source	SS	df	MS	F	p > F
Columns	210.18	1	201.184	16.79	8.71248e-05
Error	1201.5	96	12.516		
Total	1411.69	97			

6.6 CONCLUSIONS

The public transportation system plays an important role for evacuation during large-scale events. However, there are still many challenges in the modeling and analysis of the system, as it is both vast and too complex to be modeled using traditional methods.

The ACP approach is adopted by this study in order to build PPTS. Details of the modeling processes are discussed, including building an artificial system using agent-based technology and implementing the schedule plan by utilizing intelligent traffic clouds. A case study has been carried out for the 2010 Guangzhou Asian Games, and the effectiveness of PPTS is demonstrated through the evaluation of two transportation evacuation plans for the Asian Games.

This chapter presents an initial stage of our plan to improve public transportation management in Guangzhou. Currently, one PPTS which will cover the whole city is under construction. Besides the 2010 Asian Games, the employed PPTS will be used to handle critical situations such as peak traffic flows during the Spring Festival Season, transportation in the China Import and Export Commodities Fair, etc.

REFERENCES

Alfa, A.S., Chen, M., 1995. Temporal distribution of public transport demand during the peak period. Eur. J. Oper. Res. 83 (1), 137–153.

Armbrust, M., Fox, A., Griffith, R., Joseph, A.D., Katz, R.H., Konwinski, A., et al., 2009. Above the Clouds: A Berkeley View of Cloud Computing. EECS Department, University of California, Berkeley, Tech. Rep., UCB/EECS-2009-28.

Buyya, R., Yeo, C.S., Venugopal, S., Broberg, J., Brandic, I., 2009. Cloud computing and emerging IT platforms: vision, hype, and reality for delivering computing as the 5th utility. Future Generation Computer Systems 25 (6), 599–616.

Carey, M., 1999. Ex ante heuristic measures of schedule reliability. Transportation Research Part B: Methodological 33 (7), 473–494.

Ding, J., Huang, H., 2010. A cellular automaton model of public transport system considering control strategy. Journal of Transportation Systems Engineering and Information Technology 10 (3), 35–41.

Horn, M.E.T., 2004. Procedures for planning multi-leg journeys with fixed-route and demand-responsive passenger transport services. Transportation Research Part C: Emerging Technologies 12 (1), 33–55.

Hranac, R., Sterzin, E., Krechmer, D., Rakha, H., Farzaneh, M., 2006. Empirical Studies on Traffic Flow in Inclement Weather. U.S. Department of Transportation Federal Highway Administration., Publication No. FHWA-HOP-07-073.

Koetse, M.J., Rietveld, P., 2009. The impact of climate change and weather on transport: an overview of empirical findings. Transportation Research Part D: Transport and Environment 14 (3), 205–221.

Lam, W.H.K., Shao, H., Sumalee, A., 2008. Modeling impacts of adverse weather conditions on a road network with uncertainties in demand and supply. Transportation Research Part B: Methodological 42 (10), 890–910.

Li, Z.J., Chen, C., Wang, K., 2011. Cloud computing for agent-based urban transportation systems. IEEE Intelligent Systems 26 (1), 73–79.

Miao, Q., Zhu, F., Lv, Y., Cheng, C., Chen, C., Qiu, X., 2011. A game-engine-based platform for modeling and computing of artificial transportation systems. IEEE Transactions on Intelligent Transportation Systems 12 (2), 343–353.

Qu, F., Wang, F.Y., Yang, L.Q., 2010. Intelligent transportation spaces: vehicles, traffic, communications, and beyond. IEEE Communications Magazine 48 (11), 136–142.

Rietveld, P., Bruinsma, F.R., van Vuuren, D.J., 2001. Coping with unreliability in public transport chains: a case study for Netherlands. Transportation Research Part A: Policy and Practice 35 (6), 539–559.

Roumboutsos, A., Kapros, S., 2008. A game theory approach to urban public transport integration policy. Transport Policy 15 (4), 209–215.

Salicru, M., Fleurent, C., Armengol, J.M., 2011. Timetable-based operation in urban transport: run-time optimisation and improvements in the operating process. Transportation Research Part A: Policy and Practice 45 (8), 721–740.

Wang, F.Y., 2007. Toward a paradigm shift in social computing: the ACP approach. IEEE Intelligent Systems 22 (5), 65–67.

Wang, F.Y., 2008. Toward a revolution in transportation operations: AI for complex systems. IEEE Intelligent Systems 23 (6), 8–13.

Wang, F.Y., 2010. Parallel control and management for intelligent transportation systems: concepts, architectures, and applications. IEEE Transactions on Intelligent Transportation Systems 11 (3), 630–638.

Wang, F.Y., Tang, S.M., 2004a. Artificial societies for integrated and sustainable development of metropolitan systems. IEEE Intelligent Systems 19 (4), 82–87.

Wang, F.Y., Tang, S.M., 2004b. Concept and framework of artificial transportation system. Complex Systems and Complexity Science 1 (2), 52–57.

Wang, F.Y., Carley, K.M., Zeng, D., Mao, W., 2007. Social computing: from social informatics to social intelligence. IEEE Intelligent Systems 22 (2), 79–83.

Xiong, G., Wang, K., Zhu, F., Cheng, C., An, X., Xie, Z., 2010. Parallel traffic management for the 2010 Asian Games. IEEE Intelligent Systems 25 (3), 81–85.

Youseff, L., Butrico, M., Da Silva, D., 2008. Toward a unified ontology of cloud computing. IEEE Grid Computing Environments Workshop, Austin, TX, pp. 1–10.

Zhang, N., Wang, F.Y., Zhu, F., Zhao, D., Tang, S., 2008. DynaCAS: computational experiments and decision support for ITS. IEEE Intelligent Systems 23 (6), 19–23.

Zhao, H., Tang, S., Lv, Y., 2009. Generating artificial populations for traffic microsimulation. IEEE Intelligent Transportation Systems Magazine 1 (3), 22–28.

Zhu, F., Li, G., Li, Z., Chen, C., Wen, D., 2011. A case study of evaluating traffic signal control systems using computational experiments. IEEE Transactions on Intelligent Transportation Systems 12 (4), 1220–1226.

Predicting financial risk from revenue reports

7

B. Qian and H. Li

IBM Thomas J. Watson Research Center, Yorktown Heights, NY, United States

CHAPTER OUTLINE

Big Data and Smart Service Systems. DOI: http://dx.doi.org/10.1016/B978-0-12-812013-2.00007-1

7.1 INTRODUCTION

7.1.1 BACKGROUND AND MOTIVATION

We consider a practical risk minimization problem as follows: assume you are a conservative investor and your objective is to generate profit from trading stocks but with a rule stating that no risky transactions are permitted. The question then becomes clear—how do you measure a company's overall trading risk, which involves the net profit margin, the stock return volatility, etc. To address this problem, traditional methods tend to predict the financial risk of a company based on its stock price history using time series analytics. However, such a method is in itself risky as the future return of a stock depends on a set of external factors, such as the overall economic conditions at any given time, a company's recent performance, and the impact of new technology, all of which are completely ignored in this sort of time series analysis. Since the revenue report is the only information source which is publicly available, we propose using machine learning techniques to estimate the financial risk from these textual revenue reports. More specifically, the problem is defined as a "learning-to-rank" problem: (1) the ranking model adapts to the training data (a set of revenue reports along with their relative trading risks), and then (2) we apply the learnt model to all available revenue reports in order to ascertain which are the most reliable companies. Learning to rank refers to a branch of machine learning techniques which automatically construct a ranking model from the training data (Cao et al., 2007), and we aim to use such techniques to solve the aforementioned problems predominantly because our ultimate goal is to sort the companies in descending order with respect to their financial risks. Therefore, the key topic we hope to address in this chapter is the design of an efficient learning algorithm which can accurately model the relationship between the textual revenue reports and the corresponding companies' future stock prices. In the latter part of the chapter, we shall discuss this risk minimization issue from a machine learning perspective.

The objective of this chapter is to explore ways of improving existing methods in the following three ways: (1) Pairwise supervision. Pairwise training data are easier to acquire, for example it would be easier to compare the market value of two companies rather than asking for a real risk value of a single company, and this can therefore reduce the total cost of training a ranking model. (2) Nonlinearity. In practical terms it is unlikely that linear methods could produce the desired level of accuracy, consequently, nonlinear approaches are preferable if the computational complexity is not significantly increased. (3) Active learning mode. Typical learning methods would be likely to fail when training data are insufficient since their performance is highly dependent on the quality of training data (Long et al., 2010). Due to the complexity of real-world ranking applications, abundant training samples are generally required in order to achieve an expected performance. However, the acquisition of a large amount of training examples is usually both expensive and time-consuming. This provides further motivation for developing active learning, where the goal is to effectively improve the ranking performance with minimal human effort.

7.1.2 PROBLEMS AND CHALLENGES

In order to address the three principal limitations of existing works in a single learning model, we confront three distinctive difficulties: (1) Whilst training samples are treated independently in most supervised learning approaches, in the context of our ranking problem the correlation between the risk scores of different companies cannot be ignored as ranking itself is a relative problem. (2) Nonlinear problems are generally computationally intractable, which greatly limits our choice of learning models as we require our risk learning method to be solved efficiently. (3) Compared to typical active learning, which has been extensively studied in the context of querying labels in classification problems, the design of pairwise query selection strategy (used in active learning mode) is not as obvious.

7.1.3 RISK PREDICTION VIA ACTIVE PAIRWISE LEARNING

In this section, we briefly describe the approaches we have adopted to address the three challenges mentioned above, and will discuss the detailed formulations pertaining to these approaches later in the chapter. We start with a simple linear prediction function. In order to incorporate pairwise supervision into the learning framework, we propose a "large margin" orientated cost function (Joachims, 2002; Parikh and Grauman, 2011) whereby the pairwise constraints can be easily encoded (Davidson et al., 2013). To neglect the noise in training data, we soften our method using slack variables which allows the ranking hyperplane to be slightly distant on the wrong side of the training pairwise constraints. Since linear models cannot handle complicated scenarios, we kernelize our formulation to be a nonlinear model by deriving the dual of the primal optimization. So as to involve humans in the learning loop, we propose to select informative questions by finding a balance between *local* and *global* uncertainty measures. In particular *local uncertainty* (LU) is useful for those sample pairs whose relationship is unclear in the current ranking function, and *global uncertainty* (GU) measures the uncertainty of the relation between a particular sample and all the other samples. LU helps to identify the most uncertain sample pairs, while GU helps to locate the representative samples. Through combining both of the uncertainty measures, the proposed active learning strategy proves reliable in terms of identifying informative sample pairs, while ignoring uninformative outliers or noise samples.

Our work seeks to make three main contributions to the area. (1) We investigate using a pairwise learning method to perform financial risk estimation of publicly traded corporations, which can be recovered using efficient gradient-based optimization. (2) The proposed model is nonlinear due to the kernelization, but can still be solved as a linear problem. This property enables us to embrace all the advantages of nonlinearity without suffering the computational complexity that accompanies it. (3) The proposed framework is designed with a self-estimation scheme which seeks to uncover the weakness of the current prediction model, on which basis our model can actively ask humans informative questions in order to improve itself.

7.1.4 CHAPTER ORGANIZATION

The rest of the chapter is organized as follows; we begin with a discussion of related studies in Section 7.2, and then present the proposed prediction model and its dual formulation in Section 7.3. In Section 7.4, we extend our model to incorporate the context of human–machine interaction, and discuss the properties of our active query scheme in depth. Section 7.5 tests our approach in a real-world application—estimating the financial risk of publicly traded corporations using 10-K files. Finally we draw conclusions from our work in Section 7.6 and references are provided at the end of the chapter.

7.2 RELATED STUDIES

Learning to rank methods falls into three categories which differ in supervision type. (1) *Pointwise* approaches approximate a ranking problem by ordinal regression (Shashua and Levin, 2002; Crammer and Singer, 2001; Cossock and Zhang, 2006), where the group structure of data is usually ignored. (2) *Pairwise* methods transform a ranking problem into pairwise classification by adopting a binary predictor that can decide which instance is ranked higher in a pair of instances. (3) *Listwise* methods treat a ranked list as a training sample (Cao et al., 2007; Xu and Li, 2007; Yue et al., 2007), where the group structure is considered. As it is easier to answer a pairwise question than pointwise or listwise questions, we shall focus on the pairwise model in this chapter. Pairwise learning to rank has been successfully applied to many information retrieval applications. For example, Joachims (2002) applied RankSVM to document retrieval, where the training set consisted of pairs of documents derived from the click-through data; RankNet (Burges et al., 2005) has proven to be useful in large-scale web searches. A brief survey of learning to rank techniques is presented in Hang (2011).

Though extensively studied, learning to rank has not been sufficiently explored in an active learning setting. Donmez and Carbonell (2008) investigate the use of active document selection in a ranking problem, which aims to query documents which will potentially have great impact on the ranking model. Yu (2005) suggests that the most informative pair in a ranking problem is the pair whose ranking seems most ambiguous to the ranking model. Long et al. (2010) incorporate both query and document selection into the active query scheme, and present a two-stage optimization to minimize the loss of expected discounted cumulative gain. Yang et al. (2009) introduce a leveraged query strategy that maximizes the linear combinations of query difficulty, density, and diversity. A comprehensive empirical evaluation of document selection strategies is available in Aslam et al. (2009). However, existing approaches have limitations, for example the expected model change method is computationally expensive, and the uncertainty sampling method often fails if noise scattered in the data. In addition, existing methods have ignored the existence of similar objects, where a pairwise ordering proves difficult to provide. To address this, we have added a set of weak constraints to the prediction model, and enforced the estimated risks of two similar companies. A hashing method used to scale the query selection process can be found in Qian et al. (2013). A similar method as presented in Chang et al.

(2013) can be adopted in order to adjust a learned ranking function for slightly different preferences.

7.3 THE FRAMEWORK OF RISK PREDICTION

7.3.1 OVERVIEW OF THE PREDICTION SYSTEM

Fig. 7.1 illustrates the mechanism of our proposed risk prediction system, which contains two major components, i.e., a learning and a prediction model. The learning model adapts to the provided training data and produces a prediction function, which is later used to estimate risks of unseen data. The linear formulation of our approach is presented in Sections 7.3.2 and 7.3.3, and the corresponding nonlinear version is presented in Section 7.3.4.

7.3.2 PRELIMINARIES AND NOTATIONS

Given a set of n revenue reports of corporations represented in $\mathbf{R}^d$ space using n feature vectors $\mathbf{R} = \{\mathbf{r}_1, \mathbf{r}_2, \mathbf{r}_n\}$, we define a risk prediction problem so that we can sort the corporations in descending order with respect to their financial risks. Two sets of pairwise constraints are provided: (1) A set of strongly ranked pairs of corporations $\mathcal{E} = \{(i, j)\}$, such that $(i, j) \in \mathcal{E} \rightarrow$corporation i is significantly financially more stable than corporation j; (2) A set of weakly ranked pairs of corporations $F = \{(i, j)\}$, such that $(i, j) \in F \rightarrow$corporation i is slightly more financially stable than corporation j. To make the training of prediction models feasible, the initial training set cannot be empty, i.e., we require that either $\mathcal{E}$ or F is not empty at the beginning of the training. To begin with, we aim to learn a prediction function ρ with a linear projection vector p,

$$\rho(\mathbf{r}) = p^T \mathbf{r}, \tag{7.1}$$

where p can be viewed as the normal vector of a hyperplane in $\mathbf{R}^d$ space. Then the risk estimation problem is to optimize p so that maximal pairwise constraints are satisfied:

$$p^T \mathbf{r}_i > p^T \mathbf{r}_j, \quad if\,(i, j) \in \varepsilon$$
$$p^T \mathbf{r}_i = p^T \mathbf{r}_j, \quad if\,(i, j) \in \mathcal{F} \tag{7.2}$$

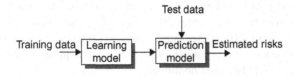

FIGURE 7.1

The flow chart of prediction model.

7.3.3 THE PREDICTION MODEL

As shown in Höffgen et al. (1995), recovering the optimal p over the constraints in Eq. (7.2) is non-deterministic polynomial-time hard (NP-hard). Alternatively, we propose to approximate the problem using a large margin approach. Additionally, we further ease the problem by using two non-negative soft margin slack variables, ζ and η. Note that completely complying with the given pairwise constraints is not preferred since real data may contain noise or outliers. Instead, a smooth separating boundary that ignores a few noisy constraints is better than one that loops around the outliers. Such relaxation allows the prediction model to create a small distance on the wrong side of the training data. To avoid oversimplified solutions in which large slacks allow any p, we add a penalty term of slacks to our formulation. The soft margin is expressed as:

Primal optimization:

$$\min_{p,\zeta,\eta} \frac{1}{2}\|p\|^2 + e\zeta \sum_{i,j} \zeta_{ij} + e_\eta \sum_{i,j} \eta_{ij}$$

$$\text{s.t.} \quad p^T \mathbf{r}_i - p^T \mathbf{r}_j \geq 1 - \zeta_{ij}, \qquad \quad if\,(i,j) \in \varepsilon; \qquad\qquad (7.3)$$

$$p^T \mathbf{r}_i - p^T \mathbf{r}_j \geq -\eta_{ij}, \qquad\qquad if\,(i,j) \in \mathcal{F};$$

$$\zeta_{ij} \geq 0; \quad \eta_{ij} \geq 0.$$

where e_ζ and e_η are two tuning parameters which act to balance the margin and training error (in terms of unsatisfied pairwise constraints). The first set of constraints in Eq. (7.3) enforces the prediction function p in order to comply with the strong constraints, and the second set of constraints enforce the weak constraints.

The optimization problem described in Eq. (7.3) is convex (Joachims, 2002), and is similar to an support vector machine (SVM) formulation but on pairwise differences $(x_i - x_j)$. Therefore, Eq. (7.3) can be solved using a revised decomposition SVM solvers, such as SVM light (Joachims, 1999). The penalty term of slack variables ζ and η is defined as the hinge loss, which is not differentiable. We may use Huber loss (differentiable) to approximate the hinge loss (Chapelle, 2007), and the optimal solution can be recovered using Newton optimization (Parikh and Grauman, 2011) with a backtracking strategy to reach a convergence.

7.3.4 NONLINEAR DUAL OPTIMIZATION

In real-world prediction problems, it is unlikely that linear methods would produce optimal performance. Consequently, nonlinear methods are preferred if the computational complexity will not be significantly raised. A nonlinear prediction function can be easily derived from a linear prediction function using linear mapping φ, which maps the data vectors onto a higher dimensional space where there is a better chance that more pairwise constraints can be satisfied. With a mapping φ, the linear prediction shown in Eq. (7.1) becomes nonlinear.

$$\rho(\mathbf{r}) = p^T \phi(\mathbf{r}) \qquad\qquad (7.4)$$

Such a method is called the kernel method, which enables nonlinearity but does not require an explicit definition for the mapping φ. To deploy the kernel method, we need to derive the duality of the problem defined in Eq. (7.3). There are two main reasons to solve our problem in the dual format: (1) the duality theory provides a convenient way to handle the constraints and (2) the dual optimization can be expressed using inner products of data vectors, thereby making it possible to apply kernel functions. According to the Lagrangian theory and Karush–Kuhn–Tucker conditions, strong duality of the primal problem (Eq. (7.3)) holds. Therefore dual optimization can be obtained using the following steps. The Lagrange primal function, denoted by L, is expressed using two multipliers γ and δ.

$$
\begin{aligned}
\min_{p,\zeta,\eta} \max_{\gamma,\delta} L = {} & \frac{1}{2}\|p\|^2 + e_\zeta \sum_{i,j} \zeta_{ij} + e_\eta \sum_{i,j} \eta_{ij} \\
& - \sum_{(i,j)\in\varepsilon} \gamma_{ij}(p^T(\mathbf{r}_i - \mathbf{r}_j) - 1 + \zeta_{ij}) \\
& - \sum_{(i,j)\in F} \delta_{ij}(p^T(\mathbf{r}_i - \mathbf{r}_j) - 1 + \eta_{ij})
\end{aligned}
\tag{7.5}
$$

$$
\text{s.t.}\quad \gamma_{ij} \geq 0; \delta_{ij} \geq 0; \zeta_{ij} \geq 0; \eta_{ij} \geq 0 \cdot
$$

Set the first-order derivatives of L on p to zero, and we arrive at

$$
\frac{\partial L}{\partial p} = 0 \Rightarrow p = \sum_{(i,j)\in\varepsilon} \gamma_{ij}(\mathbf{r}_i - \mathbf{r}_j) + \sum_{(i,j)\in F} \delta_{ij}(\mathbf{r}_i - \mathbf{r}_j)
\tag{7.6}
$$

Let $\mathbf{J}$ denote the kernel matrix and $\mathbf{r}_t$ denote a corporation t, the kernelized prediction function ρ_k can be expressed using:

$$
\rho_k(\mathbf{r}_t) = \sum_{(i,j)\in\varepsilon} \gamma_{ij}(\mathbf{J}_{it} - \mathbf{J}_{jt}) + \sum_{(i,j)\in\mathcal{F}} \delta_{ij}(\mathbf{J}_{it} - \mathbf{J}_{jt})
\tag{7.7}
$$

The dual problem is obtained by substituting Eq. (7.6) to Eq. (7.5).
Dual optimization:

$$
\begin{aligned}
\max_{\gamma,\delta} {} & \sum_{(i,j)\in\varepsilon} \gamma_{ij} \\
& - \frac{1}{2} \sum_{(i,j)\in\varepsilon} \sum_{(k,l)\in\varepsilon} \gamma_{ij}\gamma_{kl}(\mathbf{r}_i - \mathbf{r}_j)^T(\mathbf{r}_k - \mathbf{r}_l) \\
& - \frac{1}{2} \sum_{(i,j)\in\mathcal{F}} \sum_{(k,l)\in\mathcal{F}} \delta_{ij}\delta_{kl}(\mathbf{r}_i - \mathbf{r}_j)^T(\mathbf{r}_k - \mathbf{r}_l) \\
& - \sum_{(i,j)\in\varepsilon} \sum_{(k,l)\in\mathcal{F}} \gamma_{ij}\delta_{kl}(\mathbf{r}_i - \mathbf{r}_j)^T(\mathbf{r}_k - \mathbf{r}_l)
\end{aligned}
\tag{7.8}
$$

$$
\text{s.t.}\quad 0 \leq \gamma_{ij} \leq e_\zeta;\quad 0 \leq \delta_{ij} \leq e_\eta \cdot
$$

According to the duality, both the primal and dual problems are convex. The dual optimization is equivalent to a kernel SVM problem but on the inner products of pairwise differences $(\mathbf{r}_i - \mathbf{r}_j)^T (\mathbf{r}_k - \mathbf{r}_l)$. Therefore the dual problem can be solved using kernel SVM solvers, such as LIBSVM (Chang and Lin, 2011). According to the convexity, alternating the gradient-based optimization over γ and δ can also result in the global optima. In our implementation, we simply solve the above constrained dual problem using a CVX solver (CVX, 2012; Grant and Boyd, 2008), which is a Matlab package for specifying and solving convex programs.

7.4 IMPROVING THE MODEL WITH HUMANS-IN-THE-LOOP

7.4.1 OVERVIEW OF THE ACTIVE PREDICTION SYSTEM

In Fig. 7.2 we illustrate the conceptual diagram of our risk prediction framework with humans included in the loop. A learning cycle starts with the training of a prediction function. Subsequently our query selection strategy finds the most informative question and asks a human for its answer, which will later be encoded as an additional constraint to update the current prediction model. This process repeats until a desired level of accuracy is achieved or a certain stopping criterion is satisfied. Compared to the prediction system shown in Fig. 7.1, this active system requires a different query selection strategy we shall now describe.

7.4.2 QUERY SELECTION STRATEGY

Predictions which include humans-in-the-loop mainly aim to improve the prediction performance using minimal human effort. Therefore, the key question is—*How*

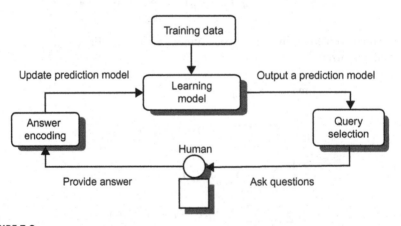

FIGURE 7.2

The prediction cycle with humans in the loop.

do we find informative pairwise queries? An informative pairwise query needs to have the following properties. (1) LU: the prediction model is uncertain about the financial rank of a pair of corporations, which implies that the difference in the risk scores between the two corporations i and j ($p^T(\mathbf{r}_i - \mathbf{r}_j)$) is small. In particular, the two revenue reports $\mathbf{r}_i$ and $\mathbf{r}_j$, $p^T(\mathbf{r}_i - \mathbf{r}_j) > 1$ indicate that our prediction model is certain that corporation i is considerably more financially stable than corporation j. (2) GU: the overall financial rank of a corporation is uncertain in our prediction model, and figuring out the rank of such a corporation can potentially engender significant change to the prediction model. In particular, if our prediction model is confused about the overall rank of a revenue report $\mathbf{r}_i$, querying on $\mathbf{r}_i$ would generally help to improve the prediction accuracy. To achieve a stable query strategy, we propose to combine the two uncertainty measures using a balancing factor z. Let $(\mathbf{r}^*_i, \mathbf{r}^*_j)$ denoting the most informative pair of corporations whose rank is to be queried in the next iteration (to improve the prediction accuracy), the leveraged query selection strategy is formulated as:

$$(\mathbf{r}^*_i, \mathbf{r}^*_j) = \arg \max_{\mathbf{r}_i, \mathbf{r}_j \in \mathbf{R}} (\mathcal{G}\mathcal{U}(\mathbf{r}_i) + \mathcal{G}\mathcal{U}(\mathbf{r}_j))\mathcal{L}\mathcal{U}(\mathbf{r}_i, \mathbf{r}_j)^z \tag{7.9}$$

where GU ($\bullet$) measures the GU of the overall rank of a pair of corporations considering all available corporations, and LU ($\bullet$) assesses the LU of our prediction model on the local rank of a pair of corporations. z is a tuning parameter used to balance the influence of the two measures, and a larger z emphasizes the LU.

7.4.3 DEFINITION OF THE LU

In our proposed prediction model, the LU is defined using the value of risk score distance, formally $p^T(\mathbf{r}_i - \mathbf{r}_j)$. In the active mode, our algorithm is more interested in pairwise financial rankings that are not clear. For example, a large $p^T(\mathbf{r}_i - \mathbf{r}_j)$ implies that our prediction function is certain on the financial rank of the two corporations i and j. Therefore, it is reasonable to query the pairs of corporations with small risk score distances. Formally, the LU can be estimated using the inverse of $p^T(\mathbf{r}_i - \mathbf{r}_j)$:

$$\mathcal{L}\mathcal{U}(\mathbf{r}_i, \mathbf{r}_j) = \left| p^T(\mathbf{r}_i - \mathbf{r}_j) \right|^{-1} \tag{7.10}$$

For the nonlinear version, the kernelized LU is expressed as shown below:

$$
\begin{aligned}
\mathcal{L}\mathcal{U}(\mathbf{r}_i, \mathbf{r}_j) = \Big| &\sum_{(k,l)\in\varepsilon} \alpha_{kl}(\mathbf{J}_{ki} - \mathbf{J}_{kj} - \mathbf{J}_{li} + \mathbf{J}_{lj}) \\
&+ \sum_{(k,l)\in\mathcal{F}} \beta_{kl}(\mathbf{J}_{ki} - \mathbf{J}_{kj} - \mathbf{J}_{li} + \mathbf{J}_{lj}) \Big|^{-1}
\end{aligned} \tag{7.11}
$$

In real applications, the criterion shown above would tend to prefer the pairs of corporations (1) whose financial ranks are unclear to the prediction function and (2) the two corporations' risk are in fact similar. Although the latter case does not constitute an informative query for active learning, the occurrence of this case would be significantly alleviated by the GU, which we shall further elucidate in the following section.

7.4.4 DEFINITION OF THE GU

Since a globally uncertain corporation is one whose pairwise financial ranks compared to all other corporations are uncertain, the GU can also be measured using a risk score distance, formally, $p^T(\mathbf{r}_i - \mathbf{r}_j)$. Assuming that there is a revenue report $\mathbf{r}_i$ whose risk score distances are exactly the same as all others, we can safely conclude that our prediction model will have no idea about where $\mathbf{r}_i$ is ranked (with respect to risk) among all these corporations, and therefore querying humans about the relative risk rank of $\mathbf{r}_i$ would greatly enrich the training data. To facilitate such queries, we adopt entropy to assess the GU. Considering the fact that in our model the risk score distances can be either negative or positive, and the sum of the values of $p^T(\mathbf{r}_i - \mathbf{r}_j)$ over $\forall \, \mathbf{r}_j \in \mathbf{R}$ is unlikely to be one. We first normalize the risk score distances so that they become non-negative and sum-to-one using the normalization equation as shown in the following:

$$\mathcal{N}(r_i, r_j) = \frac{p^T(\mathbf{r}_i - \mathbf{r}_j) - \min_{\mathbf{r}_k} p^T(\mathbf{r}_i - \mathbf{r}_k)}{\max_{\mathbf{rk}} p^T(\mathbf{r}_i - \mathbf{r}_k) - \min_{\mathbf{r}_k} P^T(\mathbf{r}_i - \mathbf{r}_k)} \tag{7.12}$$

Then, the GU can be calculated using the entropy of the normalized risk score distances, as follows:

$$\mathcal{GU}(\mathbf{r}_i) = - \sum_{\mathbf{r}_j \in \mathbf{R}, j \neq i} \mathcal{N}(r_i, r_j) \log \mathcal{N}(r_i, r_j) \tag{7.13}$$

The kernelized version of the above equation can be easily derived by substituting the kernelized p as shown in Eq. (7.6) into Eq. (7.13). In practice, by maximizing the uncertainty measure shown in Eq. (7.13) our prediction model would prefer to select the revenue reports that are located near the center of a dense area in the feature space. Such corporations are representative and potentially carry the maximum amount of knowledge, which if queried can create a better projection vector p.

7.5 EMPIRICAL EVALUATION

7.5.1 BASELINES AND ACCURACY MEASURE

In our experiment, we attempt to understand the strengths and relative performance of our approach which we refer to in this section as Ours+ Active. In particular, we wish to know how well our method compares to the two following state-of-the-art baseline methods:

1. RankSVM (Chapelle and Keerthi, 2010), a state-of-the-art ranking algorithm, which solves the ranking SVM problem in the primal format using gradient-based optimization.
2. RelativeRankSVM (Parikh and Grauman, 2011) is also an SVM-based algorithm, which allows similarly ranked objects and is solved in the primal form using Newton's method.

Our proposed model significantly outperforms these two state-of-the-art methods (as shown in Fig. 7.3). Given this, a natural question would be "Is this good performance due to our query selection strategy or the nonlinearity of our prediction model?" To investigate this we explore the following scenarios:

1. Applying our active selection strategy to the two baselines' prediction models, i.e., RankSVM + Active and RelativeRankSVM + Active.
2. Our prediction model set alongside a query selection that is solely based on LU (without GU), i.e., Ours + Local.
3. Using random query selection for all three prediction models, i.e., Ours + Random, RankSVM + Random, and RelativeRankSVM + Random.

We compare the seven approaches mentioned above on a real-world application, predicting the financial risk of publicly traded corporations using revenue reports. The parameters in RankSVM and RelativeRankSVM include an initial prediction vector p (set to zeros in our experiment), and the two options for Newton's method, i.e., maximum number of linear conjugate gradients (set to 20), and a stopping criterion for conjugate gradients (set to 10^{-3}). In our prediction model, we adopt an Radial Basis Function kernel (the length scale is selected using cross-validation), and set the tuning parameter z to 1. The penalty constant for the slack variables in all three ranking models is set to 0.1. In our evaluation, ranking accuracy was assessed using the normalized discounted cumulative gain (NDCG), defined as:

$$\text{NDCG}(\rho) = C \sum_{i} \frac{(2^{s(i)} - 1)}{\log_2(1 + i)} \tag{7.14}$$

where $s(i)$ denotes the real financial risk of corporation i, and C is a normalization constant in which circumstance a perfect risk prediction gets an NDCG score of 1. We chose to calculate NDCG scores at two different rank numbers in order to simulate the scenarios where different numbers of corporations are initially viewed by investors. Additionally, it is worth noting that we did not include *error bars* in our experimental results, rather we just reported the average performance. The reason is that in an active prediction scenario the initial training data are usually assumed to be very limited, thereby the performance over random trials can be significantly different, which makes the error bar meaningless.

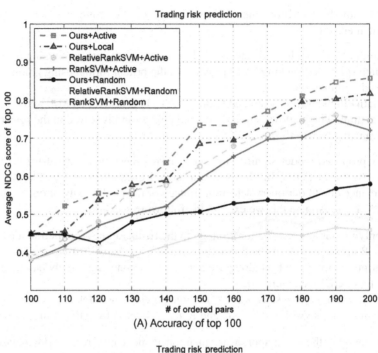

(A) Accuracy of top 100

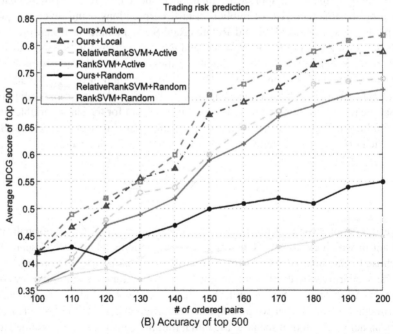

(B) Accuracy of top 500

FIGURE 7.3

Performance comparison on 10-K files (annual revenue reports). (A) Accuracy of top 100, (B) Accuracy of top 500.

7.5.2 **DATA SET AND EXPERIMENTAL SETTINGS**

The financial dataset used in our experiment consists of 19,395 textual files—10-K reports (data are publicly available at http://www.ark.cs.cmu.edu/10K/), the annual revenue reports of publicly traded corporations required by SEC (Securities Exchange Commission), published over the period of 1996–2006 from 10,492 corporations (Kogan et al., 2009). The feature extraction is deployed on the raw text files using Term Frequency–Inverse Document Frequency (TFIDF), and produces 150,360 features (sparse) for each corporation. To further speed up the computation, we project the feature vectors to a 100-dimensional space using Principal Component Analysis (PCA). In terms of investment security, our task is to rank the corporations in descending order with respect to their financial risks. Each report comes with a date of publication, which can be used to locate the stock price changes over a 12-month period before, and the 12-month period after each report. The ground truth financial risk (used to calculate NDCG scores) of each corporation was assessed using stock return volatility measurements defined in Kogan et al. (2009), based upon which the pairwise constraints (used as the supervision in our prediction model) are generated.

7.5.3 **RESULT AND DISCUSSION**

In each trial we randomly selected 100 pairs of ranked corporations as the initial training set to learn a prediction function. We then gradually added 100 additional pairwise constraints to the training set using our proposed query selection strategy or simply random querying, so that the evaluation was performed on a series of training sets with different sizes. The experiments were repeated 30 times, and the average NDCGs are reported in Fig. 7.3A (at Rank 100) and Fig. 7.3B (at Rank 500). We see that, compared with the methods using our active query strategy, along with the number of training pairs increases the ones using random querying does not noticeably improve the prediction accuracy. Additionally, querying solely based on LU does not yield results as good as those which utilize our combined querying scheme. This validates the utility of our LU and GU selection strategy, and confirms the motivation and necessity for active prediction with humans-in-the-loop, since asking humans randomly selected pairwise questions cannot efficiently improve the prediction progam's performance. It can also be observed that RelativeRankSVM in general achieves higher prediction accuracy than RankSVM, which testifies to the success of using weak constraints (similarly stable corporations). Among the three prediction models, the proposed model significantly outperforms the other two, which demonstrates the effectiveness of our nonlinear prediction function. We believe the superior performance of the proposed prediction model arises from both the nonlinearity of our model and the tolerance of weakly ranked corporations.

7.6 **CONCLUSION**

In this chapter we have proposed a financial risk prediction model based on learning to rank techniques with pairwise constraints, to make use of the publicly available revenue reports. The contributions of our learning to rank formulation are to make the prediction function nonlinear using kernel methods, and to take into consideration the existence of similar or closely ranked corporations. The proposed query strategy combines LU and GU measures, and enables querying on informative pairs of corporations whilst ignoring useless pairs such as those which could be labeled noise or outliers. We empirically show that the proposed query selection strategy performs well even when concatenated with other prediction models, demonstrating the versatility of our query strategy. These promising results shown in our experiment establish the effectiveness of our proposed model in solving a wide range of real-world problems.

REFERENCES

Aslam, J.A., Kanoulas, E., Pavlu, V., Savev, S., Yilmaz, E., 2009. Document selection methodologies for efficient and effective learning-to-rank. In: Proceedings of the 32nd International ACM SIGIR Conference on Research and Development in Information Retrieval, ser. SIGIR 2009. New York, NY, USA: ACM, pp. 468–475. [Online]. Available: http://doi.acm.org/10.1145/1571941.1572022.

Burges, C.J.C., Shaked, T., Renshaw, E., Lazier, A., Deeds, M., et al., 2005. Learning to rank using gradient descent. In: Proceedings of the 22nd International Conference on Machine learning. New York, NY, USA: ACM, pp. 89–96.

Cao, Z., Qin, T., Liu, T.-Y., Tsai, M.-F., Li, H., 2007. Learning to rank: from pairwise approach to listwise approach. In: Proceedings of the 24th International Conference on Machine Learning, ser. 2007. New York, NY, USA: ACM, pp. 129–136.

Chang, C.-C., Lin, C.-J., 2011. "LIBSVM: a library for support vector machines,". ACM Transactions on Intelligent Systems and Technology, vol. 2, 27. 1–27:27.

Chang, S., Qi, G.-J., Tang, J., Tian, Q., Rui, Y., Huang, T.S., 2013. "Multimedia lego: learning structured model by probabilistic logic ontology tree," In: Data Mining (ICDM), 2013 IEEE 13th International Conference on. Dallas, Texas, USA: IEEE, pp. 979–984.

Chapelle, O., 2007. "Training a support vector machine in the primal,". Neural Comput. vol. 19 (no. 5), 1155–1178. [Online]. Available at: http://dx.doi.org/10.1162/neco.2007.19.5.1155.

Chapelle, O., Keerthi, S.S., 2010. "Efficient algorithms for ranking with SVMs,". Inf. Retr. vol. 13 (no. 3), 201–215.

Cossock, D., Zhang, T., 2006. Subset ranking using regression. In: Proceedings of the 19th Annual Conference on Learning Theory, Pittsburgh, Pennsylvania, USA: Springer, pp. 605–619.

Crammer, K., Singer, Y., 2001. Pranking with ranking. In: NIPS, Vancouver, British Columbia, Canada, pp. 641–647.

CVX Research, Inc., 2012. CVX: Matlab software for disciplined convex programming, version 2.0.

Davidson, I., Li, H., Qian, B., Wang, J., Wang, X., 2013. Active learning to rank using pairwise supervision. In: Proceedings of the 13th SIAM Internaional Conference on Data Mining, San Francisco, CA, USA, pp. 297–305.

Donmez, P., Carbonell, J.G., 2008. Optimizing estimated loss reduction for active sampling in rank learning. In: Proceedings of the 25th International Conference on Machine Learning, ACM, Helsinki, Finland ACM, pp. 248–255.

Grant, M., Boyd, S., 2008. "Graph implementations for nonsmooth convex programs,". In: Blondel, V., Boyd, S., Kimura, H. (Eds.), Recent Advances in Learning and Control, ser. Lecture Notes in Control and Information Sciences. Springer-Verlag Limited, vol. 371, pp. 95–110.

Hang, L., 2011. "A short introduction to learning to rank,". IEICE Transactions on Information and Systems, vol. 94 (no. 10), 1854–1862.

Höffgen, K.-U., Simon, H.-U., Horn, K.S.V., 1995. "Robust trainability of single neurons,". J. Comput. Syst. Sci. vol. 50 (no. 1), 114–125.

Joachims, T., 1999. "Making large-scale SVM learning practical,". In: Schölkopf, B., Burges, C., Smola, A. (Eds.), Advances in Kernel Methods – Support Vector Learning. MIT Press, Cambridge, MA, pp. 169–184. ch. 11.

Joachims, T., 2002. Optimizing search engines using clickthrough data. In: Proceedings of the Eighth ACM SIGKDD International Conference on Knowledge Discovery and Data Mining, ser. KDD 2002, New York, NY, USA: ACM, pp. 133–142.

Kogan, S., Levin, D., Routledge, B.R., Sagi, J.S., Smith, N.A., 2009. Predicting risk from financial reports with regression. In: Proceedings of Human Language Technologies: The 2009 Annual Conference of the North American Chapter of the Association for Computational Linguistics, ser. NAACL 2009. Stroudsburg, PA, USA: Association for Computational Linguistics, pp. 272–280. [Online]. Available: http://dl.acm.org/citation.cfm?id=1620754.1620794.

Long, B., Chapelle, O., Zhang, Y., Chang, Y., Zheng, Z., Tseng, B., 2010. Active learning for ranking through expected loss optimization. In: Proceedings of the 33rd International ACM SIGIR Conference on Research and Development in Information Retrieval, ser. SIGIR 2010. New York, NY, USA: ACM, pp. 267–274. [Online]. Available: http://doi.acm.org/10.1145/1835449.1835495.

Parikh, D., Grauman, K., 2011. Relative attributes. In: International Conference on Computer Vision, pp. 503–510.

Qian, B., Wang, X., Wang, J., Li, H., Cao, N., et al., 2013. Fast pairwise query selection for large-scale active learning to rank. In: IEEE International Conference on Data Mining Series, Dallas, Texas, USA, pp. 607–616.

Shashua, A., Levin, A., 2002. Ranking with large margin principle: two approaches. In: Conference on Neural Information Processing Systems, pp. 937–944.

Xu, J., Li, H., 2007. Adarank: a boosting algorithm for information retrieval. In: SIGIR 2007: Proceedings of the 30th Annual International ACM SIGIR Conference on Research and Development in Information Retrieval. New York, NY, USA: ACM, pp. 391–398.

Yang, L., Wang, L., Geng, B., Hua, X.-S., 2009. Query sampling for ranking learning in web search. In: Proceedings of the 32nd international ACM SIGIR conference on Research and Development in Information Retrieval, New York, NY, USA: ACM, pp. 754–755.

Yu, H., 2005. SVM selective sampling for ranking with application to data retrieval. In: Proceedings of the 11th ACM SIGKDD International Conference on Knowledge Discovery in Data Mining, New York, NY, USA: ACM, pp. 354–363.

Yue, Y., Finley, T., Radlinski, F., Joachims, T., 2007. A support vector method for optimizing average precision. In: ACM SIGIR Conference on Research and Development in Information Retrieval (SIGIR), New York, NY, USA: ACM, pp. 271–278.

Novel ITS based on space-air-ground collected Big Data

G. Xiong[1,3], F. Zhu[1,2], X. Dong[1,2], H. Fan[4], B. Hu[1], Q. Kong[1,2], W. Kang[2] and T. Teng[4]

[1]The State Key Laboratory of Management and Control for Complex Systems, Institute of Automation, Chinese Academy of Sciences, Beijing, China [2]Qingdao Academy of Intelligent Industries, Qingdao, China [3]Dongguan Research Institute of CASIA, Cloud Computing Center, Chinese Academy of Sciences, Dongguan, China [4]Cloud Computing Center, Chinese Academy of Sciences, Dongguan, China

CHAPTER OUTLINE

8.1 INTRODUCTION

Most traditional methods of traffic data collection rely mainly on ground data. In fact, Big Data collected from Space-Air-Ground can improve the current ITS (intelligent transportation system) further (Liu et al., 2010; Zhang et al., 2013; Maamar et al., 2014). Aerial imagery sensors can provide sufficient resolution to sense vehicle locations and movements across broader spatial and temporal scales (Sun et al., 2014). Digital video, global positioning systems (GPS), and automated image processing are used to improve the spatial coverage, accuracy, and cost-effectiveness of the data collection and reduction (Han and Wu, 2011; Amini et al., 2014; Seo and Walter, 2014). By remote sensing, high-resolution images are available and their merit is distributed for traffic problems in a variety of cases, including illegal parking, etc. (Maamar et al., 2014). With high-resolution monochrome images collected from helicopter, 98% of the vehicles can be detected automatically when conditions allow (Puri et al., 2007). The traffic information management system was designed and developed; it can be applied to traffic control, vehicle guidance and dispatching, route planning, and infrastructure construction (Park et al., 2013). An image fusion method is proposed with bilinear resampling wavelet transform, which has good performance for preserving the spectral and spatial resolutions for remote sensing images, with the lowest loss of spectral information (Sun et al., 2014). A method is proposed to detect and track vehicles based on airship video and to calculate traffic parameters in real-time (Li et al., 2009; Sun et al., 2014). The fixed-point theory is a favorable theoretical background for the network organization, dynamic characteristics, and regularity of the Space-Air-Ground integrated network (Liu et al., 2010). A multifunctional transceiver for future ITS is proposed with two operation modes, namely, radar (sensing) mode and radio (communication) mode (Han and Wu, 2011).

However, these works are scattered and limited, and comprehensive research on novel ITS based on Big Data collected from Space-Air-Ground is necessary. Based on the Big Data collected from Space-Air-Ground, a novel ITS is studied in this chapter. In Section 8.2, the current situation and future trend of related R&D areas are analyzed. In Section 8.3, the main research contents of novel ITS are summarized. In Section 8.4, technical solutions of novel ITS are designed and its main research contents are summarized. In Section 8.5, the potential benefits of novel ITS are analyzed, and conclusions are drawn.

8.2 RELATED R&D AREAS: THEIR CURRENT SITUATION AND FUTURE TREND

Urban traffic covers a broad variety of subjects, including bus, taxi, municipal administration, passenger transport hub, integrated information service, infrastructure, etc. (Park et al., 2013). As the expansion of urban roads fails to catch up with the increasing pace of vehicle ownership, which has resulted from urban population explosion and economy expansion (Li et al., 2011), the urban traffic problem is becoming more and more serious. Traffic congestion, blockage, and accidents have become the three main problems for most large and even middle-sized cities. Researchers have explored a number of methods and technologies to solve the problems. On the one hand, urban public transportation is developed and technologies of sensing, control and network communication are used to improve its efficiency to attract more passengers. On the other hand, integrated information systems and parking guidance systems are being developed to reduce vehicles' on-road delay. This problem is very complex and important, and many related research institutes and traffic agencies have made efforts to collect and provide information about urban traffic.

8.2.1 CLOUD COMPUTING AND BIG DATA

Cloud computing is a kind of adding, using, and paying mode for related services based on the Internet (Jaworski et al., 2011; Li et al., 2011; Wang and Shen, 2011; Bitam and Mellouk, 2012; Yu et al., 2013). It is usually involved with providing dynamic and extensible resources which are often available virtually through the Internet. In the narrow sense of cloud computing, the resources are IT infrastructures, while in the broad sense they include all kinds of Internet services.

In recent years, the rapid growth of data has provided both great challenges and huge opportunities for many industries (Park et al., 2013; Yu et al., 2013). It brings the information society into the Big Data era. Usually, Big Data refers to those data sets on which the perception, acquisition, management, processing, and serving are beyond the capabilities of common machines and normal hardware and software tools. The IDC Company reports that the total amount of global data is 1.8 ZB, and it is predicted to be 35 ZB in 2020.

Big Data has its special functions in protecting digital sovereignty, maintaining society stability, and promoting the sustainable development of society and economy (Luo et al., 2013; Yazici et al., 2013; Eckhoff and Sommer, 2014; Feng et al., 2014; Liu et al., 2014; Qiu et al., 2014; Yoon et al., 2014; Zhang et al., 2014). In the information era, national competitiveness is partly reflected by the scale and use of Big Data and the ability to explain and utilize the data. For any country, falling behind in the area of Big Data usually means falling behind in many related hi-tech industries. For this reason, the American government has engaged six departments and invested 200 million dollars to launch the "Big-data R&D Plan." In this plan the NSF (National Science Foundation) has proposed the formation of a unique subject covering mathematics, statistics, and computation algorithms.

To prepare for the development trends of Big Data and provide better data analysis services for enterprises and personal users, it is urgently needed to build different kinds of Big Data platforms to meet the various requirements of all users. Unlike traditional data platforms, during the building of a Big Data platform, the characteristics of Big Data, including immense scale, varied types, rapid fluxion, dynamic hierarchy and huge value, should be especially considered. In addition, problems like sorted storage of data, openness of data platforms, intelligent processing of the data, and the interactivity between the users and the data platforms represent great challenges. Despite the difficulties, a few companies have made progress in this area, e.g., the Freebase of Google, the Probase from Microsoft, and CNKI (China National Knowledge Internet). Concerning Big Data platforms, three are typical: the Big Data analysis platform Infosphere from IBM, the uniform data management platform Teradata from the Teradata Corporation, and the Chinese first electric commerce cloud platform "Jushita," which were jointly built by T mall, Aliyun cloud engine, and Hi China.

8.2.2 REMOTE SENSING SPATIAL INFORMATION

The application of remote sensing technology from satellites is becoming broader and deeper in many industries. It is developing towards those characteristics such as multisensor, multiplatform, multiangle, and high resolution in various aspects, such as space, spectrum, time, and radiation. Miniaturization of the earth observation systems, networking of the satellites, all-time and all-weather observation of the earth have been the three main development directions. The US plans to accomplish 17 new satellite projects between 2010 and 2020, covering all the fields of earth sciences. China will send about 14 high-resolution satellites as a major special project of building the high-resolution earth observation system, which will be integrated with other observation methods, enabling all-time, all-weather, and global covering observation of the earth.

Nowadays remote sensing applications have been switched from qualitative analysis to quantitative analysis. Satellite remote sensing data have been the main data sources for the updating of topographic maps of 1:50,000, or even of smaller scale. Products of remote sensing data with different resolving and spectral characteristics coexist, which provides information insurance for resource management and disaster response. As for processing of remote sensing data, a few parallel processing systems exist, for example the Pixel Factory System from France and the Geo Imaging Accelerator GXL System from the PCI Company of the United States.

8.3 MAIN RESEARCH CONTENTS OF NOVEL ITS

Utilizing the abilities of cloud computing, such as high-performance computing, distributed storage, and concurrent multiuser interaction and high-volume throughput, this chapter tries to research critical problems for ITS applications including Big Data sensing and collection, dynamic data transmission, massive data storage, multisource data fusion, and data analysis and mining (Li et al., 2009, 2011; Deng et al., 2011; Jaworski et al., 2011; Wang and Shen, 2011; Bitam and Mellouk, 2012; Liu, 2012; Zhu et al., 2012; Luo et al., 2013; Park et al., 2013; Yazici et al., 2013; Yu et al., 2013; Eckhoff and Sommer, 2014; Feng et al., 2014; Liu et al., 2014; Qiu et al., 2014; Yoon et al., 2014; Zhang et al., 2014). By integrating spatial information, Big Data, cloud computing and Internet of Things, the data service chain that includes data collection, analysis, visualization, application, and feedback can be implemented. The relationships among various traffic elements, including people, cars, and roads, are represented in an innovative way. The goal is to realize a real-time, accurate, efficient, safe, and energy-saving transportation system.

The main contents of novel ITS include three aspects: ITS Big Data collection, ITS cloud computing supporting platform, and ITS Big Data application and service platform, as shown in Fig. 8.1.

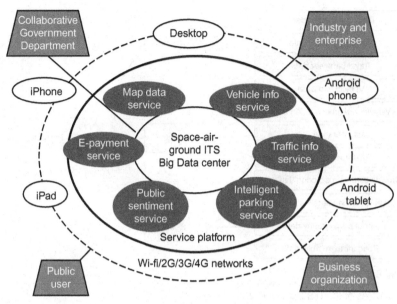

FIGURE 8.1

Main contents of novel ITS.

8.3.1 ITS BIG DATA CENTER

ITS Big Data are collected from multiple sources (as shown in Fig. 8.2), including satellite sensing data, aerial photography measuring data, unmanned aerial vehicles sensing data, and ground ITS data generated from videos, IC cards, inductive loops, and cellphones. These data are all focused on the three basic elements—people, vehicles, and roads—of transportation systems. People-related data mainly describe driving and payment behavior of drivers and travel behavior of passengers. Vehicle-related data mainly describe the basic information, real-time location, operation, and crowd sourcing road conditions. Road-related data mainly describe the geometry of road networks and characteristics of road infrastructures.

8.3.1.1 Public Transit Operation Data

Real-time passenger data, such as boarding time, alighting time, boarding station, and alighting station can be obtained through an on-bus QR code payment system based on 3G/Wi-Fi wireless network. Based on these data, real-time intelligent bus schedule and scientific bus line planning can be achieved. As a result, passengers can receive better services, i.e., safer, more comfortable, and more convenient. Since more passengers are willing to take public transit, traffic congestion can be reduced. In summary, the public transit operation data have great potential to deliver social and economic benefits.

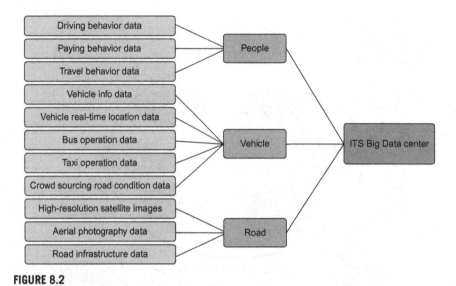

FIGURE 8.2

Data sources of the ITS Big Data center.

8.3.1.2 On-Vehicle Terminal Data

First, intelligent wireless onboard terminals are developed. Efforts are focused on the development of functional, logical, and physical system architectures by integrating the monitor, navigation, sensor, communication, and control units. These terminals are mainly used to facilitate the management of buses, taxis, and other types of vehicles. The application areas include management of driving safety, operation, quality of service, centralized intelligent schedule, electronic station boards, etc. The onboard terminal data can also meet the varying requirements of different users. Governments need the data to improve traffic control, traffic law enforcement, transit organization, and emergency management. Meanwhile enterprises need the data for logistics information, and passengers for trip guidance.

8.3.1.3 Crowd Sourcing Road Condition Data

To improve traffic conditions and to finally implement ITS, one needs huge and complex transportation data. Among these, accurate crowd sourcing data play an important role. Crowd-reported real-time vehicle speed data are processed by smart terminals and the system platform, so that vehicle speed can be detected, published, and this information then utilized and implemented in real-time. Crowd sourcing data play an important role in improving traffic conditions, saving energy, reducing emissions, and finally in implementing intelligent transportation. On the other hand, with the popularity of social media like online communities, blogs, micro blogs, and social networks, netizens are joined together to share real-world information. This provides an opportunity for obtaining road condition data from crowd sources.

Practices indicate that crowd sourcing road condition data have become an important supplementary part of real-time traffic information.

8.3.1.4 Intelligent Parking Data

With the acceleration of urbanization and rapid increase in car ownership, many problems arise accordingly. In addition to traffic congestion, the management of parking has become more and more necessary and difficult. The problems can be solved from a management perspective. Information about parking lots and parking spaces can be shared in communities with access to the Internet, 3G communication technology, and the cloud computing platform. Intelligent perception of parking space availability and platforms guiding drivers to free spaces can be developed in the process of building smart cities.

8.3.1.5 Spatial Data Collection

Spatial data are one of the content-richest forms of information since they can be collected by earth observation satellites in a much larger scale. These satellites are equipped with broad spectral observation technologies and are capable of high-resolution photography. The most accurate resolution can reach to 0.06 m, making available highly refined spatial data. There have been several imaging sensors with high performance in both spatial and spectral resolution, especially the C-SAR sensor with 1 m resolution, and the GF-5 hyperspectral sensor. The GF-5 hyperspectral sensor is claimed to have 10 m resolution, making its potential for practical purposes noteworthy. The GF-4 geostationary orbit satellite has an advantage in time resolution over other satellites. It has high application value in meteorological monitoring and emergency response. For areas requiring emergency response or timely protection, unmanned aerial vehicles are used to collect the local spatial data. By this means, emergency response times can be limited within 3 h and the collection of spatial data can be finished within 3 days.

Image data are collected mainly by ground photography and aerial photography, which are the original data for three-dimensional modeling. Ground photography includes manual photographing and streetscape scanning. Aerial photography refers to low-altitude aerial photography here, using unmanned aerial vehicles and delta-winged drones as the remote sensing platforms. Aerial photography is the major means for regional three-dimensional modeling. Multiple aerial photographic cameras are available for aerial photography, including ordinary cameras, A3, ADS40/80, the Trimble AOS inclined camera, Pictometry camera, and SWDC-5 inclined camera and so on. An example of an aerial photographic image can be seen in Fig. 8.3.

8.3.2 ITS CLOUD COMPUTING SUPPORTING PLATFORM

The Space-Air-Ground Big Data service and other related services are implemented through cloud computing (Luo et al., 2013; Yazici et al., 2013; Eckhoff and Sommer, 2014; Liu et al., 2014). The system hierarchy of the ITS cloud computing supporting platform is shown in Fig. 8.4. The system hierarchy is composed of three layers: the

FIGURE 8.3

An example of an aerial photographic image.

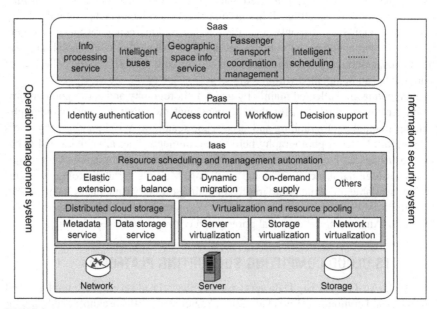

FIGURE 8.4

Hierarchy of the ITS cloud computing supporting platform.

physical resource management layer, the logic resource management layer, and the data center operation and maintenance layer.

The whole platform is composed of several subsystems, each of which provides specific types and services of information, management, and surveillance. The cloud computing virtualization platform is utilized to ensure all-time stable and efficient services. The application system and physical machine are separated by virtualization, thus the system service failing time resulting from physical breakdown will be reduced. The physical resources can also be deleted, upgraded, or changed without negative impact on the users.

8.3.3 ITS BIG DATA APPLICATION AND SERVICE PLATFORM

The ITS Big Data application and service platform is based on ITS Big Data and the ITS cloud computing supporting platform. It adopts the "central data storage and processing" and "local application and service" mode. The real-time transportation information is grabbed from ITS Big Data and analyzed together with the historical data. Intelligent predictions are made on the platform to provide decision support for users.

The ITS Big Data application and service platform mainly provides services for the government, enterprises, and public users. The platform structure is shown in Fig. 8.5. The government can use the platform for the management of transportation law enforcement. Multiple services are available, including accurate geoinformation,

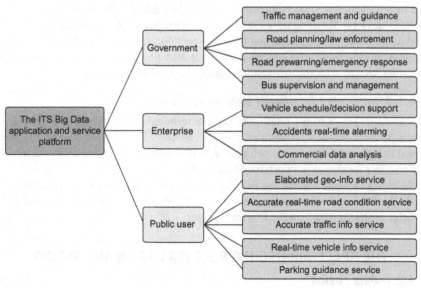

FIGURE 8.5

The ITS Big Data application and service platform.

traffic management, emergency response, on-road parking space management, and public transit supervision. Enterprises can use the platform for the accurate acquisition of geoinformation, assistance in decision-making, and the analysis of commercial data. In addition, mobile applications are developed for the public users to provide them with transportation information services. The data of public trip behavior can be gathered through the APPs (Applications). And in return the public users get improved services like accurate geoinformation, real-time traffic conditions, driving and parking guidance, etc.

Based on this platform, the industry data, computation resources, and characterized intelligence analysis results can be shared by different kinds of users. In this way, system resources and costs can be saved, and at the same time efficiency can be improved significantly.

8.4 TECHNICAL SOLUTION OF NOVEL ITS

8.4.1 THE SPACE-AIR-GROUND BIG DATA COLLECTION AND TRANSMISSION TECHNOLOGY AND ON-VEHICLE TERMINALS

8.4.1.1 The Beidou/GPS Dual-Mode Positioning and Navigation Technology

The Beidou Navigation Satellite System/GPS dual-mode positioning and navigation technology uses a kind of active dual-direction two-dimensional navigation technology. Accurate three-dimensional position data are resolved by a ground control center and then transmitted to users through satellites, instead of being directly resolved by the user devices. To navigate a car, the car's space location is first detected by the dual-mode positioning system, and then the space location is mapped to the city map location. Furthermore, the control center can also provide a user-defined distance reporting service with the differential distance algorithm.

8.4.1.2 Integrated Intelligent Vehicle Terminal

As shown in Fig. 8.6, the intelligent vehicle terminal is composed of a hard disk, sound pick-up, monitor, positioner, etc. The wireless access point function is integrated into the terminal device, which makes it possible to organize all the terminals in a wireless local area network based on Wi-Fi.

Vehicles are connected to the Big Data cloud computing center through a 3G network. Real-time information about the locations, operations, and statuses of multiple vehicles is shared based on the Big Data center.

8.4.2 THE SPACE-AIR-GROUND BIG DATA FUSION AND MINING

8.4.2.1 Data Fusion

The Space-Air-Ground Big Data, collected from multiple sources, must be fused first. The basic process of data fusion includes multisource data collection, data preprocessing, data fusion, and target parameters estimation. Data fusion is accomplished

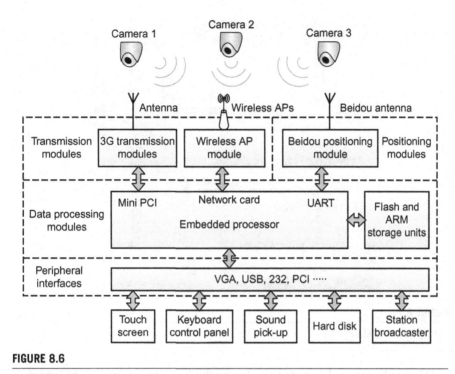

FIGURE 8.6

Structure of the intelligent vehicle terminal.

at three levels. The first is data-level fusion, which finishes data preprocessing and association. The second is characteristic-level fusion, which is supposed to predict the traffic parameters. The third is state-level fusion, which is responsible for determining the transportation state based on the current traffic flow information.

8.4.2.2 Data Mining

The knowledge we need is acquired through data-mining technologies. Data mining is a multistep process, including problem definition, data preparation, and pattern recognition and model evaluation. The transportation data-mining model is shown in Fig. 8.7.

The ETL and data preprocessing provide a clean, consistent, integrated and reduced data set for pattern recognition of transportation Big Data. The transportation data-mining model is hierarchical with four layers: the application layer, the analysis and logic layer, the algorithms and tools layer, and the data layer. The application layer provides the access point for users to call up functions of the lower layers. The analysis capability of the system is reflected by the analysis and logic layer.

The algorithms and tools layer is a set of different algorithms and tools needed for traffic flow analysis, including data-mining techniques, statistical methods, and similarity measurement methods and so on. For data-mining tasks, we mainly use the prediction and classification models.

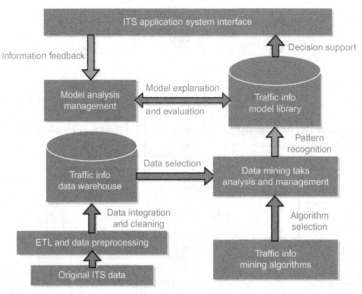

FIGURE 8.7

Transportation data-mining model.

The prediction models have three layers: the basic data layer, the characteristic attributes layer, and the state description layer. Different layers are used for different prediction targets. The basic data layer is used for traffic flow prediction. The characteristic attributes layer can be used for predictions of traffic flow properties, traffic accidents and their types, and traffic congestion. The state description layer is used for the predictions of network-wise level of service, as well as development trends and impact evaluation of traffic accidents.

Classification models are built in two steps: training/learning and testing. In the training/learning stage, a classification model is created by analyzing or learning the characteristics of the training data. In the testing stage, the classification model is tested against the labeled testing data set. A great deal of classification methods and models have been proposed, including the ID3 and C4.5 methods structured by a decision tree, the probabilistic methods NB (Naive Bayesian) and TAN (Tree Augmented Naive Bayes) based on the Bayesian rules, the Back Propagation (BP) neural network model, the CBA (Classification Based on Associations) method based on association rules, and other methods based on fuzzy logic.

Traffic flow can be classified by different characteristics. Thus, before classification, traffic data should first be reduced to only keep those related characteristics. There exists research addressing the traffic flow classification problem by fuzzy logic method or by artificial neural network (ANN). The fuzzy logic classification model is described by a set of "if … then" rules, which are understandable. The ANN method involves training a network to classify the data. But the trained ANN is often unexplainable.

8.4.3 **THE SPACE-AIR-GROUND BIG DATA PROCESSING**

8.4.3.1 Parallel Reception of Massive Data

The ITS contains massive data collection terminals. The servers are challenged with reception of massive amounts of data. Efficient and stable solutions can be achieved by a strategy involving parallel reception of data. The system architecture is shown in Fig. 8.8. The terminals and collectors communicate to the masters regularly to report their states.

1. The terminal reports its online state and connection status with the collector to the master via Transmission Control Protocol (TCP). If a terminal cannot connect to the collector, it will report the problem to the master, and the master will allocate another available collector to it.
2. The collector reports its load status and online state to the master. If the workload is too heavy, it will ask the master to allocate some workload to other collectors.
3. If the master does not receive the reports of a collector for a specific interval, the collector is thought to be breaking down. Then the related terminals will be notified to send their data to other collectors.
4. When the data storage function breaks down, the collectors will cache the data temporarily. The cached data will be sent to the GT-Data on the storage function.

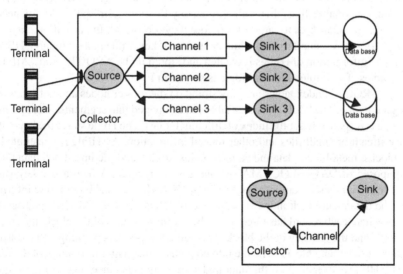

FIGURE 8.8

The inner structure of a collector.

The core function of a collector is collecting data from the data sources and transmitting them to expected destinations. To ensure data integrity, the data are cached locally on the collector before transmission and will not be deleted until the targets really received them. The collector is an integrated data-collecting tool which is composed of three core modules: source, channel, and sink. The data flow from one point to another point through these modules. The source is where external data are received by the collector. Different sources are designed to receive different kinds of formatted data. The received data are put onto different channels according to predefined rules. The channel is where data are stored. As mentioned above, the data will not be deleted from the channel until they successfully enter the next channel or terminals. Even if failure occurs during writing data into sinks, the data will not be lost and can be recovered. To this point, the system is relatively reliable. The sink consumes data in the channels and transmits them to external sources, like GT-Data or databases.

8.4.3.2 Segmental Storage of Massive Small Files

The GT-Data provides distributed storage for both small and large files. But the underlying implementations are different.

For large files, they are split into segments, which are stored in different nodes of the storage clusters. The file information and segmentation information are stored in the metadata. When reading a file, the indices of the segments of the file are firstly read from the metadata so the system knows where to read the segments. Finally these segments are merged to form the entire file.

For small files, since their amount is much larger, the size of the metadata will be too huge to be loaded in the memory. Besides, considerable storage space will be wasted. As is known, the file system has minimum space (e.g., 4 KB) occupancy for each file. For smaller files, they will still occupy the minimum space. So it is necessary to merge small files to large files before they are stored. In current practice, the GT-Data organizes small files as a binary stream of key-value pairs into large HFiles. The index information of HFiles is created and stored in the "-ROOT-" and ".META" index tables. The implementation logic is shown in Fig. 8.9.

The "-ROOT-" index tables are only stored on the master nodes and not supported by segmentation. The ".META" index table can be divided into segments, among which each one is responsible for the index of different HFiles. The HFile stores the key-value binary stream of small files and other related information. An HFile is constituted of data blocks, meta-block, data index, meta-index, trailer, and file info. Each data block is composed of DATABLOCKMAGIC and several records. A record is a key-value pair. The meta-block is composed of METABLOCKMAGIC and bloom filter information. The data/meta-block index is composed of INDEXBLOCKMAGIC and several records where each record has three parts: the starting location of the block, the size of the block, and the first key of the block. The trailer has pointers pointing to the starting location of other data blocks. The file info contains some meta-information of the files.

The HFiles are stored on the data nodes by segments since they are large files. When reading the data, the corresponding HFile is firstly located by looking up the key in the "-ROOT-" and ".META" index tables. Then the data index is found in the

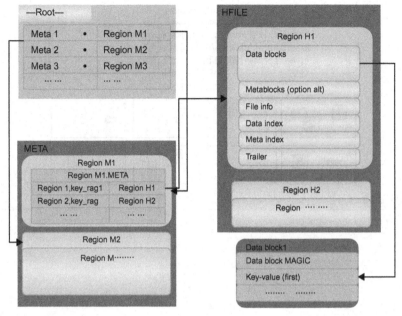

FIGURE 8.9

The segmental storage logic of massive small files.

trailer, and thus the data block. Finally the target key-value pairs can be read from the data block. In practice, the location efficiency can be improved by applying a multilevel index.

8.4.3.3 Duplication Storage of Massive Data

All the data blocks of the GT-Data files have their copies. Parameters about the size and duplication coefficient of data blocks are user-defined. A GT-Data file is written as a whole at once. It is ensured that there is only one writer at any time.

The NameNode is in full charge of data block duplication. It receives heartbeats and block status reports from each DataNode periodically. A block status report includes a list of all the data blocks on the DataNode. The storage of data block duplications of the GT-Data files is shown as Fig. 8.10.

8.4.3.4 High-Performance Reading of Massive Data

Within the GT-Data, data exchange is finished based on the wide-band network. The process of a specific data exchange is divided into data reading and data writing. The data-reading process is shown in Fig. 8.11.

The process of data reading can be described as follows:

1. Clients or users open the needed file through the open() method of the file system.

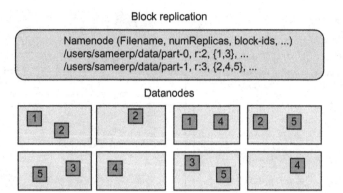

FIGURE 8.10

Storage of block replications.

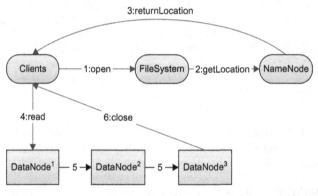

FIGURE 8.11

The data-reading process in GT-Data.

2. The file system calls the related NameNode through a predefined protocol to find the locations of the first few blocks of the file. For each block, the NameNode returns a copy of the metadata of it. Then, all the DataNodes containing the required data are sorted by their distances from the client in ascending order. In this way, data are preferentially read from the nearest DataNode for efficiency. If the client itself is a DataNode, then data are firstly read from local storage.

3. The related NameNode returns an address including the data information to the client. Then the client starts data reading by creating an FSDataInputStream instance.

4. According to the DataNode addresses of the first few blocks, the FSDataInputStream instance connects to the nearest DataNodes and reads data

from the beginning of the file. The client calls the read() method repeatedly, reading data from the DataNodes as binary streams.

5. When encountering the end of a data block, the FSDataInputStream instance will close the connection to the related DataNode, and find the optimal DataNode of the next data block.

6. When data reading is finished, the client calls close() method to close the FSDataInputStream instance.

The system is designed to be fault-tolerant. If any errors occur during the communication between the client and DataNode, the client will drop the current connection and try to locate the next DataNode containing the required data block. The broken-down DataNodes are recorded in case the client tries to connect to them again. The client also verifies the checksum of the data block received. Any errors in the data block will be reported to its DataNode before the client requests the next DataNode for the same data block.

An important achievement of this design is that the client is directed by the NameNodes to the optimal DataNodes containing the required data blocks and can receive data directly from the DataNodes. Since all the DataNodes in the clusters are connected by the data transmission lines, the GT-Data is expendable for many clients. The NameNodes only need to provide a DataNode indexing service. They do not have to provide data service as DataNodes do.

8.4.3.5 High-Performance Writing of Massive Data

Figure 8.12 illustrates how the GT-Data writes the data. The data-writing process can be described as follows:

1. The client calls the create() method of the file system to request the creation of a file.

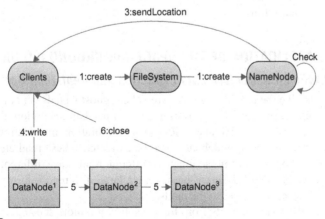

FIGURE 8.12

The data-writing process in GT-Data.

2. The local file system sends a remote request to the NameNode to create a new file in the NameNode. But the newly created file is temporarily not associated with any data blocks. The NameNode conducts a series of verification to make sure the file to be created does not exist in the system and the client has enough authority to perform the data writing. If all the verification is passed, the NameNode will record the information of the new file. The file system returns an FSDataOutputStream instance to the client for data writing. As in the data-reading process, the FSDataOutputStream instance encapsulates a DFSOutputStream instance for communication with the DataNode and NameNode. An IOExpection will be thrown if an error occurs during the file creation, indicating that the normal writing process is interrupted and an additional operation needs to be taken. The process to handle writing errors will be discussed later.

3. The client starts writing data. The FSDataOutputStream instance firstly writes the data into intermediate queues by packets, which will be read later by the DataStreamer instance. The DataStreamer's responsibility is to notify the NameNode to find the optimal DataNodes for storing the duplication of the data.

4. The FSDataOutputStream instance maintains a special packet queue, within which the packets wait to be acknowledged by the DataNode. This queue is called the waiting queue. A packet will not be removed from the waiting queue until all the DataNodes have confirmed it.

5. The client calls the close() method to close all the data streams after all the data have been written successfully.

Writing errors are taken care of as below. The writing flow is closed immediately if any error occurs. The unacknowledged data block is moved to the front of the data queue and assigned a special flag telling the NameNode that it should be deleted after the broken-down DataNode recovers. The NameNode notices that writing of this data block has not yet been finished. It arranges another available DataNode to finish the remaining data writing.

8.4.4 ITS APPLICATION OF THE SPACE-AIR-GROUND BIG DATA

8.4.4.1 Traffic Infrastructure Data Extraction and Real-Time Updating

Road elements, like the road surface, the green belt, ghost islands, and blind turning for large vehicles, can be extracted from images with <1-m resolution. From aerial images and obliquely viewed images with <10-cm resolution, information about the street lamps, well lids, and guideboards can be extracted. These road elements can have all kinds of appearances in the images. Different roads have different structures and expressions. Roads of different grades have large differences in scale. What's more, a lot of noise can appear in the landscape.

We extract the road elements from high-resolution remote sensing images. The images are analyzed from the perspective of spatial resolution. The object-oriented classification method for remote sensing images is adopted. Firstly, the images are segmented to suppress the noises and objects in the images are detected, then the target scale is carefully selected, to which the images will be transmitted. After the transmission, the object hierarchy in the image is built. Then the road information is extracted on the prebuilt road knowledge-base, in which the characteristics of different roads are described. Finally, the road lines are automatically or semiautomatically recognized on the shapes of the green belts, plant areas, and mathematical morphology. The areas of the road surfaces will also be calculated through geographic information system (GIS).

The real-time aerial photography will capture any changes to the urban roads. The changes will be recorded and reflected immediately by automatically updating the database in the ITS data center. In this way it is ensured that the users can always get the most accurate road information.

8.4.4.2 Live-Action Three-Dimensional Navigation and Intelligent Prewarning

In intelligent transportation navigation systems, the traditional two-dimensional virtual navigation is substituted by live-action three-dimensional navigation, where the virtual scenes are replaced with real screen images. An example of the live-action navigation map is shown in Fig. 8.13. The three-dimensional navigation map is not simply the three-dimensional display on the two-dimensional navigation map. It is implemented through the information communication technology based on the three-dimensional spatial data obtained. According to the collected real-world image data, scene details like color, material, texture, and lightness are carefully rendered.

FIGURE 8.13

The live-action three-dimensional navigation map.

The live-action three-dimensional scenes of the roads are displayed on the navigator. The live-action three-dimensional navigation map can break the constraints of the traditional two-dimensional map in the expression of forms. The real world can now be expressed in more detail and in a more comprehensive way.

For each area with a high accident rate, like crossings and curves, an intelligent prewarning system is built. The blind corners for large vehicles at the curves are calculated based on the high-resolution cameras and geometric calculation models. According to the length of the vehicle and the performance index, the safety evaluation result is presented to the driver before he arrives at the curve. The areas with high accident rates are highlighted in the live-action three-dimensional navigation map to warn drivers. With the intelligent prewarning system, drivers can go through the dangerous areas safely and many traffic accidents will be avoided.

8.4.4.3 Driver Behavior Analysis and Prewarning Based on the Big Data of Driving

The received data packages are processed differently according to their classes such that we can achieve all-time surveillance, alarm, command, and operation of the on-road vehicles. The collected spatial coordination data and timestamps of the vehicles are mapped on the digital map, so that we can know the real-time locations and states of the vehicles. The trajectories of the vehicles are shown in the GIS, and vehicle tracking can be implemented.

Based on the mass driving and driver behavior data, the drivers' behavior can be efficiently modeled with methods of statistical analysis. The modeling results can be applied in many areas, including a correction system for the errant behavior of new drivers, an automatic diagnostic system of driver behaviors, etc. The available analysis methods include:

1. The range analysis method: Analyzes the varying characteristics and range of the data value.
2. The time domain analysis method: Analyzes the varying frequency and varying period of the data value.
3. The correlation analysis method: Analyzes the proportional and corresponding relationships of related data.
4. The cause-and-effect analysis method: Analyzes the response relationship and response speed of related data.
5. The comparative analysis method: Analyzes the comparisons of the same performance index of the same vehicle type.

8.5 CONCLUSIONS

In the Big Data era, different kinds of massive data are available now, including remote sensing data, traffic video data, all kinds of perception data, and public sentiment data and so on. These data are collected from decentralized sources and used separately in traditional applications. Since each dataset can only describe one aspect of the real world, these traditional applications are not able to utilize the value of the data to its potential. In this chapter, we have proposed to build the Space-Air-Ground Big Data insurance system. The data are able to be updated from perspectives of scale, accuracy, and time phase. An accurate and timely data service with a dynamic surveillance system can be further implemented.

An ITS service of the mobile Internet age is supported by the cloud computing platforms and high-speed network transmission. The service is implemented through data collection by mobile clients, analysis and knowledge mining of Big Data, high-speed network transmission, and intelligent push services. Based on the real-time data, users can benefit from the more accurate navigation and parking services in the same manner that the new interconnected transportation service mode does. The administrative barriers are eliminated thanks to the information technology. The transportation data from different sources can be integrated and shared on a uniform platform to provide administrative surveillance services for the government and transportation services for enterprises and public users. The level of service of the transportation system will be further improved.

ACKNOWLEDGMENTS

This work was supported in part by the National Natural Science Foundation of China (grants 71232006, 61233001, 61304201, and 61174172); Finnish TEKES's project "SoMa2020: Social Manufacturing" (2015–2017); Chinese Guangdong's S&T project (2014B010118001, 2014A050503004); Chinese Dongguan's S&T project (2013508102018); and Dongguan's Innovation Talents Project (Gang Xiong).

REFERENCES

Amini, A., Vaghefi, R.M., De La Garza, J.M., Buehrer, R.M., 2014. Improving GPS-based vehicle positioning for intelligent transportation systems. In: IEEE Intelligent Vehicles Symposium, Dearborn, Michigan, USA, pp. 1023–1029.

Bitam, S., Mellouk, A., 2012. ITS-cloud: cloud computing for intelligent transportation system. In: IEEE Global Communications Conference, Anaheim, CA, USA, pp. 2054–2059.

Deng, A., Feng, T., Lang, M., Cai, J., 2011. Comparative study on the development of the Internet of Things in intelligent transportation between China and abroad. In: 8th International Conference on Service Systems and Service Management, pp. 1–4.

Eckhoff, D., Sommer, C., 2014. Driving for Big Data? Privacy concerns in vehicular networking. Security & Privacy, IEEE 12 (1), 77–79.

Feng, L., Feng, Y.-j., Li, K., Zhang, M., 2014. Coordinated control of traffic flow in complex-arterial networks under the big data background. In: 26th Chinese Control and Decision Conference, Changsha, China, pp. 1811–1817.

Han, L., Wu, K., 2011. Multifunctional transceiver for future intelligent transportation systems. IEEE Transactions on Microwave Theory and Techniques 59 (7), 1879–1892.

Jaworski, P., Edwards, T., Moore, J., Burnham, K., 2011. Cloud computing concept for intelligent transportation systems. In: 14th International IEEE Conference on Intelligent Transportation Systems, Washington DC, USA, pp. 391–936.

Li Q.Q., Lei B., Yu Y., Hou R., 2009. Real-time highway traffic information extraction based on airborne video. In: Proceedings of the 12th International IEEE Conference on Intelligent Transportation Systems, St. Louis, MO, USA, pp. 1–6.

Li, Z., Chen, C., Wang, K., 2011. Cloud computing for agent-based urban transportation systems. IEEE Intelligent Systems 26 (1), 73–79.

Liu, C., 2012. Intelligent transportation based on the Internet of Things. In: 2nd International Conference on Consumer Electronics, Communications and Networks, Yichang, China, pp. 360–362.

Liu, H., Zhang, J., Cheng, L.L., 2010. Application examples of the network fixed point theory for space-air-ground integrated communication network. In: International Congress on Ultra-Modern Telecommunications and Control Systems and Workshops, Petersburg, Russia, pp. 989–993.

Liu, J., Liu, F., Ansari, N., 2014. Monitoring and analyzing big traffic data of a large-scale cellular network with Hadoop. Network, IEEE 28 (4), 32–39.

Luo, T., Liao, Y., Chen, G., Zhang, Y., 2013. P-DOT: a model of computation for big data. In: IEEE International Conference on Big Data, 2013, Santa Clara, CA, USA, pp. 31–37.

Maamar, M., Liu J., Liu W., 2014. A new lightweight link quality based reputation model for space-air-ground integrated wireless sensor network (SAGIWSN). In: IEEE Workshop on Electronics, Computer and Applications, Penang, Malaysia, pp. 230–236.

Park H.W., Yeo I.Y., Lee, J.R., Jang H., 2013. Study on Big Data center traffic management based on the separation of large-scale data stream. In: Seventh International Conference on Innovative Mobile and Internet Services in Ubiquitous Computing (IMIS), Taichung, Taiwan, p. 4.

Puri, A., Valavanis, K., Kontitsis, M., 2007. Generating traffic statistical profiles using unmanned helicopter-based video data. In: IEEE International Conference on Robotics and Automation, Roma, Italy, pp. 870–876.

Qiu, R.G., Wang, K., Li S., Dong J., Xie M., 2014. Big data technologies in support of real time capturing and understanding of electric vehicle customers dynamics. In: 5th IEEE International Conference on Software Engineering and Service, Beijing, China, pp. 263–267.

Seo, J., Walter, T., 2014. Future dual-frequency GPS navigation system for intelligent air transportation under strong ionospheric scintillation. IEEE Transactions on Intelligent Transportation Systems 15 (5), 2224–2236.

Sun, Z.H., Leotta, M., Hoogs, A., Blue, R., Neuroth, R., Vasquez, J., et al., 2014. Vehicle change detection from aerial imagery using detection response maps. In: Proceedings of SPIE—The Society of Photo-Optical Instrumentation Engineers, Geospatial InfoFusion and Video Analytics IV, and Motion Imagery for ISR and Situational Awareness II, Vol. 9089.

Wang, K., Shen, Z., 2011. Artificial societies and GPU-based cloud computing for intelligent transportation management. IEEE Intelligent Systems 26 (4), 22–28.

Yazici, M.A., Kamga, C., Singhal, A., 2013. A big data driven model for taxi drivers' airport pick-up decisions in New York City. In: IEEE International Conference on Big Data, pp. 37–44.

Yoon, S.-H., Park, J.-S., Kim, M.-S., Lim, C.T., Cho, J.H., 2014. Behavior signature for big data traffic identification. In: International Conference on Big Data and Smart Computing, Bangkok, Thailand, pp. 261–266.

Yu, J., Jiang, F., Zhu, T., 2013. RTIC-C: a Big Data system for massive traffic information mining. In: International Conference on Cloud Computing and Big Data, 2013, Xiamen, China, pp. 395–402.

Zhang, F., Zhang, Y., Lu, Y., 2013. Research on hybrid layered architecture of command and control system for space-air-ground collaboration. Journal of Academy of Equipment v 24 (n 5), 74–77.

Zhang J., You, S., Gruenwald, L., 2014. High-performance spatial query processing on big taxi trip data using GPGPUs. In: IEEE International Congress on Big Data (BigData Congress), Anchorage, Alaska, USA, pp. 72–79.

Zhu Y., Zhu X., Shuxian Z., Guo S., 2012. Intelligent transportation system based on Internet of Things. In: World Automation Congress, Puerto Vallarta, Mexico, pp. 1–3.

Behavior modeling and its application in an emergency management parallel system for chemical plants

X. Liu[1,2], X. Shang[1,2], X. Dong[1,2] and G. Xiong[1,3]

[1]*The State Key Laboratory of Management and Control for Complex Systems, Institute of Automation, Chinese Academy of Sciences, Beijing, China* [2]*Qingdao Academy of Intelligent Industries, Qingdao, China* [3]*Dongguan Research Institute of CASIA, Cloud Computing Center, Chinese Academy of Sciences, Dongguan, China*

CHAPTER OUTLINE

9.1 INTRODUCTION

The emergency response plan (ERP) is a predeveloped plan or program including timely, orderly and effective emergency response and rescue activities to reduce the loss in an accident or disaster (Chen et al., 2009). It is important for emergency management; above all, it clarifies the responsibility assignments, the critical time points, the handling strategies, and the resources preparation during the feedforward, concurrent and feedback stages (Jiao and Xiong, 2008). However, most existing ERP and emergency management systems have their drawbacks. Because not all related specialists, managers, operators, and departments are invited to develop the ERP, the accident analysis is insufficient, and the formulated ERPs are often incomplete and inefficient, with ambiguous and rough descriptions. And, even worse, the released ERPs are not maintained and managed effectively, which decreases their usability and effectiveness (Xu, 2010; Wu, 2011). For example, some petrochemical enterprises manage their ERPs through MS Word documents on their intranet, which is difficult to manage dynamically. This management approach of ERPs has some disadvantages, such as, keyword search among all ERPs is unavailable, and it is not convenient and intuitive for employees to learn and master these ERPs, etc.

To effectively apply the ERP to emergency response and rescue, it is necessary to design a comprehensive ERP management system from the viewpoint of the whole lifecycle of ERPs (Wu, 2011). The emergency management is systematic engineering involving multiple disciplines, industries, and departments, and effective emergency management should be based on the analysis, control, and management of complex systems, which generally contain engineering and social complexities (Cui et al., 2010). However, the traditional emergency management is rarely carried out systematically from the viewpoint of a complex system and generally social complexity is neglected. To cope with this problem, a parallel system theory is proposed (Wang, 2004a,b,c,d, 2010). Based on the theory, an artificial system is created using agent-based modeling, and then it is possible to analyze the complex system deeply; computational experiments are performed to probe the effective operation of the emergency management mechanism, so that it can reveal the accident evolvement in the production system, which is not possible in the real world; finally, parallel execution of the actual and artificial system is implemented to establish a dynamic emergency management capability in its whole lifecycle. The abovementioned three steps constitute the artificial system, computational experiment, and parallel execution approach.

This chapter focuses on the refined decomposition technique and its application to ERP management, which is a core technique for the construction of emergency management parallel systems. The ERP management system designed by us includes the ERP preparation, releasing, elaboration, training, support of emergency operations, three-dimensional virtual drills and exercises, and ERP evaluation functions, as shown in Fig. 9.1.

In the following parts of the chapter, Section 9.2 introduces the closed-loop management of ERPs in their whole lifecycle; Section 9.3 describes the refined decomposition method of ERPs, by which the ERPs can be converted into cell activities; Section 9.4 describes the evaluation techniques based on the cell activities; Sections 9.5 and 9.6 give a brief introduction about the applications of cell activities on the ERP training and the operations support; and, finally, Section 9.7 concludes the chapter.

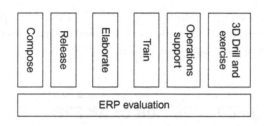

FIGURE 9.1

Structure of the emergency management parallel system.

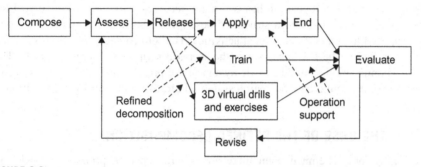

FIGURE 9.2

Life cycle of the ERPs.

9.2 CLOSED-LOOP MANAGEMENT OF ERP

The lifecycle of an ERP is shown in Fig. 9.2. First, in accordance with the emergency experience and the scientific method, the draft of ERP is developed and discussed by the related professionals from the production workshop and management offices. Second, the draft is sequentially assessed, revised, and released formally, on the basis of the standard procedure. After the release of the ERP, plant operation specialists, expert operators, and managers are gathered to perform the refined decomposition of the plan. The refined decomposition is essentially a kind of behavioral modeling for emergency handling, and it is also the foundation of the artificial systems (Liu et al., 2010). The decomposed ERPs can easily be employed in the ERP training, 3D virtual drill and exercise, operations support, etc. A platform for study and examination is built for ERP training, and the examination should cover all knowledge points and operation skills of the ERPs; 3D virtual drill and exercise is a kind of special training, by which the interactive operations among operators and computers are implemented. Operational suggestions about the next manipulation or a detailed checklist for an identified emergency case are provided by operations support during the course of virtual drills and exercises and training. The operations supports also include the decision supports after starting an ERP. The closed-loop management of ERPs is accomplished according to the evaluation and analysis of the three processes of refined decomposition, training, and practical operation.

9.3 REFINED DECOMPOSITION OF AN ERP

It is significant to refine ERPs for improving the emergency response and evaluating the usability of the ERPs. The refinement can enhance the function of the management system, the system usability, and the accuracy of the evaluation and analysis. The refined decomposition has two main purposes. First, an unstructured ERP document is converted into a structured description. Second, the coarse ERPs are decomposed to detailed operational activities. The refined decomposition is carried out according to the ERP analysis or the scenario scripts of emergency drills. The refined composition should be made by a group of professionals in brainstorm fashion. We are designing an information system platform for the refined composition.

9.3.1 THE BASE OF THE REFINED DECOMPOSITION

Generally, for a chemical plant there are general, special, production field, and temporary ERPs (Jiao and Xiong, 2008). The general ERP focuses on the global, general organization and coordination, which is not convenient for refined analysis. The organization, operational mechanism, and the SOP (standard operation procedure) are clearly defined for the other three types of ERPs, which can be refined and decomposed deeply. At present, the ERPs are usually brief procedures in many chemical plants, without concrete technical details.

The desktop drills and exercises are a common pattern of emergency training. In the desktop drill, the plant operators and managers discuss and deduce the decision-making and emergency response for an imaginary accident scenario based on released ERPs and related process flow diagrams. It is helpful for the relevant staff to remember their responsibilities and operational procedures, which are stated in the ERPs, and sequentially improve the decision-making and cooperation capacities. Since there are no site constraints and production is not affected by desktop drills and exercises, these measures are not only an effective training approach for ERP evaluation, but they are also a necessary means of emergency training. The operational procedures can be obtained based on the desktop drills for a specific emergency scenario, but the procedures may not cover all possible situations because the desktop drills are generally simple and incomplete.

The scenario scripts including scenes, roles, tasks, processes, evaluation, etc. are designed for the three-dimensional virtual drills based on the ERPs. Although the scenario scripts contain very detailed procedures, these are just one case of many possible situations and therefore the ERP decomposition should involve situations, as many as possible, except for the scenario in desktop or virtual drills.

9.3.2 THE REFINED DECOMPOSITION APPROACH

An ERP mainly consists of three parts: (1) the organization system of emergency, in which the responsibilities of involved positions are defined according to the hierarchy of a tree-like structure; (2) the emergency environmental situations, including space, time, organizing people, production technology, the external environment, etc.; (3) emergency procedures. On the basis of the above three parts, the refined decomposition of the ERPs structure the text of the plan and set the property features, so that it is convenient to do analysis and evaluation deeply and build flexible and intelligent applications. The refined decomposition approach is, accordingly, as follows.

The organization system of emergency can be broken down into three parts: node, hierarchy, and responsibility. Fig. 9.3 shows a common type of emergency response procedure, in which the contents cannot be directly used to a specific emergency. As shown in the figure, this organization system of emergency has four nodes consisting of four positions, that is, the leader of the workshop, the squad leader on duty, the operator in the control room, the first finder. The responsibilities of each position are listed. In the list, the leader of workshop is duty bound to know the truth, to direct emergency, and to report to superiors; the squad leader on duty is responsible for command and reporting; the operator in the control room is in charge of informing,

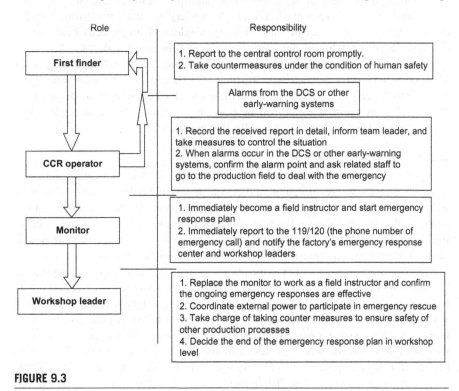

FIGURE 9.3

General emergency response plan at the workshop level.

reporting, execution and command; the first finder should report the accident and execute the command.

The emergency environmental situations include the time, space, organization, production systems, and the description of the external environment. These environmental situations are mainly used for conditional judgment of work flow. The common logics of situation judgment are OR logic, AND logic, and NOT logic. OR logic needs to meet one condition at least; AND logic means that multiple conditions must be met; NOT logic can obtain the opposite to the given conditions.

Emergency procedures consist of a group of actions to be performed, divided into two categories: human–machine behavior and interpersonal behavior. Human–machine behavior means that humans operate the equipment and implement emergency measures. Interpersonal behavior refers to the information reported, issued and transmitted between superior and subordinate, and the communication between the same levels for the tasks.

Besides starting and finishing activities, common patterns include: (1) the sequential pattern, in which the activities are arranged in time sequence and cannot be adjusted in order; (2) the parallel pattern, starting from one time node to execute multiple actions simultaneously, without affecting each other; (3) the divergence pattern, starting from one time node to execute multiple actions simultaneously, with mutual influence and interdependency; (4) the convergence pattern, starting from the different time nodes to execute the follow-up, single, and simple activities; and (5) the mixture pattern, which is a mixture composed of the above patterns.

In addition to the organization system and situations analysis, time management methodology (Project Management Institute, 2009) converts the emergency processes into the cell activities, which is the main work of the refined decomposition. Before the conversion, a variety of the possible patterns of the evolving incident should be listed and enriched by the collective brainstorming.

9.3.2.1 Cell Activities

The goal of refined decomposition is to convert the operation procedure into cell activities that define executor, aim, and course of action. Each cell activity includes only one action, which cannot be decomposed, e.g., open the valve to 50%. On the contrary, the detachable complex activities with multiple units contain verbs denoting complex actions (e.g., coordinating rescue, accident analysis) or verbs denoting multiple steps (e.g., equipment shutdown, open the standby pump).

The decomposition of cell activities has five steps: (1) activities decomposition; (2) arranging the sequence of activities; (3) estimating activity resources; (4) estimating activity duration; and (5) drawing the node network diagram of the active group with time characteristics. The principle of decomposition involves the description of human–machine behavior or interpersonal behavior; these behaviors are decomposed into multiple statements and each statement contains only a verb phrase. The phrase has the following requirements: (1) only one verb; (2) Subject-Verb-Object (SVO) order with clear reference (Xu, 2010); and (3) clear quantitative modification of the unachievable action owing to the lack of action, measured, and other information.

An active group is composed of a group of cell activities or complex activities with cooperation and the same target. The forcible dependency relationship is that activities of an active group must be executed strictly in accordance with a predetermined sequence in order to ensure safe and reliable operation. The selective dependency relationship means that activities of an active group can be adjusted in sequence, independently of each other, without any cross-reference relations. Some activities may have external dependencies, whose implementations depend on the completeness of external conditions.

In the process of implementation, the two activities in the mandatory dependency closely linked with each other are called the predecessor activity and successor activity. The predecessor can decide the beginning time and ending time of the successor. The two activities have four logical relationships: (1) finish to start means that the starting time of the successor depends on the completion time of the predecessor, which is the most common logical relationship; (2) finish to finish, that is, the successor cannot be finished before the predecessor; (3) start to finish, which is that the ending time of the successor can be determined by the starting time of the predecessor; (4) start to start, that is, the initial time of the later can depend on that of the predecessor.

Each activity has a set of properties, including activity code, type, model, its predecessor activity and the logical relationship, its successor activity and the logical relationship, the earliest starting (ES) time, the latest starting (LS) time, the earliest finishing (EF) time, the latest finishing (LF) time, duration, resources required, actors, action, object, extent, direction of information flow, situations and conditions needed to start (activity with external dependence), the waiting time for meeting the conditions (activity with external dependence), and the relevant process flow diagram.

After an emergency response procedure is decomposed and refined, all the cell activities are arranged according to the logical relationships and the patterns. Table 9.1 shows the logical relationship between the cell activities. Fig. 9.4 is the node network diagram describing Table 9.1, in which the earliest and the latest starting and ending times can be calculated (Project Management Institute, 2009). The three-point estimates technique is utilized to predict the duration and the waiting time required by meeting the conditions. The activity resource estimate refers to the material conditions needed for each cell activity, such as tools, equipment, and so on. Activities information, including actors, actions, objects, and the degree, can be obtained from the activities' descriptions. Information flow direction contains the information transmission between the devices and people in the human–machine behaviors, and between subordinates and superiors in interpersonal behaviors

Table 9.1 Logical relationship of cell activities

Activity	A	B	C	D	E	G	H
Following work	CDE	DE	G	H	H	–	–

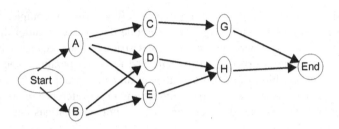

FIGURE 9.4

Node network diagram of an activity group.

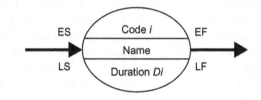

FIGURE 9.5

Activity node.

Time estimate is calculated as:

$$Dmean = (P + 4M + O)/6,$$ (9.1)

where P is the most pessimistic time; O is the most optimistic time; M is the most likely time. An estimate of the standard deviation σ is $(PO)/6$.

After estimating the duration for each activity, the whole node network diagram can be obtained, based on the logical relationship between activities. Each node of activity is generally represented as shown in Fig. 9.5.

Each node represents an activity; an arrow indicates the relationship between nodes, usually from finished node to starting node. There are four parameters with time characteristics on both sides of a node: the ES time, the LS time, the EF time, and the LF time.

9.4 APPLICATION ON ERP EVALUATION

The activity group decomposed from ERP is used as the operational rules for the operator agent in the artificial system. It also can be used for ERP evaluation, such as the Monte Carlo simulation on the ERP's execution time, usability evaluation of the ERP based on the node network of the activity group, and complexity evaluation of the ERP based on the structure of the activity group.

9.4.1 EVALUATION OF THE ERP EXECUTION TIME

Based on the Monte Carlo simulation approach, input data are randomly defined according to the probability distribution of cell activity's execution duration and to the trigger condition waiting time, and then the execution time and its probability distribution of the entire ERP are calculated. The evolvement probability of the branch activity group should be defined in the case of the activity group with external dependencies.

9.4.2 USABILITY EVALUATION OF THE ERP

The critical activity chain(s) is/are recognized based on the node network graph of an activity group. The delay of any activity in the chain may cause the delay of the emergency response as a whole and it may even result in an unpredicted heavy accident. Based on the node network graph and activity sequence bar chart, the application conflict of resource, such as human, tool, or material can be found, for example, the same executor is assigned more than two tasks at the same time. Efficiency of resource application can also be computed. The advantages and disadvantages of several ERPs for the same accident are obtained based on the evaluation.

9.4.3 COMPLEXITY EVALUATION OF ERP

9.4.3.1 Network Analysis Method

The general structure complexity of an ERP is estimated by the density ρ of the node network graph of an activity group, ρ is defined as:

$$\rho = \frac{2L}{N(N-1)} \tag{9.2}$$

where L is the number of the arrow lines in the network graph and N is the number of nodes. The node density ρ implies the relation tightness among the activity nodes, and it shows the difference between the actual distribution graph and a complete graph.

The out-centrality of the activity node network graph is defined as:

$$C(V_i) = \frac{x_{i+}}{\displaystyle\sum_{i=1}^{N} x_{i+}} \tag{9.3}$$

where x_{i+} is the out degree. The centrality shows the importance of an activity node from the structural viewpoint. The node with a large out-centrality is followed by many sequential activities, and the activity denoted by such a node should be specially monitored by the managers. The activity node with large in-centrality connects with the execution results of several precedence activities, and the workshop managers should confirm these results in particular.

9.4.3.2 Graph Entropy-Based Evaluation Method

Graph entropy is defined according to the concept of entropy in informatics, and based on graph entropy, the ERP's procedure complexity is estimated according to the graphical structure of an activity group network. The entropy H is calculated by:

$$H = -\sum_{i=1}^{h} p_i \log_2 p_i \qquad (9.4)$$

where h means the number of divided groups, and p_i denotes the probability of every group's occurrence. The greater the uncertainty of a variable, the more information is needed to make it clear, which means the entropy is larger. If a system runs in order, its entropy is small, and vice versa, if a system is disordered, its entropy is large.

The entropy graph includes first- and second-order entropy. First-order entropy is calculated according to the number of inputs and outputs (IOs) of every node. The nodes with the same number of IOs are one group, and the total first-order graph entropy is the summation of all groups' first-order entropy. The second-order entropy of a node is calculated according to the neighbor nodes. The nodes around a given node form a group, and the total second-order graph entropy is the summation of all groups' second-order entropy (Mowshowitz, 1968; Park et al., 2001; Zhang et al., 2009; Wei and Cheng, 2011). The more the activities with the same number of IOs, the smaller the first-order entropy is. First-order entropy reflects the irregularity of the ERP activity group in logical structure. The more nodes connecting with the same precedence and successor nodes, the smaller the second-order entropy is. Second-order entropy shows the procedure complexity of the ERP.

9.5 APPLICATIONS IN EMERGENCY RESPONSE TRAINING

The refined decomposition of ERPs can be used for the training of emergency response. There are three types of training based on the activity group: (1) activities are employed to demonstrate operational procedures, (2) the responsibility assignment matrix for the activity group is useful for emergency response drills and exercises (Table 9.2), and (3) the prerequisite conditions of activities and their logical relations are listed clearly.

Table 9.2 Responsibility assignment matrix of an ERP

Role activity	Indoor operator	Outdoor operator	Indoor assistant operator	Outdoor assistant operator
A	Execute	Inform	Inform	Inform
B	Report	Execute	Inform	Inform
C	Conduct	Inform	Inform	Execute

9.6 APPLICATIONS IN EMERGENCY RESPONSE SUPPORT

Activity groups can also be used to support the desktop drills and the actual emergency response. Such support is implemented based on the detailed information of every activity, for example, if the prerequisite conditions, roles, and current situations are known, the system will supply the possible operational suggestion; if the current activity is clear, the system will show the next activity; the system can also supply an operational checklist, etc.

9.7 CONCLUSIONS

As an important technique to build an emergency management parallel system, a refined decomposition method for ERPs has been proposed, and the applications on ERP evaluation, emergency response training, and emergency response support have been introduced. In the future, this method will be used to construct the rule database of operator agent in the artificial system, and it is useful for artificial system construction, computational experiment execution, and dynamic emergency management.

REFERENCES

Chen, A., Chen, N., Ni, H., et al., 2009. Modern Emergency Management Theory and Method. Science Press, Beijing.

Cui, F., Cheng, C., Wang, F., Liu, X., Li, L., Zou, Y., et al., 2010. Design of parallel management information system based on service-oriented architecture. Comput. Appl. Chem. 27 (9), 1171–1176.

Jiao, Y., Xiong, Y., 2008. Handbook of Emergency Response to Production Safety Accident in Chemical Plant. Chinese Labor and Social Security Press, Beijing.

Liu, X., Noda, M., Nishitani, H., 2010. Evaluation of plant alarm systems by behavior simulation using a virtual subject. Comput. Chem. Eng. 34 (3), 374–386.

Mowshowitz, A., 1968. Entropy and the complexity of graphs: I. An index of the relative complexity of a graph. Bull. Math. Biophys. 30, 175–204.

Park, J., Jung, W., Ha, J., 2001. Development of the step complexity measure for emergency operating procedures using entropy concepts. Reliab. Eng. Syst. Saf. 71 (2), 115–130.

Project Management Institute, 2009.. In: Wang, Y., Zhang, B. (Eds.), A Guide to the Project Management Body of Knowledge (PMBOK Guide), fourth ed. Electronic Industrial Press, Beijing.

Wang, F., 2004a. Computational experiments for behavior analysis and decision evaluation of complex systems. J. Syst. Simul. 16 (5), 893–897.

Wang, F., 2004b. Computational theory and methods for complex systems. China Basic Sci. 6 (41), 3–10.

Wang, F., 2004c. Parallel system methods for management and control of complex systems. Control Decis. 19 (5), 485–489.

Wang, F., 2004d. Artificial societies, computational experiments, and parallel systems: an investigation on computational theory of complex social-economic systems. Complex Syst. Complexity Sci. 1 (4), 25–35.

Wang, F., 2010. Parallel control and management for intelligent transportation systems: concepts, architectures, and applications. IEEE Trans. Intell. Transport. Syst. 11 (3), 630–638.

Wei, W., Cheng, C., 2011. The complexity evaluation of chemical emergency response plans based on graphical entropy. J. Saf. Sci. Technol. 7 (2), 67–72.

Wu, S., 2011. "Emergency management in whole life cycle,". Mod. Occup. Saf. 3, 47–51.

Xu, D., 2010. Problems and their countermeasures in the constitution and application of enterprise emergency rescue plans. Sci. Technol. Innov. Herald 13, 246. 246.

Zhang, Y., Wu, B., Li, Z., et al., 2009. Operation complexity measure of emergency failure operation procedure in spaceflight. J. Astronaut. 30 (3), 1225–1230.

The next generation of enterprise knowledge management systems for the IT service industry

10

R. Anand

IBM Thomas J. Watson Research Center, Yorktown, NY, United States

CHAPTER OUTLINE

10.1 INTRODUCTION

The rise of knowledge-based organizations is one of the most important business trends of the past three decades (Davenport and Prusak, 1998). A knowledge-based organization is one that creates its primary value by absorbing, manipulating, and disseminating knowledge. Knowledge-based organizations are characterized jointly by the nature of their work, the kind of employees they hire, the tools that they use, and the way they employ people.

It has been our observation that in many respects, modern IT service providers represent a close approximation to the ideal of a pure knowledge-based organization. Given the complex and dynamic environment in which they operate, their knowledge management needs are extreme by the standards of other industrial organizations.

The noted venture capitalist Marc Andreessen has stated that "software is eating the world." The implication is that, eventually, all industries will begin to resemble the IT industry. Hence, in this chapter, we use the IT service industry as a lens to characterize knowledge-based organizations and study how knowledge management tools have evolved to meet their needs. We then draw on some of the recent developments in cognitive computing to suggest how a new generation of knowledge management tools might be created to meet their needs.

10.2 IT SERVICE PROVIDERS AS KNOWLEDGE-BASED ORGANIZATIONS

An asset is defined as being anything capable of being owned or controlled to produce value. In the industrial age, the most valuable assets, such as land, machinery, and buildings, were generally tangible. However, increasingly, the most valuable asset of an organization has become the knowledge, skill, and competence of its employees (Sveiby, 1997).

Among the diverse kinds of businesses, IT service providers come closest to the ideal of a knowledge-based organization. While the term "IT service provider" is rather broad, we use the term broadly to include organizations that install, modify, deploy, and support computer systems. As such, IT service organizations differ from those involved in software product development in that they work on a diversity of custom-negotiated engagements with a set of customers and do not generally have standard software offerings of their own.

The chief asset of IT service providers is their own employees. N. R. Narayana Murthy, founder and CEO of Infosys, a major IT service provider, has observed: "Our assets walk out of the door each evening. We have to make sure that they come back the next morning."

IT employees are called on to solve complex, intellectually challenging problems on a daily basis. Consequently, it is no surprise that they are among the most qualified and highest paid among all industries (BLS, 2013).

Let us now consider the characteristics of work performed by IT service providers. This exercise will play a key role in helping us identify their knowledge management requirements.

10.2.1 TASK COMPLEXITY

One of the main kinds of tasks for IT service workers is the creation and maintenance of computer software. Software has been characterized as "the most complicated man-made artifact and system" (Zhu, 2012). As a result of the fundamental nature of computing, documentation about computer systems is necessarily incomplete. Every time a computer program is modified, the programmer needs considerable contextual knowledge about the program in order to be able to make the change. This includes knowledge about the program itself, the operating system, and the customer's needs. Furthermore, the programmer also needs to understand the thought processes of the original programmers who created the program originally.

10.2.2 CROSS-DISCIPLINARY COLLABORATION

With the explosion of different programming languages, operating systems, and library frameworks, it has become impossible for IT workers to have both a broad and deep knowledge of the field. Consequently, IT workers tend to have specialized knowledge. Any significant project is likely to require a multiplicity of specialists. However, despite specialization, workers need a sufficient knowledge of other fields so as to know how to ask for help.

10.2.3 COMPLEX INTERACTIONS

At some stages during a customer engagement, complex interactions between teams of employees are often involved. In many IT service providers, there are distinct sales and delivery teams. Sales teams are responsible for locating customers and negotiating deals with them. The delivery team is responsible for actually providing the services. The handoff between the sales and delivery teams is often problematic for a number of reasons. Firstly the sales team may not have acquired information properly from the customer—the information may be incomplete or incorrect. Secondly, the customer information may not be transferred properly between the sales and delivery organizations. Further complications arise from the fact that both teams have multiple employees and may even be located on different continents. In order to ensure a smooth handover, very sophisticated knowledge management tools are necessary.

10.2.4 FLUID ORGANIZATIONAL STRUCTURE

The constantly changing nature of technologies and customer base invariably impacts organizational structure. Whenever a new technology is introduced or a new customer acquired, new departments are often created. Employees are constantly being transferred from mature departments to these newly formed departments. The size of teams and departments will often vary considerably over their lifespan, depending on business needs. Finally, when emergencies occur, employees are often reassigned temporarily to help deal with urgent problems. Finally, another source of organizational churn is employee turnover. Considering that knowledgeable employees are often valuable due to their skills, the market often rewards them handsomely for switching jobs. The departure of a key, especially senior, employee can often result in considerable organizational restructuring.

10.2.5 **INFORMATION TRANSFER RESTRICTIONS**

IT service providers have access to sensitive, often strategic, information possessed by their customers. This results in some significant restrictions on the use of this information.

- Service providers are themselves generally not allowed to use the customer's data for their own purposes.
- IT service providers must manage the data of customers in isolation. That is to say, the data from one customer must not be leaked to another customer, even by accident. IT service providers often have a large and diverse customer base and it is often the case that some of the customers may be mutual competitors. Such situations mandate the need for extreme care in information management.

10.2.6 **DUAL STATUS OF EMPLOYEES**

The employees of an IT service provider often have a dual role as virtual employees of the customer. For example, it is routine for IT service provider employees to have email accounts from both their own employer and from the customer. As a consequence of such arrangements, the barrier between the proprietary knowledge of the customer and the service provider cannot be clearly delineated and is often porous.

10.2.7 **TIME CONSTRAINTS**

It is common for customers to stipulate certain levels of service known as service-level agreements. For example, a time limit, say 1 day, is specified as the time limit for fixing a severity 1 defect in a piece of software. To achieve such levels of performance, employees need a considerable amount of information and also access to other employees who may have worked on similar problems in the past.

10.2.8 **CONTINUOUS EDUCATION**

As a result of the rapid evolution of the IT field, IT service organizations face an especially great challenge in keeping their employees up to date with the latest technologies. Even though employees may be highly educated at the time of recruitment, they need continuous education in the form of on-the-job training to stay productive. However, time spent in education is time away from the customer. Maintaining the balance between education and service is difficult.

10.3 **REQUIREMENTS FOR KNOWLEDGE MANAGEMENT**

Knowledge is defined as ... facts, information, and skills acquired by a person through experience or education.

For an individual, knowledge acquired in the course of employment is what gives him or her the ability to get their work done and create value. Our goal is to extend the concept of "knowledge" to the level of an organization. Two considerations are important in this regard:

- *Scale*: Knowledge management is, in essence, the process of enabling an organization as a whole to benefit from knowledge acquired by an individual member.
- *Origin*: The most valuable knowledge within an organization generally is that which is *internally* generated. Now, knowledge can indeed be purchased from external sources but such knowledge is also likely to be available to competitors. Internally generated knowledge is therefore one of the main sources of strategic advantage.

Based on our characterization of IT service providers, we are now in a position to articulate a set of requirements for knowledge management. Broadly, we can divide the knowledge management space into three areas:

- *Knowledge acquisition*: The first step in knowledge management is to acquire knowledge.
- *Knowledge maintenance and curation*: After initial acquisition, facts may change and some aspects of the acquired knowledge may have to be modified based on new experiences.
- *Knowledge delivery*: The challenge is to provide knowledge in the right form and at the right time in a way that will help them complete a task.

We shall examine requirements related to these three aspects of knowledge management in greater detail below.

10.3.1 KNOWLEDGE ACQUISITION

Let us consider the following common scenarios involving knowledge creation and acquisition:

1. An employee of an IT service provider creates an organization chart for a customer that includes annotations indicating how decision-making authority is distributed. Such charts help the employee's fellow team members quickly locate the correct person in the customer organization obtain approval for certain tasks that they must perform.
2. An employee takes a course and learns a new skill, for example, a popular new programming language. As a consequence of this new skill, the employee becomes valuable as a potential resource for new customer engagements that involve this programming language.
3. An employee solves a complex problem for one customer and devises a procedure to prevent its recurrence.
4. An employee uses data-mining tools to analyze a large number of problem tickets to identify a common cause for problems related to updating software

running on customer workstations. The employee then writes a memo that explains certain problem areas to avoid when performing such upgrades.

In all of these cases, some potentially useful knowledge has been created or acquired. In order to make this knowledge available to the wider organization, this knowledge has to be recorded in some way. Several problems arise in this regard:

- A worker may simply not be aware that something is worth recording. For example, in Scenario 3, the employee may not be aware that the recorded procedure could be of value to others and may fail to record the procedure in a publicly accessible manner. One requirement for a knowledge management system is therefore to help employees determine when a piece of knowledge is worth acquiring. In other words, it is often important to be able to request that a particular kind of knowledge be acquired.
- Knowledge cannot be separated from people involved with it: Even after knowledge has been acquired, there may be deficiencies or other clarification might be required by a future consumer of the knowledge. It is therefore necessary to track the provenance of all of the acquired knowledge.
- Information *about* employees can be valuable knowledge in and of itself. In Example 2, the real knowledge of organizational importance is the fact that an employee has gained proficiency in a programming language.
- There is often a tension between knowledge acquisition and speed of execution. In Example 3, it may take considerable time and effort for the employee to record the procedure with sufficient accuracy so as to allow others to follow the procedure. There is a need to reduce the barriers to recording knowledge—whether this is by technological assistance or by suitable incentive.
- When capturing knowledge, it must be captured in some kind of a language (which could be textual or diagrammatic) with the help of a tool. Both the language and the tool must be suited for the job—that is, the tool must have enough expressive power to capture the knowledge accurately while at the same time be easy to use.
- In addition to capturing the knowledge itself, it is also important to record the context in which it was captured. This includes who captured the knowledge, which customer was being served, the relevant technologies, etc. This is needed for the purpose of recording the provenance. As such, it can facilitate credit assignment or to obtain clarifications.

10.3.2 KNOWLEDGE MAINTENANCE AND CURATION

After knowledge has been acquired, it starts to lose value almost immediately unless it is maintained or curated. We have identified several category requirements related to knowledge maintenance that we discuss in this section:

- Metadata management
- Generalization

- Correctness
- Temporal issues
- Access control

Metadata management: In order to make the acquired knowledge discoverable and consumable, metadata must be added. This is, of course, a very well-studied area and numerous approaches exist (Simmhan et al., 2005; Sakr et al., 2011). One special requirement in our context is that there is a need to enable periodic refactorization of metadata. In other words, metadata itself may need to be periodically reviewed and modified as necessary.

Generalization: Knowledge acquired is often highly specific to a particular customer or to a particular technology. In order to make the knowledge more consumable, it often needs to be generalized. Generalization takes two forms:

- Generalization over domains: If an employee has recorded a procedure for fixing a software problem on one version of an operating system, it is desirable to also record the procedures for other versions of the operating system. It is therefore often desirable to extend the domain for a piece of knowledge. This kind of domain extension must be guided by the demand for the generalization.
- Generalization over customer engagements: If an employee solves a problem for one customer, it is very likely that the solution may be relevant for other customers as well. Indeed, this kind of knowledge acquisition is the key component of the business model for IT service providers. Expertise gained from serving one customer carries over to other customers. One critical requirement in this regard is that the solution must be neutralized—that is, all customer-specific information must be removed to avoid leakage of information between customers.

Correctness: For knowledge to be useful, it must reflect the reality of the business. As is the case with metadata, the correctness of acquired knowledge has to be established periodically. In the case of frequently used knowledge, this can be achieved by creating a social network-based community including the producers and consumers of knowledge. In the case of less frequently used knowledge, some kind of automated technique must be used to establish correctness.

Temporal issues: Some items of acquired knowledge have limited validity over time. As a part of knowledge maintenance, expired knowledge must be removed from current search results. On the other hand, it is frequently valuable to search over historical data. For example, it might be useful to know what was the procedure for dealing with a particular class of problems one year ago—for comparison with the current procedure for the same problem.

Access control: Given the sensitive nature of some of the collected information, customers may impose stringent restrictions on the propagation of the information within the IT service provider organization. On the one hand, standardized heavy-handed access control rules will stifle the sharing of knowledge. On the other hand, it is simply not scalable to have a fine-grained access control list for every fact in the knowledge base. Thus, there is a need for intelligent and flexible access control mechanisms that use sophisticated rules to determine what knowledge can be propagated safely.

10.3.3 KNOWLEDGE DELIVERY

For knowledge to be useful, it needs to be made available to employees in the right context at the right time. Let us now consider the requirements for effective knowledge delivery:

- *Search*: One of the key mechanisms for employees to locate relevant knowledge is through search. However, search within the enterprise remains problematic (Dmitriev et al., 2010). Part of the problem here is that relevance ranking is difficult within an enterprise. The real requirement is for semantic search in the context of knowledge management. This is due to the smaller amount of data.
- *Contextual delivery*: In some cases, it may not even occur to employees that some item of information is available. Or it is possible that they are very busy. In either case, we would like the knowledge delivery system to monitor what the user is doing and offer relevant information as appropriate.
- *Demand generation*: Being able to request information is as important as acquiring it. In other words, the knowledge management system must keep track of demands for information.
- *Mode of delivery*: Current state of the art is text-based delivery. However, it is very likely that for more complex kinds of information, it will have to be broken down automatically into smaller pieces and presented to the knowledge consumer in a piecemeal format. Interactivity is desirable. The user can ask for explanations.

10.4 CURRENT STATE OF KNOWLEDGE MANAGEMENT

Early knowledge management systems in the 1980s and 1990s were generally centralized, human-mediated systems that required the services of full-time knowledge curators. The curators were responsible for collecting, managing, and disseminating information throughout their organizations. One of the key problems with this early approach was both the centralization and the need for full-time dedicated staff. However, given the state of technology, this approach was unavoidable.

In recent years, a powerful suite of technologies collectively referred to as Web 2.0 has become the means for implementing a new generation of web-based knowledge management tools. The key attributes of the Web 2.0 approach with respect to this chapter are decentralization and crowd-sourcing.

Web 2.0 technologies reduce the barriers to sharing information by providing knowledge management tools to all employees in an organization, thereby providing them with the means for sharing information relatively easily. Furthermore, no central authority needs to approve additions to the knowledge base. The impact of

Web 2.0 tools like Wikis has been studied by academic researchers (Grace, 2009). Overall, these tools have definitely assisted in advancing the state of the art in knowledge management.

While Web 2.0 technologies are a good start, several significant problems have been observed:

- Lowering the barriers to recording information has resulted in a great increase in the volume of information captured. Consequently, the problem of locating useful information has become even harder. Text (i.e., keyword) search is the primary technique for locating information in Web 2.0 knowledge bases. While search engines such as Google and Bing have been successful on the Internet, enterprise search remains a significant problem (Dmitriev et al., 2010). The key problem is the lack of relevance. Algorithms like Page Rank simply do not work well within the enterprise. Finally, much of the data in Web 2.0 repositories is simply not searchable due to it being pictorial in nature or recorded in formats such as PDF that can be hard to search.
- There is a significant problem with correctness and stale data being captured in Web 2.0 systems. In practice, workers sometimes simply dump all of their documents into these document repositories without regard to duplication or relevance. Related to this problem, it can be difficult to track the provenance of a piece of information.
- Usage statistics are very hard to obtain. That is to say, it is not easy to determine how often a piece of information has been accessed.
- Natural language is not always the best way to record some kinds of knowledge, especially procedures, but this is often the only choice available. Consider, for example, a procedure to correct an error in a customer invoice. There are likely to be numerous conditional steps in such a procedure. A person who has not been trained in programming may lack the ability to capture a sophisticated procedure like this in a document.

It must be noted that several new techniques based on social networks have been proposed as a new way to manage some kinds of knowledge. The basic approach of these tools can be summarized as being a way to avoid directly capturing knowledge but rather to keep track of those employees who have expertise in a particular topic (Vridhachalam, 2010).

When an employee needs information, the intent is that he or she will use the expertise locator to identify a person who could help the knowledge seeker. The fundamental problems with this approach are:

- It is difficult to accurately characterize expertise in people in a succinct manner.
- This approach is fundamentally not scalable, since expertise is often concentrated among a few people in an organization. The time of these experts becomes a valuable commodity.

Another kind of a Web 2.0 tool that has become popular is question–answer exchanges. The basic approach was established by the Internet website StackExchange.

com. Questions can be posted by anyone and answers are contributed by subject matter experts. To ensure the quality of answers, all users are allowed to edit or critique the answers. To encourage participation, users are rewarded in merit points that can be used to signal expertise. A number of companies such as IBM have deployed such systems internally with a view to promote information sharing among employees.

At their heart, all of the new information management techniques in the Web 2.0 family inherently depend on human cognitive processing to be effective. Given the current emphasis on lean organizations, however, there are limits to the availability of full-time staff to curate the contents of Web 2.0 applications. Furthermore, the volume of data is so great that human intervention may not even be possible.

10.5 KNOWLEDGE MANAGEMENT IN THE ERA OF COGNITIVE COMPUTING

In the last 10 years, approximately from the mid-2000s, there have been a number of notable innovations in technologies related cognitive computing. These include:

- *Machine learning*: While machine learning is not a new field, several new techniques including kernel methods and deep learning have been developed.
- *Natural language processing*: Many new techniques based on statistics and machine learning have been applied to the field of natural language processing. In the past, natural language processing systems were, in general, painstakingly handcrafted. With the advent of new techniques such as statistical parsing and vector-based semantic representation, much less manual labor is necessary to create sophisticated applications that can process vast streams of natural language.
- *Knowledge extraction from Big Data*: Many new techniques for extracting facts from large corpus have been developed. In particular, techniques such as mapreduce have enabled the use of data sets that are many terabytes in size. Halevy et al. (2009) make the case that the availability of vast Internet-scale data sets along with relatively simple algorithms have enabled the creation of novel natural language processing systems that have the potential to reduce the need for human labor in knowledge management.

In this section, we describe some of these new applications of cognitive computing and suggest how they may help address the problems of knowledge management.

10.5.1 UNSTRUCTURED DATA

In any modern organization, the key problem of knowledge management is that manual curation of knowledge does not scale. The main reason for this is that the data generated by an organization are not structured—they exist in the form of emails, Word documents, and PDF files. In order to extract useful information from such documents, mere text search is not sufficiently powerful. Within an organization's data, unlike the Internet, relevance cannot be determined by analyzing hyperlinks.

This problem is addressed by technologies from the IBM Watson suite of products. Watson is a collection of technologies for managing, querying, and interactively exploring unstructured information. Starting as a research project at IBM, T. J. Watson Research Center in 2006, the initial goal of the Watson project was to create a sophisticated question-answering system that could work with unstructured data. This capability was publically demonstrated in a well-known Jeopardy match on television in which Watson defeated several champions. Watson has now expanded beyond question answering to become a suite of products.

The Watson question-answering system works by parsing a query and then using the extracted information from the query to search intelligently through a corpus of documents. Multiple candidates are identified—which are then ranked and sorted via relevance computations. The quality of the answers rivals that of human-curated knowledge bases.

10.5.2 LEARNING BY OBSERVATION

While systems such as Watson are highly capable of extracting knowledge from collected data, there is a separate challenge in capturing *procedural* knowledge. That is to say, capturing and disseminating the procedure to perform a task. While it is often feasible to create a script in a programming language to perform a task, the difficulty arises from the fact that not everyone can write such scripts.

The key requirement is therefore a system that can observe the performance of a task and then extract an abstract general procedure from observations. This is clearly a difficult problem that is at the very limits of what is currently feasible. This problem has received much attention by researchers in a number of diverse fields including AI, software engineering, and robotics.

In the field of robotics, for example, the work of Bentivegna et al. (2004) is representative of research into autonomously learning physical tasks. Their system can learn to play physical games such as air hockey by watching human players.

With respect to the problem of capturing typical knowledge-worker tasks, PLOW (Allen et al., 2007) is a notable project. PLOW is a system that learns executable task models from a single collaborative learning session consisting of demonstration, explanation, and dialog.

10.5.3 VIRTUAL AGENTS

As we noted earlier in this chapter, it is often difficult for a knowledge worker to know when to ask for help and what information is available. We see the field of conversational virtual agents as the key means for implementing this functionality.

A virtual agent can act as a personal assistant for a knowledge worker. One of the key functions of such an agent is to create a behavioral model of the person it is serving and furthermore use observationally obtained information to preemptively deliver relevant and useful information at the right moment.

Work by Zhao et al. (2014) is representative of work in this field. They have studied the problem of how a computer system can attain rapport with a human worker. This work has been applied to the area of tutoring students, but it also has general applicability to all knowledge-based work.

10.6 CONCLUSIONS

In this chapter, we have identified the key characteristics of a knowledge-based organization using IT service providers as the archetype. Furthermore, we have identified knowledge management as one of the key gating factors for creating competent and responsive knowledge-based organizations of the future.

The first phase of knowledge management relied on manual curation of knowledge by experts. The second era is characterized by the use of crowd sourcing. We have argued in this chapter that the fourth era of knowledge management will be based on new developments in the field of cognitive computing. Specifically, we have proposed that natural language processing, Big Data management, and personalized virtual agents are the foundational technologies for the future. We anticipate that these technologies will have a dramatic impact on worker productivity and effectiveness in the future.

REFERENCES

Allen J., Chambers N., Ferguson G., Galescu L., Jung H., Swift M., et al., 2007. PLOW: a collaborative task learning agent. In: Proceedings of the AAAI Conference.

Bentivegna, D.C., Atkeson, C.G., Cheng, G., 2004. Learning tasks from observation and practice. Robotics and Autonomous Systems 47, 163–169.

BLS 2013 National Occupational Employment and Wage Estimates United States, http://www.bls.gov/oes/current/oes_nat.htm#00-0000.

Davenport, T.H., Prusak, L., 1998. Working Knowledge: How Organizations Manage What They Know. Harvard Business School Press, Boston, MA.

Dmitriev P., Serdyukov P., Chernov S., 2010. Enterprise and desktop search. In: Proceedings of the 19th International Conference on World Wide Web, ACM: Raleigh, North Carolina, USA, 1345-1346

Ferrucci, D.A., 2012. Introduction to "this is watson". IBM J. Res. & Dev. 56 (3), 1:1–1:15.

Grace, T.P.L., 2009. Wikis as a knowledge management tool. Journal of Knowledge Management 13 (4), 64–74.

Halevy, A., Norvig, P., Pereira, F., 2009. The unreasonable effectiveness of data. IEEE Intelligent Systems 24 (2).

Sakr, S., Liu, A., Batista, D.M., Alomari, M., 2011. A Survey of large scale data management approaches in cloud environments. IEEE Communications Surveys & Tutorials 13 (3) third quarter.

Simmhan, Y., Plale, B., Gannon, D., 2005. A survey of data provenance in e-science. SIGMOD Record 35 (3).

Sveiby, K.E., 1997. The New Organizational Wealth: Managing and Measuring Knowledge-Based Assets. Berrett-Koehler Publishers, San Francisco, CA.

Vridhachalam M., 2010 *Building an enterprise expertise location system*, http://www.ibm.com/developerworks/webservices/library/ws-soapattern/?ca=drs.

Zhao, R., Papangelis, A., Cassell, J., 2014. Towards a dyadic computational model of rapport management for human-virtual agent interaction. Lecture Notes in Computer Science, 8637. Intelligent Virtual Agents (IVA), Springer, Cham Heidelberg, New York, Dordrecht London, 514–527.

Zhu H., 2012. Position statement: can software design benefit from creative computing? In: Computer Software and Applications Conference (COMPSAC) IEEE 36th Annual.

Expertise recommendation and new skill assessment with multicue semantic information

11

J. Wang, K.R. Varshney, A. Mojsilović, D. Fang and J.H. Bauer

IBM Thomas J. Watson Research Center, Yorktown, NY, United States

CHAPTER OUTLINE

11.1 INTRODUCTION

Globalization, recognized as the process of extending social relations worldwide, has driven economic growth in the past few decades. In addition, globalization has pushed many large multinational corporations to transform from collections of several domestically based organizations to globally integrated and cross-cultural enterprises (Palmisano, 2006). In particular, advances in transportation and telecommunications infrastructures served as the first major impetus for such a globalization trend. More recently, the rise of social networking on the Internet has made social interaction across world-space easier and more frequent. For example, the world's largest social network, Facebook, consists of >1 billion users with over 1 trillion connections and LinkedIn, the world's largest professional social network, reached 200 million members in January 2013.

Social networks provide efficient ways for people to communicate and collaborate, and help businesses be more competitive and successful. Therefore, there is also

Big Data and Smart Service Systems. DOI: http://dx.doi.org/10.1016/B978-0-12-812013-2.00011-3

an increasing use and need of social network and social media technologies inside every enterprise and corporation, which leads to a more connected, interactive, and enabled workforce (Raghavan, 2002; McAfee, 2006; Wu et al., 2010).

Traditionally, governments are the employers with the largest workforces. For example, the US Department of Defense is the world's largest employer with around 3.2 million employees. However, globalized business drives workforce growth of nongovernmental employers since companies tend to require more employees to work directly with local clients (Prahalad and Ramaswamy, 2004). Among the 20 largest employers from the Fortune Global 500 by number of employees, it is no surprise that companies from traditional industries, such as retail and energy, tend to have large workforces since they are labor-intensive. In addition, technology companies, like International Business Machines and Hon Hai Precision Industry, also have considerable workforce size due to their growth in the global market.

There are many emerging challenges for human resource (HR) management and workforce analytics and optimization in modern multinational corporations. To address these challenges, the fast growth of data sources like enterprise social networks can be utilized to help corporations manage, transform, engage, and plan for their workforces. In particular, social networking naturally captures information about the activities, interactions, and knowledge of employees in a digital form that can be mined for insight and business process improvements (Ehrlich et al., 2007; Chelmis et al., 2012; Lin et al., 2012; Varshney et al., 2013).

Knowledgeable employees are not interchangeable because they each have specialized expertise and skills; this has an important role in a corporation's business, especially in service industries with much client interaction. Hence, it is critical to capture and understand the individual specialties of employees for successful human capital management and operation in large enterprises. For instance, if the expertise of each employee can be comprehensively cataloged, the assignment of projects can be extremely efficient and accurate since the desired experts can be called upon to meet clients' needs. From a more strategic perspective, an accurate understanding of employees' skill information can be used to plan for an enterprise's long-term business goals.

However, existing HR management tools are insufficient in terms of handling such challenging issues in both scalability and depth (Varshney et al., 2013). First, although employees can be easily categorized by their organization charts and reporting chains, it is difficult to characterize the employees by specific functions they carry out or knowledge they have. An expertise or skill taxonomy within a company is one structure for representing the various functional abilities or knowledge that employees may have (Ilgen and Hollenbeck, 1991). Such taxonomies can be used for various business processes (Hu et al., 2007; Naveh et al., 2007).

Although it is important to capture skills information in a structured format, it is fairly time-consuming since constructing a skill taxonomy and assessing employees against it relies heavily on manual processing. Especially for a modern multinational corporation, since the number of employees can be hundreds of thousands and even several million, and the skills carried by the workforce could cover a very wide range of fields, it is extremely challenging to develop such a complex skill taxonomy on such a scale. Second, even if such a taxonomy could be built and populated to organize and index employees by their expertise, search and retrieval of experts using the skill taxonomy is not straightforward. This is mainly because the enterprise's skill taxonomy often consists of specific technical terms and there exists a clear semantic gap between those terms and natural search keywords. So it is necessary to map the technical skill terms to a common set of concepts.

Acknowledging all of these challenges and opportunities, this chapter focuses on automatic expertise assessment using various types of semantic sources, each of which reveals a different cue of skill, knowledge, and expertise. As illustrated in Fig. 11.1, we particularly treat the expertise assessment as a recommendation problem, where we utilize several prediction techniques for solving such a problem. First, we conduct a basic matrix completion (BMC) task using a set of incomplete observed skill assessments. Then we explore the social context and skill semantics to perform collaborative filtering, content filtering, and a hybrid approach to predict the skills of employees. Empirical study using a real-world employee data set from a multinational Fortune 500 corporation clearly demonstrates the strengths and weaknesses of each method. The results indicate that a further study for such a problem should be directed towards combined models with multicue semantic information.

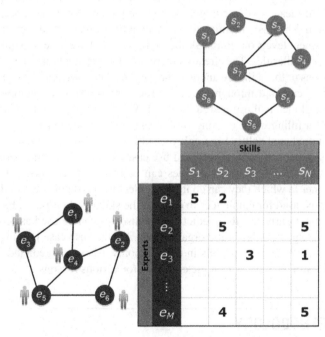

FIGURE 11.1

Illustration of skill prediction problem formulation using multicue semantic information.

The remainder of this chapter is organized as follows. Section 11.2 briefly reviews the problem of expertise assessment and the corresponding use cases. Section 11.3 presents the methods used for predicting experts' skills. Section 11.4 provides experimental validations and comparative studies, and, finally, Section 11.5 concludes the chapter and discusses further work.

11.2 SKILL ASSESSMENT AND USE CASES

In this section, we set forth the concrete workforce analytics problem that we are considering and discuss the use cases that a solution to the problem would enable.

In this work, we consider a corporation with an existing expertise taxonomy of hundreds or thousands of fine-grained skills with detailed textual descriptions that have been created and curated manually. Within this structure of skills, employees have assessment scores that indicate their level of mastery of the skill, ranging from no expertise at all, to having acquired the skill, to having mastered the skill, to being so skilled that the employee is viewed as a thought leader. However, due to the multitude of skills and the semantic gap discussed in Section 11.1, most employees are not assessed on most skills. If we think of employees as rows and skills as columns in a table, with skill assessment values as entries of table cells, then a large fraction of the cells are empty. The problem we tackle is to fill in the empty cells through analytics-based means in order to get a complete picture about the expertise within the corporation. The basic premise for such analytics is that similar employees have similar assessment levels on similar skills. Moreover, we have access to multiple cues to define these similarities. The already-entered skill assessments are one cue, the textual descriptions of the skills are another cue, and the data about employee knowledge and interaction captured through enterprise social networking technology is a third cue. The overall idea is illustrated in Fig. 11.1. We discuss the precise mathematical formulation for filling in the missing skill assessments in Section 11.3.

Based on predicted values for employee skill assessments, there are several business processes that can be improved and use cases satisfied (Varshney et al., 2013). First, the predicted values for employees can be recommended to them in a user-friendly manner in which they can confirm or reject the prediction. Second, a similar interface can be used for employees to endorse the skills of their peers. For planning and management purposes, the predictions themselves can be used as proxy values for characterizing expertise in the organization. Another use case is using analytics to construct new or emerging skills in the taxonomy. Also, the predicted values can be used in locating experts within the company for various reasons.

11.3 METHODOLOGY

We first give a brief introduction of the notations used in this chapter. Assume we have a set of employees $\{e_i\}_{i=1}^{M}$ and that there are a total of N skills for assessment. The skill level of an employee e_i for the jth skill is denoted by m_{ij}, hence the employee-skill matrix $M = \{m_{ij}\} \in R^{M \times N}$ indicates all of the skill assessments. Given a partial observation of the skill assessment as $\tilde{M}$, the goal for skill assessment is to complete the underlying matrix M.

Without considering any context, the problem of skill assessment can be treated as a matrix completion problem, where the objective is to complete the missing values in the employee-skill matrix $M \in R^{M \times N}$ under certain structural assumptions on M. Here we describe two related methods: matrix factorization and low-rank matrix estimation. Matrix factorization-based approaches assume that the target matrix can be decomposed into two matrices $W \in R^{L \times N}$ and $H \in R^{L \times N}$ as $M = W^{\mathrm{T}} H$ (Koren et al., 2009). Given a partially observed matrix $\tilde{M} = \{\tilde{m}_{ij}\}$ with $O = \{(i,j)\}$ indicating the set of matrix cells with observed values, a basic formulation of matrix factorization can be written in a square loss form as:

$$\arg\min_{W,H} \sum_{(i,j)\in O} \left\| \tilde{m}_{ij} - w_i^T h_j \right\|^2$$

where w_i, and h_i, are the ith and jth column vectors of the hidden matrices W and H, respectively.

As a classical latent factor model, the above minimization problem can be interpreted as the representation learning of both user and item features in an unknown feature space R^L with L as the latent dimension. A similar formulation has been widely used for designing modern recommendation systems (Resnick and Varian, 1997; Ricci et al., 2011), where a very successful application is recommending movies to the customers of the on-demand Internet streaming media company Netflix (Bennett and Lanning, 2007). In our particular application of skill assessment, the employees are the users and the skills are the items. Imposing non-negativity constraints on both the W and H matrices leads to another well-known variant: non-negative matrix factorization (Lee and Seung, 1999, 2001). In addition, probabilistic algorithms have been applied to matrix factorization modeling; the resulting probabilistic matrix factorization methods have been shown to be effective in handling large-scale applications as they scale linearly with the number of observations (Salakhutdinov and Mnih, 2008a, 2008b).

The low-rank matrix approximation approach assumes that the underlying rank of the target matrix is low. Intuitively, the users and items are clustered in a small number of groups. Hence, given a partial observation, it is possible to recover the target matrix directly. Although matrix factorization and matrix rank minimization methods have different explicit formulations, they are closely related and sometimes equivalent (Recht et al., 2010; Ma et al., 2011). For instance, Ma et al. (2011) propose an iterative approach, namely fixed-point continuation with approximate singular value decomposition to solve the following matrix rank minimization problem:

$$\min_{M} \mathrm{rank}(M)$$
$$\mathrm{st} \, m_{ij} = \tilde{m}_{ij} \quad \text{for} \quad (i,j) \in O$$

Matrix factorization-based solutions are also regarded as model-based collaborative filtering approaches because the resulting predictions are based on a certain form of statistical modeling (Su et al., 2009). Though such model-based approaches show promising results in many applications, one of their disadvantages is that the training cost is usually fairly high when handling large-scale data sets.

Memory-based approaches are another popular category for performing such predictions due to implementation ease and computational efficiency. Typically, one can first use the observed skill assessment data to compute similarity between employees and skills. Then the nearest neighborhood mechanism can be applied to perform either item-based or user-based top-N prediction (Su et al., 2009). For example, the similarity between two employees e_i and e_j can be computed using Pearson correlation as

$$sim(e_i, e_j) = \frac{(\tilde{m}_i - \bar{m}_i)^{\mathrm{T}} (\tilde{m}_j - \bar{m}_j)}{\sqrt{\|\tilde{m}_i - \bar{m}_i\|^2 \|\tilde{m}_j - \bar{m}_j\|^2}}$$

where $\bar{m}_i$ and $\bar{m}_j$ represent the average skill rating for the ith and jth employee across all skills. Here $\tilde{m}_i$ and $\tilde{m}_j$ are the observed skill assessment for the ith and jth employee. The similarity between skills can also be calculated using the partially observed matrix $\tilde{M}$. However, such neighborhood-based algorithms rely on the sufficient completeness of the observed assessments. In realistic scenarios, usually only a very small portion of employee-skill cells are filled with assessed values; thus, the estimation of the similarity could be extremely unstable.

However, in the application of expertise assessment, besides the partially observed expert-skill matrix, rich semantic information about the employees and skills can be acquired. For instance, as mentioned earlier, the usage of enterprise social networking creates a platform for employees to discuss their projects and research topics. Mining such social media data can help derive the social proximity between employees. For example, the employees' social activity on technical communities and microblogs can be extracted to form semantic information, which can be used to estimate their skill background. Assume we can extract the semantic representation e_i for the ith employees. Then the social proximity between any two employees can be estimated using such representations. Simply the vector cosine-based similarity can be computed as

$$sim(e_i, e_j) = \frac{e_i^{\mathrm{T}} e_j}{\sqrt{\|e_i\|^2 \|e_j\|^2}}$$

Then a user-based collaborative filtering algorithm can be used to estimate an unknown skill assessment m_{ik} as

$$m_{ik} = \frac{\sum_{(j,k) \in O} sim(e_i, e_j) \tilde{m}_{jk}}{\sum_{(j,k) \in O} sim(e_i, e_j)}$$

Intuitively, the skill assessment for the kth skill on the ith employee is the weighted sum of the skill assessment of all the similar employees on the same skill. The above prediction is essentially a weighted nearest-neighbor method in the employee space if we truncate the similarity between e_i and his or her similar employees and only choose the most similar ones.

In addition, the skill can be further analyzed by using its descriptions and definitions. Such analysis can help derive semantic features for each skill. Then we can compute the semantic similarity between skills. Let us assume the skills are represented by feature vectors as $\{s_i\}_{i=1}^{N}$. Similarly, the semantic similarity $\text{sim}(s_i,s_j)$ between two skills s_i and s_j can be computed accordingly. Hence, the skill assessment can also be estimated using the skill similarity as

$$m_{ik} = \frac{\sum_{(i,j)\in O}\text{sim}(s_j,s_k)\tilde{m}_{ij}}{\sum_{(i,j)\in O}\text{sim}(s_j,s_k)}$$

Finally, since both employee and skill can be represented by semantic features, it is straightforward to combine both pieces of information to perform two-way prediction as

$$m_{ik} = (1-\mu)\frac{\sum_{(j,k)\in O}\text{sim}(e_i,e_j)\tilde{m}_{jk}}{\sum_{(j,k)\in O}\text{sim}(e_i,e_j)}$$
$$+ \mu\frac{\sum_{(i,j)\in O}\text{sim}(s_j,s_k)\tilde{m}_{ij}}{\sum_{(i,j)\in O}\text{sim}(s_j,s_k)}$$

where μ is a parameter that indicates the relative weights given to each type of semantic information.

11.4 EMPIRICAL STUDY

To perform an empirical study using the aforementioned prediction approaches, we acquired a set of employee data from a multinational Fortune 500 corporation. Below we start by introducing the data and experimental settings, followed by the evaluation results.

We collected data for a total of 2618 employees who assessed 471 unique skills. Hence, we have an employee-skill matrix with the size 2618×471. The number of assessed skills for each employee ranges from 6 to 180 with an average number of skills of 40. The popular skills have up to 615 experts and the rarest skill has only 47 assigned experts. Fig. 11.2A shows the distribution of the number of associated employees per skill and Fig. 11.2B shows the distribution of the number of skills per employee, where Birnbaum–Saunders, inverse Gaussian, and log-normal distributions all give good approximation of the empirical histograms.

For employee's semantics, we crawl the content from enterprise social networks, including research/project communities and microblogs, and the associated textual

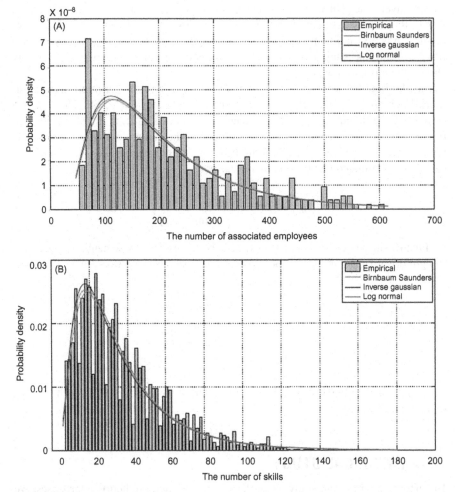

FIGURE 11.2

The distributions of (A) the number of skills per employee and (B) the number of associated employees per skill.

tags. Based on the frequency of the online social activities, a relevance score is estimated for each textual tag for the employee. Figs. 11.3 and 11.4 demonstrate examples of the extracted employee and skill semantic information in the form of a weighted keyword representation, where the size of the word indicates the strength of the relevance for that keyword.

Clearly, such a semantic representation provides an informative description of the employee. In this case, this particular employee very likely has database, data analysis, and social networking-related skills since his or her online activities cover

FIGURE 11.3

An example of the employee's semantic information on the enterprise social network represented by keywords.

FIGURE 11.4

An example of the skill's semantic information represented by keywords.

related topics. In our study, we constructed a semantic dictionary with a total of 5701 keywords to represent each employee's semantic information. Based on such a representation, we can compute the online social similarity, as described above. Meanwhile, for each skill, we build similar semantic representation with a 2514-keyword dictionary and compute the skill similarity.

To show the effectiveness of the computed semantic similarity of employees and skills, we plot the curve of semantic similarity between employees $\text{sim}(e_i, e_j)$ versus the values of $\text{sim}(m_i, m_j)$ in Fig. 11.5A, and the skill semantic similarity $\text{sim}(s_i, s_j)$

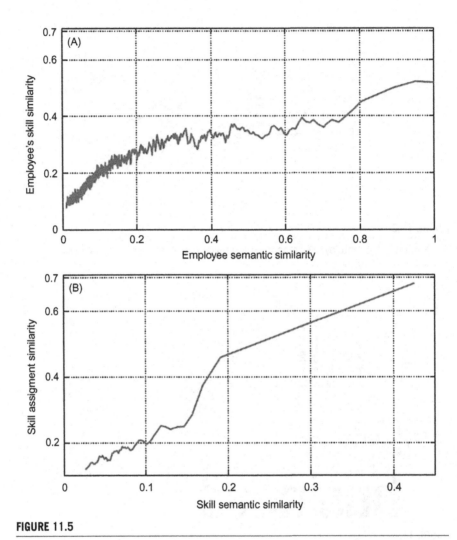

FIGURE 11.5

Evaluation of the effectiveness of (A) employee semantic similarity and (B) skill semantic similarity for the prediction of skill assessment.

versus the values of $\text{sim}(m_i, m_j)$ in Fig. 11.5B. Here, m_i and m_j are the ith and jth column vectors, representing the assessment level of the ith and jth skills across the employee population. It is straightforward to conclude that the computed semantic similarities of employees and skills are correlated to the skill assessment. In other words, similar employees tend to share a similar set of skills and similar skills tend to be associated with similar employee populations.

To validate the performance of the aforementioned methods here, we simply view skill assessment as a binary prediction problem, where the goal is to predict whether an employee has certain skills. Since the employee-skill matrix is very sparse with only around 3–4% nonzero elements, we measure the prediction error by the average of the false-positive rate and false-negative rate as:

$$\alpha = \frac{\text{False Positive}}{\text{False Positive} + \text{True Negative}}$$

$$\beta = \frac{\text{False Negative}}{\text{True Positive} + \text{False Negative}}$$

$$\text{error} = \frac{1}{2}(\alpha + \beta)$$

where α and β are the false-positive and false-negative rates, respectively. In addition, we randomly split the cells in the M matrix sixfold and use cross-validation to compute the average errors.

We evaluate the following methods: (1) BMC using the low rank approximation (Ma et al., 2011), (2) BMC combined with skill semantic information (BMC-SSI), (3) BMC combined with employee semantic information (BMC-ESI), and (4) BMC combined with both types of semantic information (BMC-BSI). Since the BMC method gives the prediction in the continuous values, we need to binarize the predicted values to generate the results. In particular, we use the training data to estimate the ratio of positive and negative values in the expert-skill matrix. Such estimates are then used to compute an adaptive threshold value to generate the binary predictions for the test subset, where the positive/negative ratio is the same as the training subset. To combine the predictions from BMC with semantic information for BMC-SSI, BMC-ESI, and BMC-BSI, we use a simple after fusion approach by applying a weighting and normalization scheme (Jain et al., 2005).

Fig. 11.6 demonstrates the prediction performance measured by the error rates. Clearly, both semantic information of employees and skills help to improve the

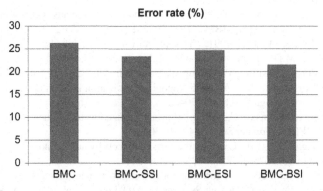

FIGURE 11.6

Prediction performance measured by the average error percentage for different approaches.

performance of the BMC methods, and using both sets of semantic information can further boost the performance. In addition, the performance gain by using the skills' semantic information is higher than that using employees' semantic information, which is also consistent with the observation in Fig. 11.5.

11.5 CONCLUSION

In this chapter, we address the problem of automatically assessing employees' expertise, which plays an important role in human capital management and workforce analytics. In particular, we treat the assessment of employees' expertise as a matrix completion problem with the rows and columns representing individual employees and skills. In addition to the well-known matrix completion techniques, we propose to explore the professional social network to retrieve multicue semantic information for both employees and skills. Empirical study using real-world HR data corroborates that the extracted multicue semantic information can help boost the performance of skill assessment. One of our future directions of research is to design a generic prediction model to combine the matrix structure information and the semantic information for robust skill assessment.

REFERENCES

Bennett, J., Lanning, S., 2007. The Netflix prize, In: Proceedings of the KDD Cup Workshop, San Jose, CA, pp. 3–6.

Chelmis, C., Sorathia, V., Prasanna, V.K., 2012. Enterprise wisdom captured socially. In Proceedings of the IEEE/ACM Int. Conf. Adv. Soc. Netw. Anal. Min., Istanbul, Turkey, pp. 1228–1235.

Ehrlich, K., Lin, C.-Y., Griffiths-Fisher, V., 2007. Searching for experts in the enterprise: combining text and social network analysis. In: Proceedings of the ACM Conf. Supporting Group Work, Sanibel Island, FL, pp. 117–126.

Hu, J., Ray, B.K., Singh, M., 2007. "Statistical methods for automated generation of service engagement staffing plans,". IBM J. Res. Dev. 51 (3/4), 281–293.

Ilgen, D.R., Hollenbeck, J.R., 1991. "The structure of work: job design and roles,". In: Psychology, M.D., Dunnette, Hough, L.M. (Eds.), Handbook of Industrial and Organizational. Consulting Psychologists Press, Palo Alto, CA, pp. 165–207.

Jain, A., Nandakumar, K., Ross, A., 2005. "Score normalization in multimodal biometric systems,". Pattern Recogn. 38 (12), 2270–2285.

Koren, Y., Bell, R., Volinsky, C., 2009. "Matrix factorization techniques for recommender systems,". IEEE Computer Society 42 (8), 30–37.

Lee, D.D., Seung, H.S., 1999. "Learning the parts of objects by non-negative matrix factorization,". Nature 401 (6755), 788–791.

Lee, D.D., Seung, H.S., 2001. "Algorithms for non-negative matrix factorization," Advances in Neural Information Processing Systems 13. MIT Press, Cambridge, MA. 556–562.

Lin, C.-Y., Wu, L., Wen, Z., Tong, H., Griffiths-Fisher, V., Shi, L., et al., 2012. "Social network analysis in enterprise,". Proc. IEEE 100 (9), 2759–2776.

Ma, S., Goldfarb, D., Chen, L., 2011. "Fixed point and Bregman iterative methods for matrix rank minimization,". Math. Program. 128 (1–2), 321–353.

McAfee, A.P., 2006. "Enterprise 2.0: the dawn of emergent collaboration,". MIT Sloan Manage. Rev. 47 (3), 21–28.

Naveh, Y., Richter, Y., Altshuler, Y., Gresh, D.L., Connors, D.P., 2007. "Workforce optimization: Identification and assignment of professional workers using constraint programming,". IBM J. Res. Dev. 51 (3/4), 263–279.

Palmisano, S.J., 2006. "The globally integrated enterprise,". Foreign Aff. 85 (3), 127–136.

Prahalad, C.K., Ramaswamy, V., 2004. The Future of Competition: Co-Creating Unique Value with Customers. Harvard Business School Press, Boston, MA.

Raghavan, P., 2002. "Social networks: from the web to the enterprise,". IEEE Internet Comput. 6 (1), 91–94.

Recht, B., Fazel, M., Parrilo, P.A., 2010. "Guaranteed minimum-rank solutions of linear matrix equations via nuclear norm minimization,". SIAM Rev. 52 (3), 471–501.

Resnick, P., Varian, H.R., 1997. "Recommender systems,". Comm. ACM 40 (3), 56–58.

Ricci, F., Rokach, L., Shapira, B., 2011. "Introduction to recommender systems handbook,". In: Ricci, F., Rokach, L., Shapira, B., Kantor, P.B. (Eds.), Recommender Systems Handbook. Springer, New York, NY, pp. 1–35.

Salakhutdinov, R., Mnih, A., 2008a. "Probabilistic matrix factorization," Advances in Neural Information Processing Systems 20. MIT Press, Cambridge, MA.1257–1264.

Salakhutdinov, R., Mnih, A., 2008b. Bayesian probabilistic matrix factorization using Markov chain Monte Carlo. In: Proceedings of the International Conference on Machine Learning, Helsinki, Finland, pp. 880–887.

Su, X., Khoshgoftaar, T.M., 2009. "A survey of collaborative filtering techniques,". Adv. Artif. Intell. 2009, 421–425.

Varshney, K.R., Wang, J., Mojsilović, A., Fang, D., Bauer, J.H., 2013. Predicting and recommending skills in the social enterprise. In: Proceedings of the International AAAI Conference on Weblogs and Social Media, Cambridge, MA.

Wu, A., DiMicco, J.M., Millen, D.R., 2010. Detecting professional versus personal closeness using an enterprise social network site. In: Proc. SIGCHI Conf. Hum. Fact. Comput. Syst., Atlanta, GA, pp. 1955–1964.

On the behavioral theory of the networked firm

12

G. Nyman[1], J. Peltonen[2], M. Nelson[3], J. Karjalainen[2],
M. Laine[2], T. Nyberg[2] and H. Tuomisaari[2]

[1]*University of Helsinki, Helsinki, Finland* [2]*Aalto University, Espoo, Finland*
[3]*Stanford University, Palo Alto, CA, United States*

CHAPTER OUTLINE

12.1 BACKGROUND

In the second edition of their classic book on the behavioral theory of the firm, Cyert and March (2001) make the following comment on the network structures and analysis: "… standard organization charts are inadequate and misleading representations of organizations, but they have not, as yet, yielded a generally accepted alternative conception of the basis for network structures." This is still true today and the ubiquitous growth and development of global networks is introducing novel theoretical and practical challenges for realistic network modeling and analysis. There is significant economical and theoretical pressure to find these "alternative conceptions" of the behavior of present and future networked firms. The evolution of dynamic value networks as the firm environment has not made the challenge easier. Here we introduce our approach to constructing a behavioral theory of the networked firm (BTONF).

12.2 **INTRODUCTION**

An ideal behavioral theory consists of a description of the *architectural platform* (social, biological, technological, economical), an *environment* where the behavior of interest occurs, a conceptual and empirically accessible description of the *behaving actors*, and the *observables* that allow measuring and modeling of the behaviors and their drivers. The aim of a BTONF is to model its emerging economic behavior and decision making in genuine networked contexts, internal and external alike (cf. Padgett and Powell, 2012). Network analysis is not a rare business practice today and the realism and computational benefits of the network models are fast maturing as tools boosting the performance and growth of firms and other organizations. At the same time, however, the networked life of firms practically escapes the theoretical attempts to cover this complex and multiple-domain organizational evolution. This is a challenge both to theoreticians and the management of modern firms.

Internal (intrafirm) and external (interfirm) relationships are being transformed, especially due to technological and media progress. Powell (1990) emphasized the relational nature of networks and described the key features that differentiate between hierarchies, markets, and networks as forms of economic organization, e.g., their normative basis, means of communication, methods of conflict resolution, degree of flexibility, and mixing of forms. Most dynamic Business-to-Consumer (B2C) examples of the development of network relationships today come from travel, hotel, book, entertainment business contexts and it is not infrequent for firms to manage a number of different networks in their operations. Communication technologies, the new digital life of citizens, consumers, and firms and especially social media today are adding new functions and forms to the networked firms. Furthermore, "the networked firm" as a concept is already becoming "the multinetwork firm," a complex phenomenon to model, and not least because of the changing boundaries between the firm, its allies and the market.

Consider, for example, the evolution of the publishing industry, especially newspapers and magazines, where digitalization has introduced a number of business and consumer networks, each with their own dynamics and domain, interaction and interdependence, ranging from computerized production, sales, and marketing, like in CreateSpace (https://www.createspace.com/), to different interaction channels for consumers, customers, and subcontractors. It no longer makes sense to refer to a "network" without specifying exactly what its domain and architecture are and what the ecosystem where it resides is.

Network innovations, including social innovations within and between firms and their clients, have become a significant strategic factor, a long-term and scalable asset (Barabasi, 2003). Amazon has become the praised example of a pure networked retailing firm, living on a multinetwork-based business model: first, it is a hub for a massive third-party vendor network, second, it maintains its own effective logistics and stock network, and third, its main competitive edge has rested on reaching, managing, and maintaining the customer network through high-quality network services, tools, and even network-compatible products like Kindle. Indeed, Amazon demonstrates some of the main potentials of a modern networked firm: internal networking, networking with the customers, vendors, and logistics providers. Each one of these components of the firm network has its own architecture, business dynamics, and the role in value capture, but they have to be interfaced, coordinated, and tuned for the entire value network environment. And then, of course, the life of the customers has become digitally guided, with its new social architecture and patterns of human behavior.

Industrial innovators are almost by definition dependent on the capability of the innovating actors to change. They must learn to benefit from external contributions and valuable material and immaterial resources outside the focal firm (Adner and Kapoor, 2006), all this happening through their networks of exchange (cf. Burt, 1992). In strategic alliances and partnering, network-related dependencies have a long history (cf. Movrey et al., 1996) and they are now an essential aspect of open innovation in general (cf. Chesbrough, 2003) and in value network contexts (cf. Vanhaverbeke et al., 2006).

Considering these extensive developments, it is no surprise that there is no unique network theory to be directly applied in the analysis of firm behavior. The reasons are obvious: any candidate theory should be grounded on relevant empirical observations and measurements of the economic behavior occurring within and between the networked organizations. This in itself is a huge challenge considering the behavior dynamics and breadth and depth of the problem. At the moment, there is a large variation in the way network properties or functions of a firm are described and how different network architectures are used in modeling. The existing network approaches to firm behavior appear largely incompatible and Baum and Ingram (2002), for example, point out that such a theory is indeed motivated by a "disconnect" between the observations and prevailing economic theory.

Another challenge is that the network relationships are asymmetric: evolution of a networked firm is not only a feed-forward phenomenon, where the network extends and spreads from a nodal firm towards its customers and partner organizations—also significant reverse directions exist and are an essential aspect of any firm network. Walter et al. (2001), for example, take the supplier perspective to supplier–customer relationship management and demonstrate how the direct functions of customer relationship management are being increasingly supplemented by indirect functions (related to, e.g., innovation, market, scouting, and customer access). The true network architectures are many and here we focus on the prototypical and well-represented ones to be used in the analysis of the emergence, economical behavior, and decision-making in the networked firm.

12.3 NETWORK BEHAVIORS IN FIRMS

The first major phase in constructing a network theory of the firm is the description of its basic elements (units, connections), the content of the connections (flow of signals, information, people, materials, skills, orders, and payments), the connection mechanism, and how the strength of connection or flow through units is expressed. Furthermore, it is necessary to consider what kind of clusters, cliques, or closures occur, what are the possible local and global activities or processes, what kind of internal and external connectivity exists, what are the formal and informal clusters, what are their possible reciprocities, what kind of network learning mechanisms or feed-back processes exist and, finally, how do networked firms emerge. In summary, even the simplest network functions are formally and practically extremely complex: they can vary from straightforward communication channels and practices to collaborative decision-making, innovating, resourcing, and strategic alliances where a number of different metrics can be used to characterize network form, functions, and performance.

From the classic firm perspective, the relevant networked behaviors can be roughly divided into two according to their system characteristics. First there are the firm behaviors having general closed system properties and operating under uncertainty in the domains of imperfect markets. Second, there are behaviors occurring as a direct or indirect result of the external networking of the firm and having general open system characteristics. The former behaviors can be considered as human and social factors related to decision-making and focusing on variables that contribute to the way firms span their goals, expectations, and declare their organizational choices (cf. Cyert and March, 1963, 2001). The latter behaviors can be the transformed or new forms of behavior, which emerge as a result of adaptation to the network demands of the classic firm.

However, an increasing number of firms have their origins outside the classic firm form and the current examples like Google, Facebook, cell phone, and e-commerce operators, and various network service providers are inherently networked and practically live on and in the network markets and through networked operations and partnering. Their pure network character has major behavioral consequences upon their decision-making and other psychological processes, caused by the distributed and adaptive nature of the firm. Constructing a behavioral theory of such firms is an ambitious goal and here we consider only some of the challenges and introduce the main elements of the behavioral theory in this context.

12.4 FUNCTIONAL NETWORK CHARACTERISTICS

Social network analysis has been frequently applied in the study of interfirm networking aiming at recognizing the significant personal and other relationship patterns like transactions, resource, or information flow within and between firms and organizations in general. The complex nature of network ties was understood early and different types of ties have been studied as connective phenomena (cf. Freeman, 2004). These include similarities, for example, in location, membership, or some other attribute, and social relationships such as kinship, and especially variable roles like affective or cognitive ones, interaction, and flow of information or people (Borgatti et al., 2009).

Response type. As a natural evolution of classic firm organization and function, Cross and Thomas (2009) describe two general types of function in networks having both external and internal (input–output) connectivity: customized and routine network responses. Especially the former one is aimed at a strategic advantage relying on efficient and dynamic network-supported problem-framing, coordination of the firm's activities, and decision-making, i.e., capturing value through the internal network. This division also allows the analysis of how the firm deals with ambiguous problems and established problems. The latter one, is, as its definition implies, more like a straightforward input–output process mapping providing effective service and other responses relevant to the firm and its clients.

Weak and strong ties. One of the early insights about the complexities of network connections and their dynamics was the observation concerning the functional difference between weak and strong ties (Granovetter, 1973) and it was even suggested that they form the de facto links of individuals to society (Granovetter 1983). However, the definition of a "tie" depends on the network context and numerous examples exist in the literature on how to operationalize it and make it quantifiable (e.g., frequency or recency of contacting or activation between network units/individuals, close friends vs. acquaintances, neighbor distance, etc.).

A specific modeling challenge is the impact of individual role sets in determining the actual function of the network ties (Coser, 1975). Any networked firm must conceptualize its organizational behavior with the help of a chart and a functional management system, which it can use to perceive itself and its behavior. The networking firm needs an awareness of its (new) network behaviors and properties of which the weak ties are an excellent example: it is difficult to be aware of their outward-directed impacts just as it is difficult to see under which influences they have inward effects from other networks. Weak ties offer an opportunity to build bridges from one network constellation to another, and they have the special potential to bridge network clusters having different profiles and character. However, because of their "weak nature" they can also be a significant risk factor, difficult to perceive early enough as factors influencing the intra- and interfirm dynamics.

Multiple network structures. Network "units" are by no means simple entities. Padgett (2006), for example, makes this clear in differentiating between "simple networks" on the one hand, by referring to those consisting of only identical units and having a specific topology, and the "multiple networks" on the other, described as "sets of single networks that overlap through sharing nodes." In the latter he includes assemblages of persons and skills able to channel almost anything relevant, like information, goods, services, favors, regulations, or money in reverse through the set of nets. In other words, nodes can have different roles and positions in the network complex.

A number of technological factors drive the development towards multiple and dynamic structures, e.g., media technologies, cloud services and applications, diverse and special mobile applications, and open x. In the very near future, "Internet of Everything" as it is called by Cisco (2013), and "social manufacturing" (cf. Shang et al., 2013) will boost this development. A question remains: how will networks develop in this dynamic environment and what dominant behavioral drivers and economical incentives will keep the motivation of the units in such networks to start, maintain, and reproduce their relevant roles in the networks? Padgett calls this "life" but it could just as well be called "multiple life."

Multilayer network. Perhaps the most complex and currently the most expressive organizational network representation is the multilayer, multiple-network framework, described by Padgett and Powell (2012), which they have applied in a number of business and social contexts ranging from, e.g., the historical analyses of organizational emergence in 14th century Florence to the political parties in 19th century Germany and up to the postsocialist development in Russia and China. In essence, their multilayer analysis refers to the network emergence, and related actor domains but also to the way interdomain spread of inventions and innovations (or prevention of them) becomes possible. This can happen via people having multiple, domain-compatible roles and activities and the ties they have been able to build both within and between domain layers. Hence, these evolving networks are also temporally dynamic in nature and it is not only a matter of individual roles and connectivity that guides the emergence but there are significant short- and long-term dynamics that can span any spatial extent. This complexity has been eloquently crystallized in the following: "For us, nodes and ties in social networks are not reified dots and lines; they are the congealed residues of history—in particular, the history of iterated production rules and communication protocols in interaction" (Padgett and Powell, 2012).

12.5 THEORETICAL CHALLENGES

When highly relevant, but complex flows of content are "injected" into the organizational network model, the relationships between the units, their connections, and the unit activities themselves become difficult to express formally and the representational challenges cannot be overestimated. The classic description of the firm by its strategy, processes, communication network, actors, behaviors, and branding, for example, is not easy to map on any uniform network model with its specific architecture and uniform elements in addition to the technology, platform, operators involved, and the actual networked actors. Furthermore, any network theory of the firm relies on an explicit description of the context where it is applied. Considering this, it is not an exaggeration to note that the most profound, and so far an unsolved, problem is how to model and represent the behaviorally relevant content and meanings in the network model—either at an individual or organizational level—so that it could optimally serve both theoretical and practical needs of firms. While the aim is to find an economy of representation, there are several reasons why empirically measurable, organizational phenomena of decision-making and other aspects of economic behavior are genuinely problematic.

First, the network representation itself is problematic and new theoretical models will probably emerge to include and model the most relevant, often complex and inherently multidimensional firm behaviors. It is not at all clear what the behavioral elements to be modeled are, what kind of representations and network models are to be used for them, and how to formally represent motivated and contextual human behavior in these models. For example, King and Walker (2014) introduced the idea of a field-model, a "relative" to social network models describing the way the interacting actors influence each other within their power field, which the authors call strategic action fields. While it remains unclear and speculative how the spread of power influences actually takes place in this preliminary model, it aims at finding a new functional representation for the connected actions, influences, and interaction, a shift from a network world to a field world.

Second, the connectivity within and between firms evolves fast, while new technologies and organizational models change the nature of this connectivity. Because of the fast-changing technology—the speed by which social media changes is an excellent example of this—the network connections of tomorrow will be different from the connections of today.

Third, the methods and models of network data collection and analysis have improved significantly within only a few years' time and made data collection possible in real time, with extremely large samples of increasingly rich content (cf. Pentland, 2014; Mayer-Schönberger and Cukier, 2014). This can have significant impacts on model development as well. At the same time, the theoretical developments in the study of "deep" learning networks may offer new application insights and directions for the modeling and analysis of organizational and emerging multilayer systems (cf. Bengio, 2009; Bengio et al., 2013).

Finally, firm environments are becoming dynamic, evolving from value chains to extensive and distributed value networks and an increasing amount of interfirm influences exist and come through indirect channels of networking, instead of the, e.g., traditional direct partnership- and subcontractor-type of influences (Walter et al., 2001). The shift and transformation towards dynamic and indirect networks concerns the consumers, citizens, and firms alike, and hence any theory of a networked firm must include the firm itself and its internal networks, interfirm networks, and their value network environment.

Here we want to lay the general foundations for the behavioral modeling, observation, and measurement of the networked firm. To do this it is necessary to look at the potential of different network models for a behavioral analysis of the firm. We use different stereotypical network models as "lenses" to firm behavior in order to find relevant model representations for firms living in dynamic value network environments.

12.6 NETWORK ARCHITECTURE AS A LENS TO FIRM BEHAVIOR

Network models have acquired their dominant role as a paradigm because of their mathematical and technological background and, hence, hardly any alternatives exist. However, while computationally advanced, these models not only serve as platforms for the analysis of firm behavior and performance—they also form a lens through which the behavior of the modeled firm actually becomes observed: choose a network model and you choose which behavioral phenomena you want to observe and which you will leave unobserved.

Indeed, network architectures are many and different and not all models have the same descriptive or explanatory potential in the analysis of firm behavior. At least the following differences exist: (1) general architecture of the model, (2) definition of the behavioral units and domains of the firm, (3) the nature of the individual and firm relationships, and (4) the language describing network behaviors and network development. In Table 12.1 we have compared five prototypical network types including the game-model although it is not typically seen as a network system. Other architectures do exist but we have selected these because of their general properties and their extensive theoretical background.

The following archetypes have been selected as our lenses to firm behavior: (1) Simple feed-forward network consisting of a layer of connected, classical units (actors) and their relationships (e.g., McClelland and Rumelhart, 1986; Kranton and Minehart, 2001). It is based on feed-forward and/or recurrent connections with variable connection weights, typical in social network descriptions. Its main characteristic is the ability to learn valuable input/output pattern relationships via different "learning rules." (2) Self-organizing network (Kohonen, 1982; Braha et al., 2011) resembling a simple network but with unsupervised learning and rules that impose structural changes in the network topology as a function of its behavior history, internal and external (e.g., competition) alike. Its main characteristic is to produce specific and functionally valuable architectural changes as a result of this learning. (3) Multilayer network with multiple, stacked domains (e.g., economy, kinship, politics) where units are people roles and the unit relations are defined by the constitutional ties within each specific domain, i.e., in each network layer. Its main characteristic is to represent network behavior on different functionally specific layers but also dynamic role-based unit interaction between different layers (Padgett and Powell, 2012). (4) Field model where actors with power positions span an action field (King and Walker, 2014). (5) Game system that we treat here as a special kind of dynamic, story-based network, including the actors and their roles and other elements of the game story, like the genre, style, and drama structure (e.g., Corbo et al., 2007; Laine et al., 2012). Its main characteristic is to represent and bind networked relationships in the form of a story and its dramatic elements and functions that follow from its basic properties and reward system. The game lens can be seen as a generalized version of the multilayer model with its inherent dramatic components that closely resemble the domain-specific functions in each layer of the multilayer model.

12.7 TOWARDS A BEHAVIORAL THEORY OF THE NETWORKED FIRM

The description of the performance of a networked firm refers either directly or indirectly to the firm behaviors as conceptualized and described by Cyert and March

Table 12.1 Comparison of different network types and their potential for the BTONF (cf. Kohonen, 1982; Kranton and Minehart, 2001; Braha et al., 2011; Laine et al., 2012; Padgett and Powell, 2012; King and Walker, 2014)

	Network type				
	Feed-forward	**Self-organizing**	**Multilayer**	**Field**	**Game**
Core property	Input/output functions	Competitive organization	Domain layers	Positioning in action field	Drama setting
Model strength	Routines Functions Competition	Learning Emergence Competition	Content Power relations Role impact	Actors Power influence Position	Behaviors Roles Motivations Dynamics
Model weakness	Mechanical Reactive	Emerging model Empirical fit	Computations Learning	Computations Organization	Computations Theory
Model benefit	Input/output Metrics	Structures Change mechanism	Cross-layer Holistic Multidimensions	Customer perspective Integrative	Simulation Learning Reverse engineering
Lens to behavior	I/O behaviors Relationships Performance	Mutual perceptions Competition Adaptation	Roles Domain life Cross-cultural	Values Power Activism Perceptions	Individual Social Motivation Skills

(1963). Here we have considered some of them, but in a networked context in order to see how different network types affect major aspects of firm behavior.

The networked firm as a coalition expresses itself to the observer through the behaviors represented in the specific network type the observer has chosen to use as his lens to firm behavior. Coalitions tend to develop and be transformed as a function of, e.g., the internal and external network connectivity, rewarding, experiential history in general, and relationship interaction, and not all network models are equally powerful in revealing this. Coalition boundaries can become dynamic and fuzzy and the scope of observation of their dynamics and the resulting architectural interpretation will depend strongly on the type of network used in the analysis. This has been recognized in the studies on the formal and informal relationships (Cross and Thomas, 2009) and in the studies on strong and weak ties in social networks (Granovetter 1973). In constructing the BTONF, it is important to identify and represent the most influential types of actor relationships and their potential to the relevant learning (e.g., Uzzi, 1997).

Individual and conflicting goals of a networked firm can emerge and appear in new forms as a result of increasing distribution, permeable boundaries in and outside the firm, the dynamical value networks, as impacted by social technologies. This can change the way goals are set and it influences, for example, production, inventory, sales, marketing, and even profits (Cyert and March, 1963).

In the simple feed-forward model, the goals can be seen as guiding and underlying or being embedded in the automatic input–output relationships or routines that the networked firm learns. From this perspective the goal-setting can be reactive in nature and suffer from any communication noise causing uncertainties and misunderstandings.

In the self-organization model, locally specialized communities (e.g., suboptimization) can emerge and become the sources of goal degradation, reformulation, and suboptimal interpretation. Clearly, the concept of "goal" in such an evolving, networked firm requires reconsideration. As an example, the multiple and often conflicting goals could be metaphorically considered as the firm's (multiple) behavior attractors or as formal properties of the (performance, decision -related) multidimensional landscape of the network behavior and the decision pathways available. On the other hand, using the game network perspective it becomes possible to represent many of the complexities involved such as the goals and interactions. This is due to its way of representing, e.g., the multiple actors' story-based motivations, actions, and intentions.

A tendency to suboptimal decisions can be understood in a rather similar manner in all network models. Local coalitions or automatic input/output responses are reinforced by the specific connections and learning/reorganizing properties of each network. By modeling this behavioral process, it is possible to find out what promotes or prevents suboptimal development. As the boundaries of the coalitions become fuzzy, finding a direction for common organizational action may become difficult and can lead to an emphasized but difficult-to-observe "quasi resolution of conflicts" occurring between coalitions (Cyert and March, 1963). A networked environment can then weaken the member commitment and even make leaving the coalition a viable option.

Perceptual constraints in problem-solving in the networked firm can occur as biases in their opportunity perception and sense-making. We use here the concept of *opportunity perception* to describe a higher process of organizational perception and resource allocation than mere "attention." Several other sources are relevant as well, related to the situational, story- or domain-based context of the perception mechanisms.

Resistance to radical change is strongest under uncertainty, especially when the firm has learned to rely on established behavior models and practices. Despite the efficient communication potential of the network, in typical network-based learning an inbuilt resistance can occur due to the slow distributed (converging) learning processes. According to the multilayer model, this kind of friction or even stagnation can be avoided by disruptive human connections between the layers so that new knowledge can be diffused and exchanged between the specialized domains. Change readiness can become better, if stability can be broken by such nonstandard connections or by changes in the stabilizing relationships. In standard computational learning network models, it is well known that some learning algorithms can lead to so-called local (suboptimal) minima where further learning is difficult without proper means to move out from the stagnated state (McClelland and Rumelhart, 1986). Behaviorally, there is a specific need to recognize the individual and organizational key elements in the networked firm that promote and resist change.

12.8 ON THE EMERGENCE OF MULTIPLE NETWORKS

Padgett and Powell (2012) introduce eight different forms of network emergence through which networking organizations (firms) change and are transformed in a multiple-network environment. The division is supported by a rich set of empirical examples reflecting historical, regional, political, and business contexts, where network transformation and modification take place and can be well-documented. These changes are called network folding mechanisms of organizational genesis. When folding takes place it puts the firm under a number of change pressures as is increasingly typical in present organizations and especially in firms living on the latest network technology and building much of their evolution on the adoption and acquisition of network platforms, operations, partnerships, or businesses. During the transformation processes, the organization undergoes changes concerning both the organization (firm) and the people involved, and hence new risks and opportunities emerge.

By applying the modified classification of the folding forms we have presented a hypothetical description of the impacts of the different types of network folding processes on the organization, its members (individuals), and the behavioral dynamics that result from the transformation (Table 12.2).

Table 12.2 Hypothetical behavioral impacts of multiple-network development in firms

Behavioral impact of multiple-network (MN) emergence in firms			
Type of MN emergence	**Organizational impact**	**Individual impact**	**Dynamic impact**
Adoption/new use of the "old practices" by the MN	New social practices	Learning, unlearning	Trust building problems
	Cultural tensions	Role changes	New coalitions
Integration of partner and people diversity	Organizational image	Goal awareness	Subcultures
	Value pressures	Role, identity changes	Silent/passive resistance
	Power balance	Rewarding, incentives	Competition
	Cultural tensions	Personal networks	
Incorporation of an "external" subnetwork (and detachment from its home base) into the MN	Organizational image	Goal awareness	Subcultures
	Value pressures	Role, identity changes	Silent/passive resistance
	History change	Power position	
	Cultural tensions	Personal networks	
Migration of functional networks into a new MN	Organizational image	Goal awareness	Subcultures
	Communication model	Role, identity changes	
	Cultural tensions	Power position	
Displacement of conflicts to provide an opportunity for fusion	Cultural tensions	Power resistance	Trust building problems
	Breaking of social capital	Personal network	Encapsulation
Purge the old network ("upper rank") and replace it with a new one	Power conflicts	Uncertainty (e.g., career)	Trust building problems
	Cultural tensions	Personal networks	Opposition, harming
	New coalitions		Loss of balance
Privatization and business groups	Organizational image	Goal awareness	Power conflicts
	Value transform	Rewarding, incentives	New coalitions
		Expectations	
Robust action and multivocality	Cultural tensions	Goal awareness	Persuasion
		Expectations	Manipulation

The classification is adopted and modified from the eight network-folding mechanisms introduced by Padgett and Powell (2012, pp. 12–26).

12.9 **CONCLUSIONS**

To the classic Cyert and March (1963) theory, a BTONF should add the description of behaviors that result from the networked nature of the firm. However, theories of networked behavior in general and the psychology thereof especially are still immature although evolving fast in, e.g., social network analysis, such as the recent developments in the (physical) statistics of social behavior (cf. Castellano et al., 2009; Pentland, 2014) and as demonstrated in the study of networked influences such as vitality and meme spread (Weng et al., 2013) in modern media like Facebook and Twitter. These new paradigms have made possible the use of huge data sets in the studies on network psychology.

It is no exaggeration to claim that theories of network psychology are still superficial. There remains much to learn about the psychological platforms of firms and their networks, how decisions are faced and made and conflicts resolved in networked life, and how firms learn to perceive opportunities for value creation, value offering and capturing, and in general, to prosper on the networked world. Different network models rest on different aspects of firm behavior and especially the development towards multiple-network systems has made this a challenging theoretical and practical problem.

How can compatible theoretical frameworks be constructed to model both the networked firm and its value network? Here we suggest the following general approach. First, the frameworks should build on mathematically well-formulated and/or simulated candidate network models (even metaphors), which excel in identifying and representing the firm's key behaviors. Second, the potential relevance of the models should be evaluated, for example, against an empirically feasible framework such as that offered by Cyert and March (1963,2001), describing the behaviors related to decision-making, resource allocation, goal formation, emergence of expectations, choice behaviors, and control processes in the firm. As we have noted above, networking introduces novel phenomena into the firm behaviors and, as a consequence, the applied network models should be sensitive to these. On the other hand, each network model has its specific constraints in this mapping: selecting a network model is like designing a lens to observe firm behavior (cf. Table 12.1). The selection of the network model guides the construction of the empirical mapping between the network properties and the actual, individual or organizational behaviors and related processes in the firm.

Here we introduce guidelines for building a BTONF: (1) Build on a behavioral theory framework that has relevance in the life, psychology, and performance of the networked firm. This concerns the concepts, variables, and measures to be used in the behavior analysis and modeling of the firm, (2) The framework should be grounded in the observable and measurable reality of the firm as an organization and as a community of different, individual human beings, (3) Innovate and introduce novel behavioral candidate concepts that can be assumed to have a solid grounding in the real behavior of the firm—and tune them further by testing them empirically, especially using qualitative methodology. For example, the game-based model includes several valuable behavioral features of a rather complex psychological nature and which do not yet have a scientifically solid foundation. However, there is practice-related evidence suggesting that they underlie many successful game design practices, e.g., the gamer's sense of presence, immersion, and interaction in the gameplay, performance, narrative, drama, engagement, incentives (cf. Takatalo et al., 2010), (4) Construct the empirical mapping scheme according to which behavioral phenomena in the networked firm can be empirically observed, (5) Derive network behavior metrics for the firm in the context of the value network. Look for network behavior models and representations that overcome typical network model deficiencies such as problems in representing goals, roles, agent motivations, intentions, complex content, and actions.

Extensive connectivity is natural for any modern firm but the question remains how a firm can find a strategically valuable way of behaving in its value network environment? For example, where in the firm's active network are the best opportunities for value creation and capture and how does the networked firm perceive these opportunities? How and why should the firm extend its network (cf. Table 12.2)? What new behavioral incentives are required (cf. Hulkko-Nyman et al., 2013)? How should the firm invest in networking?

We have emphasized the importance of finding a feasible network model to serve as an observational lens to the firm behavior: not all models are equally useful. In addition, a significant second-order complexity is introduced when looking at a networked firm in its value network environment, both being complex adaptive systems and interacting. For example, it is known that for some firms the value network has involved significant and fast positive feedback phenomena, creating strong nonlinearities and difficult-to-predict opportunities for sudden market dominance (Arthur, 1999). The firm should adopt optimal ways to learn about itself as a networked system and about the complex environment where it lives. Studies on the use of simulation games in teaching complex system analysis seem to suggest that students and professionals can gain insight into the strategic properties of complex adaptive systems and also understanding and foresight of their behavior (van Bilsen et al., 2010). We can speculate about the possibilities of educating a firm by a suitable combination of real-world data and simulation of its decision-making behavior and processes in the value network environment.

Firms need to find the right type of network analysis and management model for supporting their relevant behaviors and opportunity perception. On the other hand, the theory of value networks is only evolving and to the best of our knowledge there is no unique way to match these two aspects of network theory, the network perspective to the firm and to its value environment. A well-grounded BTONF can act as an observational lens through which a firm can gain realistic and relevant understanding of its network behaviors and guide its strategy and operations in the value network environment.

ACKNOWLEDGMENTS

We thank the DYNET team for collaboration in preparing this chapter. This work is supported in part by NSFC (Natural Science Foundation of China) projects 61233001, 71232006 and Tekes—the Finnish Funding Agency for Technology and Innovation project 2439/31/2012.

REFERENCES

Adner, R., Kapoor, R., 2006. Innovation Ecosystems and Innovator's Outcomes: Evidence from the semiconductor lithography equipment industry, 1962–2004. Unpublished INSEAD working paper.

Arthur, W.B., 1999. Complexity and the economy. Science 284, 107–109.

Barabasi, L., 2003. Linked: How Everything Is Connected to Everything Else and What It Means for Business, Science, and Everyday Life. A Plume Book, New York.

Baum, J.A.C., Ingram, P., 2002. Interorganizational learning and network organization: toward a behavioral theory of the firm. In: Augier, M., March, J.G. (Eds.), The Economics of Choice, Change, and Organization: Essays in Memory of Richard M. Cyert. Edward Elgar, Cheltenham, UK, pp. 191–218.

Bengio, Y., 2009. Learning deep architectures for AI. Foundations and Trends in Machine Learning 2 (1), 1–127.

Bengio, Y., Courville, A., Vincent, P., 2013. Representation learning: a review and new perspectives. IEEE Trans. Pattern. Anal. Mach. Intell. Vol 35, 1798–1828.

Borgatti, S.P., Mehra, A., Brass, D.J., Labianca, G.G., 2009. Network analysis in the social sciences. Science 323, 892–895.

Braha, D., Stacey, B., Bar-Yam, Y., 2011. Corporate competition: a self-organized network. Soc. Networks 33, 219–230.

Burt, R.S., 1982. Towards a Structural Theory of Action: Network Models of Social Structure, Perceptions, and Action. Academic Press, New York.

Burt, R.S., 1992. Structural Holes: the Social Structure of Competition. Harvard University Press, Cambridge, MA.

Castellano, C., Fortunato, S., Loreto, V., 2009. Statistical physics of social dynamics. Rev. Mod. Phys. 81, 591–646.

Chesbrough, H.W., 2003. Open Innovation: The New Imperative for Creating and Profiting From Technology. Harvard Business School Press, Boston, MA.

Cisco, 2013, IoE AT-A-Glance, http://www.cisco.com/web/about/ac79/docs/IoE/IoE-AAG.pdf.

Corbo, J., Corbo, A., Calvó-Armengol, A., Parkes, D.C., 2007. The importance of network topology in local contribution games.. Deng, X. Graham, F.C. (Eds.),. In: Internet and Network Economics, 4858. Springer, Berlin, Heidelberg, pp. 388–395. Previously published in Lecture Notes in Computer Science.

Coser, R., 1975. The complexity of roles as seedbed of individual autonomy. In: Coser, L. (Ed.), The Idea of Social Structure: Essays in Honor of Robert Merton. Harcourt Brace Jovanovich, New York, NY.

Cross, R., Thomas, R.J., 2009. Driving Results Through Social Networks. Jossey-Bass, A Wiley Imprint, SanFrancisco, CA.

Cyert, R.M., March, J.G., 1963; 2001. A Behavioral Theory of the Firm. Prentice Hall, Englewood Cliffs, NJ.

Freeman, L.C., 2004. The Development of Social Network Analysis: A study in the Sociology of Science. Empirical Press. Vancouver.

Granovetter, M., 1973. The strength of weak ties. Am. J. Sociol. 78 (6), 1360–1380.

Granovetter, M., 1983. The strength of weak ties: a network theory revisited. Sociol. Theor. 1, 201–233.

Hulkko-Nyman, K., Nyman, G., Nelson, M., Nyberg, T., 2013. Incentives in dynamic value networks—challenges and a theoretical research proposal. Service operations and logistics, and informatics (SOLI). In: 2013 IEEE International Conference, Dongguang, China, 2013.

King, B.K., Walker, E.T., 2014. Winning hearts and minds: field theory and the three dimensions of strategy.. Strategic Organization 12 (2), 134–141.

Kohonen, T., 1982. Self-organized formation of topologically correct feature maps. Biol. Cybern. 43, 59–66.

Kranton, R.A., Minehart, F., 2001. A theory of buyer–seller networks. Am. Econ. Rev. 91 (3), 485–508.

Laine, T., Paranko, J., Suomala, P., 2012. Using a business game concept to enhance servitization: a longitudinal case study. Managing Service Quality 22 (5), 428–446.

Mayer-Schönberger, V., Cukir, K., 2014. Big Data. An Eamon Dolan Book, Mariner, Boston/ New York.

McClelland, J.L., Rumelhart, D.E., 1986. Parallel Distributed Processing: Explorations in the Microstructure of Cognition. Volume 2: Psychological and Biological Models. MIT Press, Cambridge, MA.

Movrey, D.C., Oxley, J.E., Silverman, B.S., 1996. Strategic alliances and interfirm knowledge transfer. Strategic Manage. J. Vol. 17, 77–91.

Padgett, J.F. 2006. Organizational genesis in Florentine history: four multiple-network processes (unpublished manuscript).

Padgett, J.F., Powell, W.W., 2012. The problem of emergence. In: Padgett, J.F., Powell, W.W. (Eds.), The Emergence of Organizations and Markets. Princeton University Press, Princeton, NJ.

Pentland, A., 2014. Social Physics. The Pengui Press, New York.

Powell, W.W., 1990. Neither market nor hierarchy: network forms of organization. Res. Organ. Behav. 112, 295–336.

Shang, X, Liu, X, Xiong, G., Cheng, C., Ma, Y., Nyberg, T., 2013. Social manufacturing cloud service platform for mass custiomization in apparel industry. Service Operations and Logistics, and Informatics (SOLI), In: 2013 IEEE International Conference, Dongguang, China, 2013. See also the Economist, report 2012. A third industrial revolution. Economist, April 2012.

Takatalo, J., Häkkinen, J., Kaistinen, J., Nyman, G., 2010. Presence, involvement and flow in digital games. In: Bernhaupt., R. (Ed.), Evaluating User Experiences in Games: Concept and Methods. Springer-Verlag, London Limited.

Uzzi, B., 1997. Social structure and competition in interfirm networks: the paradox of embeddedness.. Admin. Sci. Quart. 42 (1), 35–67.

van Bilsen, A., Bekebrede, G., Mayer, I., 2010. Understanding complex adaptive systems by playing games. Inform. Educ. 9 (1), 1–18.

Vanhaverbeke, W., Cloodt, M., 2006. Open innovation in value networks. In: Chesbrough, H., Vanhaverbeke, W., West, J. (Eds.), Open Innovation: Researching a New Paradigm. Oxford University Press, New York, pp. 258–281.

Walter, A., Ritter, T., Gemunden, H.G., 2001. Value creation in buyer–seller relationships: theoretical considerations and empirical results from a supplier's perspective. Ind. Market. Manag. 30, 365–377.

Weng, L., Menczer, F., Ahn, Y.-Y., 2013. Virality prediction and community structure in social networks. Sci. Rep. 3, 2522 (www.nature.com/scientificreports).

Index

Printed in the United States
By Bookmasters